History

for the IB Diploma

The Cold War

Author and series editor: Allan Todd

Cambridge University Press's mission is to advance learning,
knowledge and research worldwide.

Our IB Diploma resources aim to:
- encourage learners to explore concepts, ideas and
  topics that have local and global significance
- help students develop a positive attitude to learning in preparation
  for higher education
- assist students in approaching complex questions, applying
  critical-thinking skills and forming reasoned answers.

CAMBRIDGE
UNIVERSITY PRESS
www.cambridge.org

CAMBRIDGE UNIVERSITY PRESS
Cambridge, New York, Melbourne, Madrid, Cape Town,
Singapore, São Paulo, Delhi, Mexico City

Cambridge University Press
The Edinburgh Building, Cambridge CB2 8RU, UK

www.cambridge.org
Information on this title: www.cambridge.org/9780521189323

First published 2011
Reprinted 2012

Printed in Italy by L.E.G.O. S.p.A.

A catalogue record for this publication is available from the British Library

ISBN 978-0-521-18932-3

Dedication
In memory of
Cyn
(1947–2010)

Death ends a life,
not a relationship
(A. C. Grayling)

Contents

1 Introduction

This book will examine the various aspects of what was known as the **Cold War** – a historical and global phenomenon that began around the time of the end of the Second World War in 1945. It lasted until the collapse of the communist bloc in Eastern Europe, and then the Soviet Union itself, in the years 1989–91.

Overview

Essentially, the Cold War can be seen as a 50-year worldwide struggle between two rival states – the United States of America and the Union of Soviet Socialist Republics – and their allies: the West v. the East. The two main states were often referred to as '**superpowers**', though several historians claim that only the USA was a truly global superpower for most, if not all, of the Cold War.

The Cold War was a struggle which, at one time or another, involved many different countries across the various regions of the world. While the two main protagonists never actually fought each other directly, it was nonetheless a total war in that the economies and foreign policies of both states were, to differing degrees, significantly geared to it. This commitment also affected the citizens of the states involved – again differentially – in terms of living standards, civil and political freedoms, and aspects of culture.

Cold War The term used to describe the tension and rivalry between the USA and the USSR between 1945 and 1991. Originally used in the 14th century about the conflict between Christian and Islamic states, 'cold war' refers to relations that, although hostile, do not build up into a 'hot war' (involving actual military conflict). The term was popularised in the years 1946–47 by US journalist Walter Lippmann and US politician and businessman Bernard Baruch.

superpower First used in 1944, this term refers to a country considered so powerful, because of its economic and military resources, that it can largely dictate and control international events to serve its own interests.

JAMES BOND IS BACK! 007

IAN FLEMING'S
FROM RUSSIA WITH LOVE
TECHNICOLOR

Cold War spy novels and films became very popular, especially in the West; the fictional James Bond was probably the world's best-known spy

However, the Cold War was not always 'cold'. In some states and regions across the world, 'hot wars' were fought, or local civil wars became entangled in the greater geopolitical aims and moves of the two main Cold War players. As well as large-scale military conflicts in parts of Asia – such as Korea, Vietnam and Afghanistan – many other vicious small-scale wars broke out in Africa and the Americas. In Europe no wars were fought after 1945, but several significant crises occurred – for instance, over Berlin. Also, some attempts to liberalise regimes in Eastern Europe resulted in Soviet military or political interventions.

Cold War or 'Great Contest'?

Some historians, however, see the Cold War as a specific and more intense phase of a longer-term ideological and political conflict between two opposed social and economic systems: capitalism v. communism. This conflict had been in existence since November 1917, when a revolution in Russia resulted in the Bolsheviks (Russian communists) taking power. According to the historian Isaac Deutscher, what followed were attempts by capitalist states to 'strangle' this threat to their system by both military and economic means. At the same time, the Bolsheviks and other communist parties strove to support or spread revolution to other parts of the world.

Themes

To help you prepare for your IB History exams, this book will cover the themes relating to the Cold War (Topic 5 in Paper 2), as set out in the IB *History Guide*. For ease of study, the four major themes will be examined in the order below:

- the nature of the Cold War
- the origins of the Cold War
- the development and impact of the Cold War
- the end of the Cold War.

Chapters 2–7 will explore these themes, focusing on the main issues. Units within each chapter will deal with events and developments in different parts of the world – especially in Europe and Asia, but also in the Americas and Africa.

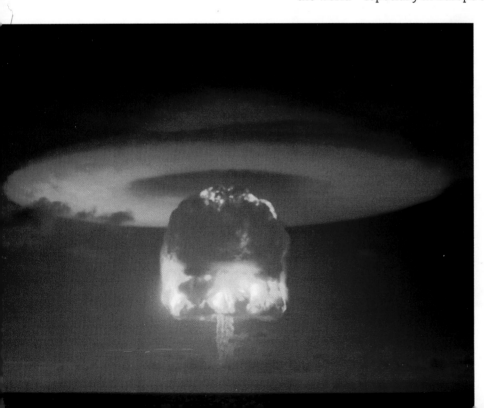

All the main events, turning points and key individuals will be covered in sufficient detail for you to be able to access the higher markbands – provided, of course, that your answers are both relevant and analytical!

One of the most significant events of the Cold War was the Cuban Missile Crisis of 1962, when the world came close to nuclear war. There were those who genuinely believed that the horror of atomic weapons experienced by the Japanese cities of Hiroshima and Nagasaki in August 1945 would be inflicted on European and American cities. The image of nuclear mushroom clouds haunted many people for the duration of the Cold War.

A photograph of a US atomic bomb test; from 1945, when the US dropped two atomic bombs on Japan, until 1949, the US had a monopoly on nuclear weaponry

Other key events include US involvement in the Vietnam War and the Soviet intervention in Afghanistan. Important aspects and concepts, such as the Truman Doctrine and containment, the arms race and Mutually Assured Destruction (MAD), the Domino Theory, détente and arms control, will also be examined.

Where appropriate, each chapter will contain visual and written sources, both to illustrate the events or issues under examination, and to provide material for exam-type questions. These will help you gain practice in dealing with the questions you will face in History Papers 1 and 2.

The nature of the Cold War

Chapter 2 will explain what the Cold War entailed and present the views of different historians about its nature (including the arms race) and how it affected the citizens of the states involved. It will examine the impact of the Cold War on the United Nations and on less-developed countries, such as those in the Non-Aligned Movement. It will also study the ideological differences between the major players, as well as the differences – and similarities – between capitalism and communism.

The origins of the Cold War

Chapter 3 will explore the various long- and short-term factors involved in the start of the Cold War, and will examine the different opinions of historians as to when and why it could be said to have started.

The development and impact of the Cold War

Chapters 4–6 will look at the global spread and impact of the Cold War, with the focus not just on Europe but also on countries in parts of Asia, the Americas and Africa.

The end of the Cold War

Chapter 7 will explore the final years of the Cold War and the reasons it came to an end, including Soviet weaknesses, the role of individual leaders and developments in Eastern Europe.

Theory of knowledge

Alongside these broad key themes, most chapters contain Theory of knowledge links to get you thinking about aspects that relate to history, which is a Group 3 subject in the IB Diploma. The Cold War topic has clear links to ideas about knowledge and history. A recent phenomenon, the Cold War was highly political, and ideology was important both for its key players and for the historians writing about it at the time and since its end about 20 years ago. Thus the questions relating to the availability and selection of sources, and to interpretations of these sources, have clear links to the IB Theory of knowledge course.

For example, when investigating aspects of the origins of the Cold War, or the motives of individuals (such as Stalin or Truman) or states (such as the USSR or the USA), historians must decide which primary and secondary evidence to select and use – and which to leave out – to make their case. But in selecting what they consider to be the most important or relevant sources, and in making judgements about the value and limitations of specific sources or sets of sources, how important are these historians' personal political views?

The Cold War was not always 'cold'. In some states and regions across the world, 'hot wars' were fought, or local civil wars became entangled in the greater geopolitical aims and moves of the two main Cold War players.

Is there such a thing as objective 'historical truth'? Or is there just a range of subjective opinions and interpretations about the past that vary according to the political interests and leanings of individual historians?

You are therefore encouraged to read a range of books offering different interpretations of the causes and course of the Cold War, in order to gain a clear understanding of its historiography. It is also important to be aware that since 1985 – and especially since 1991 – many archives have been opened up that contain sources and information unavailable to historians writing before those dates.

IB History and regions of the world

For the purposes of study, IB History specifies four regions of the world:

- Europe and the Middle East
- Asia and Oceania
- the Americas
- Africa.

Where relevant, you will need to be able to identify these regions and to discuss developments that took place within them. Remember, when answering a question that asks you to choose examples from *two* different regions, you *must* be careful – failure to comply will result in limited opportunities to score high marks.

> The four IB regions are shown on this map, along with some of the states covered by this book.

8

| The Americas | Asia and Oceania | Africa | Europe and the Middle East | USSR until 1991 |

Exam skills needed for IB History

Throughout the main chapters of this book, there are various activities and questions to help you develop the understanding and the exam skills necessary for success. Before attempting the specific exam practice questions at the end of most chapters, you might find it useful to refer to Chapter 8 *first*. This suggestion is based on the idea that if you know where you are supposed to be going (in this instance, gaining a good grade) and how to get there, you stand a better chance of reaching your destination!

Questions and markschemes

To ensure that you develop the necessary understanding and skills, each chapter contains a number of comprehension questions in the margins. In addition, three of the main Paper 1-type questions (comprehension, reliability/ utility, and cross-referencing) are dealt with at the end of Chapters 2–7. Help for the longer Paper 1 judgement/synthesis questions, and the Paper 2 essay questions, can be found in Chapter 8 – the final exam practice chapter.

For additional help, simplified markschemes have been put together in ways that should make it easier to understand what examiners are looking for in your answers. The actual IB History markschemes can be found on the IB website.

Finally, you will find examiners' tips and comments, along with activities, to help you focus on the important aspects of the questions and answers. These should help you avoid simple mistakes and oversights which, every year, result in even some otherwise good students failing to gain the highest marks.

Terminology and definitions

In order to understand Cold War propaganda produced by the USA and the USSR, and the various historical arguments and interpretations of the conflict, you will need to understand the meaning of such terms as 'democracy' and 'totalitarian', 'left' and 'right', 'communist' and 'capitalist', as well as the ideas of the corresponding left-wing and right-wing ideologies. You will then be able to understand and focus on the arguments, tensions and propaganda that existed throughout the Cold War from 1947 to 1991.

At first glance, this appears to be straightforward – certainly, many people feel sure they know what these terms mean. However, it is important to understand both the historical applications of these terms and their meaning in the context of the Cold War. Terms such as 'communism', 'capitalism', 'totalitarian' and 'democracy' are explained more fully in Chapter 2. As regards 'left' and 'right', the origins of this political terminology can be traced back to the early stages of the French Revolution in 1789. At this time, the most **radical** political groups sat on the left side of the National Convention, while the most **conservative** ones sat on the right; the **moderate** political groups sat in the middle.

Communism is seen – both by its adherents and by those opposed to this ideology – as being on the far (or extreme) left. Communists view capitalism as being either moderate or far right, depending on the political circumstances and the prevailing forms of rule. For example, communists see both the modern USA and Nazi Germany simply as different political forms of capitalism. However, supporters of capitalism usually see it as moderate and firmly linked to democracy.

radical, moderate, conservative Radicals (from the Latin word *radix*, meaning 'root') are those people who want significant and fundamental changes to a system, and for these changes to take place quickly. Moderates lean towards smaller-scale changes over a longer period and at a more gradual pace. Conservatives tend to want things to remain much the same, and oppose fundamental changes.

This is further complicated by the fact that there is more than one strand of communism; consequently, both historical players and historians have often meant different things despite using the same term. During the Cold War, for example, when Western politicians spoke about communism, they meant the form of rule in contemporary Russia – i.e. a one-party state. However, some communists have long claimed that the way Stalin ruled the Soviet Union was far removed from the ideas of Karl Marx, and even from the form of rule under Lenin and Trotsky's leadership in the first few years after the Bolshevik Revolution.

The history of the term 'totalitarian' is also complex. During the Cold War, some political commentators and historians used the term to emphasise their claim that Stalinist Russia was as bad as – or even worse than – Hitler's regime in Nazi Germany. These writers and politicians argued that the West needed to be every bit as vigilant and aggressive against the Soviet Union during the Cold War as the Allies had been against Nazi Germany. However, other historians have argued that the label 'totalitarian' did not fit the USSR at this time. They say that policies based on such false arguments and assumptions played a large part in exacerbating East–West relations, given the Soviet Union's fears following the Second World War.

SOURCE A

Stalin's police state is not an approximation to, or something like, or in some respects comparable with Hitler's. It is the same thing, only *more* ruthless, *more* cold-blooded … and *more* dangerous to democracy and civilised morals.

Eastman, M. 1955. Reflections on the Failure of Socialism. New York, USA. Devin-Adair. p. 87.

hegemony From an ancient Greek word meaning 'leadership' or 'dominance', hegemony is especially used of one state or country having dominance over a region, or the world as a whole.

However, some historians have pointed out the importance of noting that such totalitarian theories were first developed by US theorists during the late 1940s and early 1950s, at a time when the US was arguably already involved in its own 'drive towards global **hegemony**'.

Several historians and political commentators from the 1960s onwards pointed out that equating the Soviet Union with Nazi Germany was essentially a crude attempt to sway public opinion in the US and the West to accept permanent war preparations and military threats against the Soviet Union (see Source B).

Such 'totalitarian theories', which gave strong support to US foreign policy, are particularly associated with the political theorists Hannah Arendt, Carl Friedrich and Zbigniew Brzezinski. Friedrich and Brzezinski published *Totalitarian Dictatorship and Autocracy* in 1954. Brzezinski went on to publish several other titles before becoming a foreign-policy adviser to US presidents.

SOURCE B

The logic is clear. What is needed is a heavily-armed state on a permanent war-alert and ready to strike at the first sign of aggression. Now all these statements would make sense on one condition: that Nazi Germany and the USSR are in fact two faces of the same beast, a totalitarian Janus. The entire thrust of the totalitarian theorist has been to prove the existence of such a monster.

Ali, T. 1988. *Revolution From Above: Where Is the Soviet Union Going?* London, UK. Hutchinson. p. 160.

Janus Janus was the Roman god of beginnings and ends, and of doorways and all openings. He was depicted with two faces, seeing both the end of something old and the start of something new – hence January was dedicated to him.

History and changing perspectives

Since the end of the Cold War and the collapse of the USSR in 1991, historians have been able to access a wealth of Soviet archive material that had previously been wholly unavailable or only available in part (although some files had been opened to both Soviet and Western historians from 1985, under Soviet leader Mikhail Gorbachev's policy of *glasnost*, see page 191). As the years have passed, US government documents have also been made public, and many key players have published memoirs and diaries. All this has allowed historians to cross-check and either corroborate or dismiss earlier interpretations of significant moments and factors in the Cold War.

For instance, on 19 April 2002, an article by Andrew Alexander appeared in the *Guardian* newspaper in Britain, entitled 'The Soviet threat was a myth' (see Source C on page 12). In fact, Alexander is a journalist for the British newspaper the *Daily Mail*, which took a consistently right-wing, anti-Soviet position during the Cold War. In the article, he came to the conclusion that 'Stalin had no intention of attacking the west. We [the West] were to blame for the cold war.'

One interesting aspect of this article is the journalist's use of the term 'orthodox' in relation to different historical interpretations and perspectives concerning the Cold War. In order to score highly in Paper 2, you will need to show some awareness and understanding of the historiography surrounding the Cold War.

This topic involves fundamental political aspects and attitudes – such as the struggle of the 'Free West' against the 'Evil Empire' (as one US president described the Soviet Union), or the battle between communism and capitalism. It should not be surprising, therefore, that there are several almost diametrically opposed explanations of the origins and subsequent development of the Cold War. Historians, like most other people, are rarely completely neutral when dealing with important or controversial issues. For this reason you should be aware, where relevant, of the political sympathies – and even ideological agendas – of historians and politicians writing about the Cold War. As you begin to read around the subject, you will come across 'orthodox', 'revisionist', 'post-revisionist' and even 'post post-revisionist' perspectives.

journey to Damascus
According to the Bible's New Testament, Saul was an official persecutor of the early Christians. He was on his way to Damascus to arrest some of Jesus Christ's followers when he had a vision, after which he became a Christian himself and took the name Paul.

Taliban The Taliban was one of several extreme fundamentalist Islamist terrorist groups, funded by the US, which fought Soviet troops in Afghanistan. For a time they ruled Afghanistan, until driven from government by the US invasion that followed the events of 9/11. See Chapters 6 and 7 for further information on the Taliban.

SOURCE C

On a long and reluctant 'journey to Damascus', as I researched the diaries and memoirs of the key figures involved, it dawned on me that my orthodox view of the cold war as a struggle to the death between Good (Britain and America) and Evil (the Soviet Union) was seriously mistaken. In fact, as history will almost certainly judge, it was one of the most unnecessary conflicts of all time, and certainly the most perilous. ...

Truman had adopted an aggressive attitude to Russia the previous October. ... The programme would be based on 'righteousness'. There could be 'no compromise with evil'. ... He added that no one would be allowed to interfere with US policy in Latin America.

So Russian interference in countries essential to its safety was evil. But exclusive US domination of its own sphere of influence was righteous. ...

The fact that the cold war continued after Stalin's death does not, as some claim, prove the Soviets' unchanging global ambitions. The [Soviet/ Warsaw Pact] invasions of Hungary in 1956 and of Czechoslovakia in 1968 were brutal acts, but were aimed at protecting Moscow's buffer zone. The same may be said of the Soviet invasion of Afghanistan in 1980 [sic] (as a result of which, with the help of the CIA, the Taliban came into existence). In none of these cases was there a territorial threat to the west.

Alexander, A. 'The Soviet threat was a myth'. Published in the Guardian, *19 April 2002. A longer version appeared in the* Spectator.

Summary

By the time you have worked through this book, you should be able to:

- show a broad understanding of the nature of the Cold War, both within the major states involved and on a global scale
- understand and explain the various factors behind the origins of the Cold War, and be able to evaluate the different historical interpretations surrounding them
- show an awareness of the impact of the events of the Cold War in various regions of the world, and in turn how developments in different parts of the world impacted on the Cold War elsewhere
- understand the complexities of international relations resulting from both a bi-polar (USA and USSR) and a multi-polar (USA, USSR, China) framework
- understand the key events and turning points in the Cold War, from its origins through to its final stages
- understand and explain the various factors involved in the ending of the Cold War.

2 Nature of the Cold War

Introduction

Before dealing with the origins and development of the Cold War, it is necessary to establish the most significant features of its nature. Most historians consider that the Cold War ended in either 1989 or 1991, so for most students it is a phenomenon that ended either just before or just after they were born. Some political commentators and historians saw the Cold War like a massive chess game, with major implications not just for those 'playing the game', but also for the rest of the world. Some people even believed the Cold War would lead to the destruction of the entire world. Certainly there were occasions on which nuclear weapons were deployed during the various crises that marked the different stages of the Cold War. Some of those involving US nuclear weapons are shown in Source A on page 14.

Outlining the main aspects of the nature of the Cold War is not straightforward, especially as historians do not always use the term in the same way. However, something most historians agree on is that, for much of the time, the Cold War presented itself as a regional and global contest between two rival states and their respective allies: the USA and the West v. the USSR and the East. How this rivalry varied over time, and the broader effects it had on different aspects of 20th-century life and history, will be examined in the following pages.

Key questions

- What is meant by the term 'Cold War'?
- What were the main phases of the Cold War?
- What were the main features of the Cold War?

Overview

- After the Second World War, a Cold War developed between what became known as the East and the West. This Cold War lasted until 1991. Historians, however, disagree over exactly when it started and the dates of its different phases.
- Historians also disagree over the essential nature of the Cold War, so there are many different explanations for the phenomenon.
- Part of the Cold War involved a contest between two superpowers – the USA and the USSR. However, not all historians see this as a contest between equals.
- There were many aspects to the Cold War, including a propaganda war based on the different ideologies of the two superpowers.
- The Cold War affected many aspects of politics and society in the countries involved, particularly the operation of the United Nations.
- Other features of the Cold War included: an arms race; cultural, scientific and sporting competition; spying and covert activities; and public fears about a Third World War.

Timeline

1917 **Nov:** Bolshevik Revolution in Russia

1918 **Jan:** US president Woodrow Wilson delivers his 'Fourteen Points' speech

1919 **Mar:** Comintern founded

1941 **Aug:** Atlantic Charter issued

1942 **Jan:** Declaration by United Nations agreed

1943 **Nov:** Tehran Conference

1945 **Apr:** UN established

 Aug: US drops A-bombs on Hiroshima and Nagasaki

1950 **Jun:** Start of Korean War

1955 **Apr:** Non-Aligned Movement (NAM) founded

1956 **Oct:** Suez Crisis

 Nov: Hungarian Uprising crushed

1960 **Jul:** Start of crisis in the Congo

1961 **Sep:** Belgrade Conference of NAM

1965 **Apr–Sep:** Kashmir dispute between India and Pakistan

1967 **Jun:** Arab–Israeli War

1971 **Oct:** Communist China recognised by US as official representative for China in UN

1973 **Oct:** Arab–Israeli War (Yom Kippur War)

1974 **Apr:** Revolution in Portugal

 Jul: Turkey invades Cyprus

1975 **Nov:** Civil war begins in Angola

1978 **Mar:** Israel invades Lebanon

1979 **Dec:** Soviet forces sent into Afghanistan

1980 **Jul–Aug:** Olympic Games in Moscow

1984 **Jul–Aug:** Olympic Games in Los Angeles

1989 **Apr–Dec:** Collapse of regimes in Eastern Europe

1991 **Dec:** End of the USSR and the Cold War

SOURCE A

Incidents in which US Strategic Nuclear Forces were involved, 1946–73.

Incident	Date
US aircraft shot down by Yugoslavia	November 1946
Inauguration of president in Uruguay	February 1947
Security of Berlin	January 1948
Security of Berlin	April 1948
Security of Berlin	June 1948
Korean War: security of Europe	July 1950
Security of Japan/South Korea	August 1953
Guatemala accepts Soviet bloc support	May 1954
China–Taiwan conflict: Tachen Islands	August 1954
Suez crisis	October 1956
Political crisis in Lebanon	July 1958
Political crisis in Jordan	July 1958
China–Taiwan conflict: Quemoy and Matsu	July 1958
Security of Berlin	May 1959
Security of Berlin	June 1961
Soviet emplacement of missiles in Cuba	October 1962
Withdrawal of US missiles from Turkey	April 1963
Pueblo seized by North Korea	January 1968
Arab–Israeli War	October 1973

Blechman, B. and Kaplan, S. 1978. Force Without War. Washington, DC, USA. The Brookings Institution. p. 48. Quoted in Halliday, F. 1989. The Making of the Second Cold War (2nd ed). London, UK. Verso. p. 50.

What is meant by the term 'Cold War'?

SOURCE B

The cold war was a period of intense antagonism between the two superpowers – the United States and the Soviet Union – lasting from 1945 to 1991. Because there was no direct armed conflict between the two continental giants the description 'cold war' remains an accurate one. Now that it is over, and we know the outcome, it is tempting to re-define this period of recent history as the 'long peace'.

Mason, J. 1996. The Cold War: 1945–1991, London, UK. Routledge. p. ix.

This quotation from John Mason's introduction seems to summarise the essence of the Cold War; however, it actually raises several more complicated issues. These include:

- definitions of the main characteristics of 'cold war'
- the actual starting date
- the meaning of the term 'superpower'.

Perhaps the most contentious point is the suggestion that the period 1945–91 can be seen as the 'long peace'. While this description may arguably be applied to Europe and North America, and to relations between the USA and the USSR, the inhabitants of many countries in Asia, the Americas and Africa might question the application of the word 'peace' to their experience of 20th-century Cold War history.

Interpretations of 'cold war'

The term 'cold war' had been used before 1945 to describe situations characterised by extreme international tension between states, but which avoided tipping over into 'hot wars' (those in which direct fighting took place).

After 1945 – and especially after 1947 – the term was quickly applied to the deteriorating relationship between the USSR and the USA/the West. In this context it is particularly associated with US journalist Walter Lippmann (see page 5).

When considered in relation to the events of the second half of the 20th century, the term 'cold war' has a dual meaning:

a 'cold' in the sense that relations between the main protagonists were paralysed or frozen, and so not friendly or 'warm'

b 'cold' in the sense that although relations were bad, they were not so bad as to have led to a full-blown 'hot' war in Europe. However, at different times this 'cold' war also involved very bloody 'hot' wars between the main players' allies in regions beyond Europe.

One problem faced by students studying the Cold War is that different historians mean slightly different things by the term. Some use it in a broad sense – referring to the tensions and conflict between the two camps throughout the whole post-war period from 1945 to 1991. Some even argue that the name 'Cold War' refers to the globalised or international social conflict between capitalism and communism that had existed since the Bolshevik Revolution of November 1917. This will be considered in Chapter 3.

Other historians apply the term only to particularly tense periods in the years following 1945. In this sense, the name 'Cold War' refers to phases that are halfway between the two extremes of all-out 'hot' war, and **détente** (periods of accommodation, co-operation and agreements).

Applying the name 'Cold War' to the *whole* period between 1945 and 1991 can give the false impression that relations between East and West during this time remained essentially the same. In fact, there were significant variations in East–West relations with regard to aspects such as threats of direct conflict between the main protagonists, 'hot' wars around the regions of the world, the arms race, and co-operation.

Fact
'Cold war' was a term first used by the 14th-century Spanish writer Don Juan Manuel, who distinguished between 'hot' and 'cold' wars when describing the conflict between Christendom and Islam. In 1893, the term was used by Eduard Bernstein, a German Marxist leader of the socialist SPD, to describe the arms race that was developing between the new state of Germany and its neighbours, Britain, France and Russia, during the late 19th century.

Question

What do you understand by the terms 'cold war' and 'superpower'?

détente This is a French word which means a lessening of tensions and an increase in co-operation. It is normally applied to the period 1969–79, although there were several other attempts between 1945 and 1991 to improve relations between East and West.

15

Consequently, this book will examine the history of the years 1945 to 1991 by dividing it into five periods, as follows:

1 1946–53 First Cold War
2 1954–68 Fluctuating Relations
3 1969–79 Détente
4 1979–85 Second Cold War
5 1985–91 The Final Stages

1985–91 Final Stages of the Cold War
A new period of co-operation, ending with the break-up of the Soviet Union.

1979–85 Second Cold War
Relations decline again over developments in the Developing World and nuclear weapons, although a stalemate is reached.

1969–79 Détente
A period in which the USA and USSR reach several agreements in an effort to avoid war.

1954–68 Fluctuating Relations
Relations between the two superpowers go through a period of antagonism and retreat.

1946–53 First Cold War
Disagreements between the USA and USSR over Germany and Eastern Europe and the developing nuclear arms race lead to growing tensions.

1941–45 Co-operation in the Second World War
The USA and the USSR work together to defeat Germany.

The main stages of the Cold War, 1941–91

What were the main phases of the Cold War?

As we will explore in Chapter 3, historians disagree about the origins of the Cold War. They also differ in their interpretation of the conflict's time-scale and the chronology of its different phases – not only when it began (suggested dates include 1917, 1944, 1945, 1946 and even 1948), but also when it ended. Some argue that it ended in 1989, with the collapse of the Eastern European states and the various international agreements. Others consider the date of its official ending to be 1991, when the USSR itself collapsed.

Most historians, however, accept that there was a First Cold War, which began sometime after the end of the Second World War and which ended at some point in the 1950s. Debate continues over whether there were a further one or two periods of the Cold War.

The important thing to grasp is that while there has been continuous underlying rivalry and conflict between two different economic and social systems since 1945 (or even 1917), there have been fluctuations throughout the period and the process, with periods of relaxation and improved relations – often referred to as a '**thaw**' or détente.

thaw This refers to a lessening of tensions in Cold War relations, compared to a previous period of hostility. It is particularly associated with the years 1953–55, immediately following Stalin's death.

Nature of the Cold War

Most historians would accept the summary of the essential nature of the 20th-century Cold War put forward by the US historian Anders Stephanson:

*   Both sides appeared to accept for most of the period that, ultimately, coexistence with the other political and social system was impossible, and so were determined to weaken each other by any means short of all-out war – including the establishment, training and arming of terrorist groups.
*   As a result of what was increasingly a bi-polar conflict – at least until the 1950s, when the emergence of Communist China made it a multi-polar one – there was an intense arms race between the USA and the USSR and its allies, involving both conventional and nuclear weapons.
*   As part of this 'cold' conflict, both sides suppressed or sought to control their internal dissidents (the 'enemy within'), and were often prepared to ally themselves with regimes and movements that conflicted strongly with their stated political ideology and beliefs.

Italian soldiers arrest communist activists during the strikes and demonstrations against the Marshall Plan in 1948

Question

How do you think this photograph relates to the West's claim to have a greater tolerance of political dissidents than that shown by the USSR?

17

Iron Curtain This is the term used to describe the boundary between capitalist Western Europe and communist Eastern Europe. Winston Churchill described this divide as extending from Stettin in the Baltic to Trieste in the Adriatic. As the Cold War intensified, the frontiers – especially in Germany – became physical and visible to both sides.

However, according to historians such as Fred Halliday, the Cold War periods proper had some additional aspects. Halliday identified six main features:

1 conventional and especially nuclear weapons build-up and arms race
2 intense propaganda, including the suppression of accurate or balanced information in both competing states; in particular, the West tried to depict the USSR as a 'totalitarian' equivalent of Nazi Germany, while the USSR painted capitalism as an inherently warmongering system
3 no common ground or successful negotiations, and a deep division between the two camps across the '**Iron Curtain**'
4 conflict between capitalism and communism, which often spilled over into the 'Third World'
5 tightening of controls and repression of dissidents in both camps
6 East–West conflict was paramount.

Détente

Détente can be seen as having seven main features:

1 a retreat from the all-out arms race
2 repeated public calls for peace
3 a pursuit of agreed levels of armament – although no substantial disarmament occurred, some limits were set on the arms race
4 a greater tolerance of the other social order, and more interest in and accurate information about its character
5 agreements on the Developing World and Europe – achieved by summits, long-running conferences and visits by heads of state, all in marked contrast to the paralysis of the frozen hostility of the Cold War

Question

Does this map suggest that the security fears of the USSR in the decade following the end of the Second World War were justified?

This map shows the alliances of the USA and the USSR in the 1950s; at this time, the USSR felt 'surrounded' by Western allies

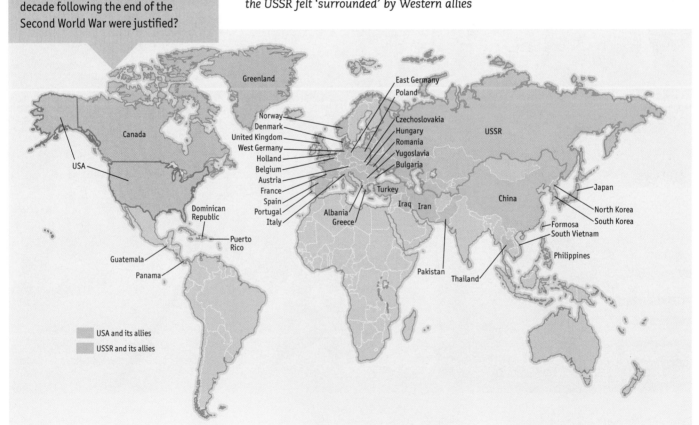

6 attempts by the West in particular to extricate itself from Developing World confrontations, and to attempt to draw a line in the face of the revolutionary forces it had been combating
7 looser emigration controls in the Eastern bloc in the early 1970s, following on from the internal 'thaw' that started in Russia following the death of Stalin.

Overall, during such periods of détente, there were attempts by both sides to separate the various international tensions that had periodically been bound together by the long-standing conflict between the rival social systems of East and West.

The rival 'camps'

As we have seen, the most obvious signs of the Cold War proper were the division of Europe by the Iron Curtain between East and West, an ideological contest, and an arms race which at times seemed to threaten nuclear annihilation. This was accompanied by the emergence of two hostile political and military alliances – the West's **NATO** (1949) and the East's **Warsaw Pact** (1955).

		NATO	Warsaw Pact
Armed forces		8 million	7.7 million
Tanks		16,000	38,000
Bombers		2260	1600
Submarines		292 (incl. 32 nuclear)	507 (incl. 12 nuclear)
Cruisers		66 (1107 escorts)	30 (189 escorts)
Battleships and aircraft carriers		76	0
Intercontinental ballistic missiles		450	76
Medium-range ballistic missiles		250	700

The relative strengths of the two military alliances in 1963

> **Question**
>
> What were the main features of the periods during the Cold War known as the 'thaw' and 'détente'?

> **NATO** This is the military alliance organised by the West in response to the perceived threat from the Soviet Union, following its takeover of Eastern Europe and the Berlin Crisis of 1948–49. Initially, the Western European states had formed the Brussels Treaty Organisation in 1948, but this became the North Atlantic Treaty Organisation (NATO) when the USA joined and assumed leadership in January 1949.
>
> **Warsaw Pact** This was the defensive military alliance formed six years after the formation of NATO. Technically known as the Warsaw Treaty Organisation (WTO), it was established shortly after West Germany was allowed to join NATO and rearm in May 1955. This alarmed the USSR, prompting an alliance with its satellite states in Eastern Europe.

19

Third World This term was at first used to describe those countries in the Americas, Asia and Africa that were economically un- or under-developed. The First World was made up of economically advanced capitalist states in the West (Europe and the USA), while the Second World encompassed those states (mainly European) in the communist bloc. More recently, the term 'Developing World' has replaced the use of 'Third World'.

Question

Look at the map on page 18 again and compare it to the map here. Why might the US have been concerned about some of the developments shown by these sources?

As the Cold War developed, the 'conflict' widened, drawing in many other countries. Both sides were keen to establish alliances, although the USA was really the only superpower able to construct a truly global network. As we will examine later, several historians thus see the Cold War as essentially an unequal contest from its very beginning.

Direct 'hot war' between the two superpowers was avoided, but there were many international crises during the Cold War, and several vicious 'hot wars' involving the allies, or 'client states', of the rival superpowers in the so-called **Third World**.

The Cold War also had an impact on various international institutions, especially the United Nations.

This map shows some of the Cold War conflicts and interventions in the Developing World, 1952–89

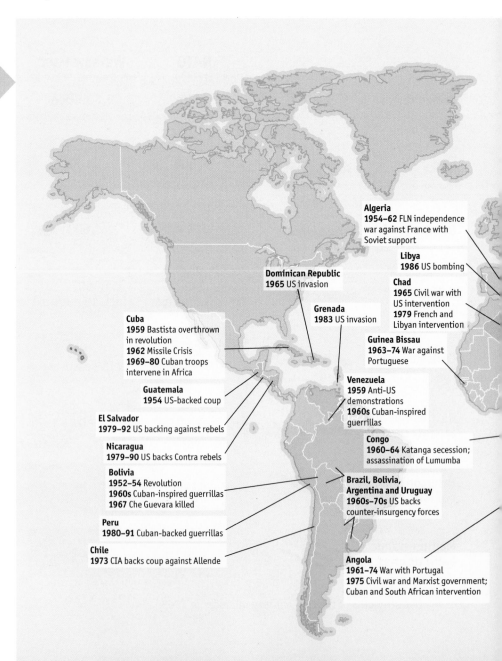

Algeria
1954–62 FLN independence war against France with Soviet support

Libya
1986 US bombing

Dominican Republic
1965 US invasion

Chad
1965 Civil war with US intervention
1979 French and Libyan intervention

Grenada
1983 US invasion

Cuba
1959 Bastista overthrown in revolution
1962 Missile Crisis
1969–80 Cuban troops intervene in Africa

Guinea Bissau
1963–74 War against Portuguese

Venezuela
1959 Anti-US demonstrations
1960s Cuban-inspired guerrillas

Guatemala
1954 US-backed coup

El Salvador
1979–92 US backing against rebels

Congo
1960–64 Katanga secession; assassination of Lumumba

Nicaragua
1979–90 US backs Contra rebels

Bolivia
1952–54 Revolution
1960s Cuban-inspired guerrillas
1967 Che Guevara killed

Brazil, Bolivia, Argentina and Uruguay
1960s–70s US backs counter-insurgency forces

Peru
1980–91 Cuban-backed guerrillas

Chile
1973 CIA backs coup against Allende

Angola
1961–74 War with Portugal
1975 Civil war and Marxist government; Cuban and South African intervention

SOURCE C

Ever since World War II, when America assumed a leadership position in the capitalist world, nuclear weapons have been seen as the symbol and effective guarantee of that role, as the bastions of US security in the conflict with the USSR. ... US security throughout the 1950s and 1960s rested upon a real superiority. ...

US government officials [in the 1980s] deny they are pursuing military superiority. Instead the talk is of 'modernisation' ... of 'restoring the balance' when the word 'balance' refers to a previous *imbalance* in the USA's favour.

Halliday, F. 1989. The Making of the Second Cold War, London, UK. Verso. p. 48.

Direct 'hot war' between the superpowers was avoided, but there were many international crises, and several vicious 'hot wars' involving allies, or 'client states', of the rival superpowers in the so-called Third World.

21

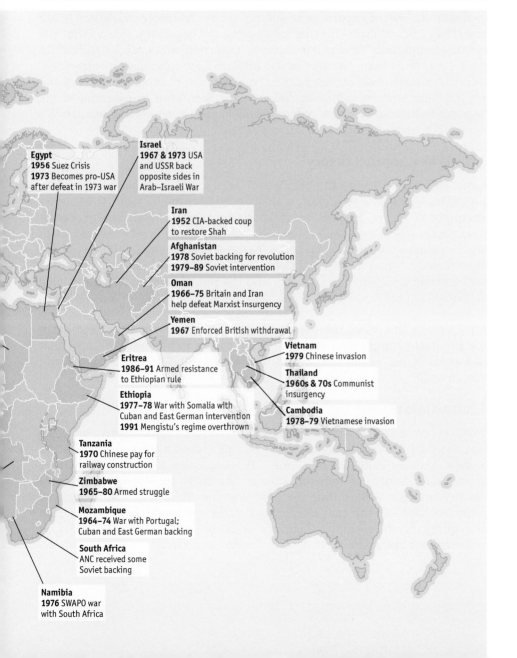

Egypt
1956 Suez Crisis
1973 Becomes pro-USA after defeat in 1973 war

Israel
1967 & 1973 USA and USSR back opposite sides in Arab–Israeli War

Iran
1952 CIA-backed coup to restore Shah

Afghanistan
1978 Soviet backing for revolution
1979–89 Soviet intervention

Oman
1966–75 Britain and Iran help defeat Marxist insurgency

Yemen
1967 Enforced British withdrawal

Eritrea
1986–91 Armed resistance to Ethiopian rule

Ethiopia
1977–78 War with Somalia with Cuban and East German intervention
1991 Mengistu's regime overthrown

Vietnam
1979 Chinese invasion

Thailand
1960s & 70s Communist insurgency

Cambodia
1978–79 Vietnamese invasion

Tanzania
1970 Chinese pay for railway construction

Zimbabwe
1965–80 Armed struggle

Mozambique
1964–74 War with Portugal; Cuban and East German backing

South Africa
ANC received some Soviet backing

Namibia
1976 SWAPO war with South Africa

communism A social and economic system which, according to Marx and Engels, should be based on the ownership, control and self-management of all major parts of an economy (land, industries, banks) by the whole of society, not just the wealthy capitalist classes. This classless society would be preceded by a socialist stage of development in which, for the first time since early human history, the ruling class would be the majority (i.e. working) class.

capitalism A social and economic system based on the private ownership of all major parts of an economy by a dominant or ruling minority class of individuals, families, companies and/or wealthy shareholders, who make all the important decisions concerning investment, production and employment. The state and society as a whole has no or very little say over such issues. Often also called a market or a free enterprise economy.

Military-Industrial Complex
This refers to the top US military leaders (the Pentagon) and large US armaments companies. Some people, including Eisenhower, expressed concern that the M-I-C worked together to persuade US presidents that increased defence expenditure was vital to respond to the Soviet 'threat' when, in fact, it was not.

Fact
Halliday suggests that the Second Cold War stemmed from the economic dominance of capitalist firms in California and those associated with the defence industry. He also links it with the rise of Christian fundamentalism and the New Right in the USA.

What were the main features of the Cold War?

The main theories

Historians have developed at least three major interpretations concerning the reasons for the Cold War. Not surprisingly, there are also multiple – often conflicting – assessments of its nature. The eight main theories are explained below.

1 The Russian menace

Many have seen the Cold War as essentially a series of crises and conflicts resulting from Russian expansionism and Soviet **communism**, which the 'free' West struggled to contain. Hence the actions taken by the US and its allies were merely defensive measures against the threat of Soviet tyranny.

2 US imperialism

Others have taken the opposite viewpoint. Instead of Moscow being the heart of an 'evil empire', the threat came from Washington, which was attempting to spread the evil of expansionist and predatory monopoly **capitalism** – and essentially US capitalism – in order to achieve global hegemony. This was not just over the 'communist' enemy, but also over its Western allies. Most significantly, the US was more than prepared to use military force to achieve its objectives, whether through invasion, the backing or instigation of coups, or training and arming 'terrorists'. In fact, such actions have been seen as essential to the **'Military-Industrial Complex'**, which is said to need enemies and war in order to maintain high profitability in late capitalism.

3 West–West conflict theory

Some historians consider the Cold War to be a much more complex conflict, suggesting that it was essentially a smokescreen for the US while the country attempted to secure domination of the Western world. By placing the Soviet Union in the role of 'evil empire', the US sought to control developments both in Western Europe and in Japan and other parts of Asia. Arguably, this can be seen most notably during the Second Cold War (1979–85), a period that coincided with economic problems in the West and the rise of independent nationalist movements in the Developing World.

According to this view, the events of the Cold War were an extension of the inevitable competition and conflicts between rich capitalist states that had certainly led to the First World War, and possibly to the Second World War as well.

4 Intra-state theory

This theory, closely related to the West–West conflict theory, suggests that the Cold War was essentially the playing out on an international stage of developments in the internal domestic economies and social formations of the most important individual states. As such, the foreign policies of the USA and the USSR during the Cold War should be seen as attempts by politicians and – in the case of capitalist states – of groups of companies, to use international events as opportunities to resolve internal tensions and overcome competitors.

5 Class-conflict theory

Although similar to the West–West and intra-state theories, the class-conflict theory is much more clearly based on Marxist analysis and the centrality awarded to national and international class struggle. Hence the Cold War and the tensions between the superpowers should be seen as a result of the historic conflict between capitalism and communism. Adherents of this theory see the Cold War as both the result of these tensions and a cover or excuse to intervene militarily in areas considered important. Such US interventions during the Cold War could be 'sold' to the general public in the West as merely defensive responses to deliberate attempts by Moscow to spread its 'evil empire' and pernicious ideology, even when evidence suggested the USSR had played no role in them.

6 Superpower theory

Another interpretation of the Cold War is linked to the emergence of superpowers after 1945, and sees the essential nature of the Cold War as the attempt by two superpowers not to vanquish each other, but to carve up the world between themselves. This view is associated in particular with Mao and Communist China, and supporters of their version of Marxism–Leninism. Developed in the 1960s, this theory had an important impact on the Cold War. The rise of Communist China, and especially its dispute with the USSR in the 1960s, created a multi-polar aspect to the Cold War, and eventually saw both the USA and the USSR trying to gain China's support in their struggles and rivalries.

During the Second World War, the term 'superpower' was first used to describe the three major members of the Grand Alliance. However, the USA was in a league of its own, and by 1945 it was clearly the most powerful state that the world had ever seen. Many commentators, and later historians, began to use the term 'global superpower' to describe the USA and USSR in the period after 1945. However, it is debatable whether both these states can really be seen as *global* superpowers. Although the USSR was clearly a *regional* superpower, given the relative decline and weakness of other European states, it was really only the USA that could be termed a truly global superpower.

The USA

During the Second World War, the US economy had grown tremendously. By 1945, its productive capacity was greater than that of all other states combined. The US economy was also strong enough to intervene in the war-shattered economies of Europe, both to alleviate the problems these states were facing, and to improve the trading position of US companies and the economic strength of the US as a whole.

By 1945, the USA had the world's most powerful air force and navy. It also had a growing network of military bases across the world. Though its army was much smaller than that of the Soviet Union, between 1945 and 1949 it was the only state to own nuclear weapons.

The USSR

Despite the economic growth of the USSR during the 1930s, the country had been set back dramatically during the Nazi invasion and occupation. In many areas, it was necessary to begin again. Economically, the USSR was no match for the USA in 1945 – in particular, the efficiency and productivity of its factories were much lower.

Fact
As an example of the multi-polar nature of the Cold War, in the 1970s the USA under Nixon was able to achieve rapprochement with Beijing, putting pressure on the USSR, which then had to secure its borders against an erstwhile ally. As a consequence, the USSR was more willing to consider deals with the USA to lessen tensions in Europe and around the world.

Fact
Given its stronger economy, its much greater wealth and productive capacity, the USA was determined to ensure that pre-war tariff systems and trade blocs were replaced by 'liberal' or 'open' free-trade conditions. Under such conditions, the mechanics of a world capitalist market economy would operate to the advantage of the most efficient companies – most of which were based in the USA.

23

Fact
The Soviet Red Army had liberated most of its Eastern European neighbours from Nazi occupation, and was now based in these countries. This gave the USSR clear military domination in a very unstable area.

Karl Marx (1818–83) Marx was a German philosopher and historian who developed the materialist concept of history, arguing that class struggle and conflict were the most important factors behind social and economic – as well as intellectual and political – change. Along with his close collaborator Friedrich Engels (1820–95), he wrote *The Communist Manifesto* in 1848, which urged the industrial working classes in developed capitalist states to bring about revolution in order to achieve a socialist and then a classless communist society, based on greater freedom and abundance. His ideas inspired many revolutionaries, including Lenin and Trotsky.

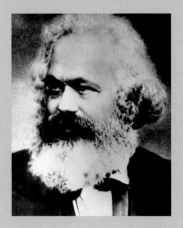

In order to defeat the Nazi invaders, Stalin had built up the world's largest land army. However, this was less well trained than the armies of the West. Also, the USSR had suffered approximately 30 million deaths during the war, and was exhausted.

Finally, the USSR did not develop nuclear weapons until 1949 – four years after the USA had deployed its first nuclear device. For most of the Cold War, the USSR's nuclear technology trailed that of the USA.

7 Arms race

Other Cold War historians have seen it as essentially driven by a new factor that emerged only in 1945 – nuclear weapons. They take the view that the Cold War was dominated by attempts by both superpowers to stop and even reverse the arms race as an issue of paramount importance to the survival of the human race. At times, the 'logic' of nuclear 'defence' seemed beyond the control of political leaders, and both sides carried different degrees of responsibility for escalating the nuclear arms race at different times.

8 North–South divide

The last major theory put forward by some historians focuses on developments in, and the growing importance of, what was for many years called the Third World. This theory suggests that the history of the period after 1945 was mainly a series of conflicts between powerful states such as the USA and the USSR over the control of weaker countries, which were of economic or strategic importance to them – or as a way of weakening their superpower rival. The issue was complicated by indigenous or local political movements in the Third World, which were intent on taking control themselves. These groups were often prepared to oppose superpowers, or to use them for their own ends.

Clash of ideologies – myths and realities

Having examined some of the main historical and political theories about the nature of the Cold War, we will now look at some of its practical manifestations in the period 1945 to 1991.

An important aspect of the underlying nature of the Cold War was that it was a war of ideology and propaganda, with each side or camp making its proclamations in an uncompromising and absolutist way. On the basis of analyses made by **Karl Marx** and **Vladimir Ilyich Lenin**, the Soviet Union believed that the development of capitalist competition invariably led to periodic economic crises and, as a consequence, to regional and global wars. It thus saw victorious worldwide communist or socialist revolutions as the only hope for world peace and adequate living standards for all.

The USA, on the other hand, believed that capitalism, a market economy and individual political rights would secure good living standards for all, and that the only way to achieve world peace was to contain and eventually 'roll back' communism wherever it existed. In this area alone, then, their respective and conflicting ideologies seemed to lead the two powers down a road to inevitable collision.

There were thus several similarities as well as significant differences between these two social systems. In reality, during the 1920s and 1930s – and after 1945 – there were many variations of these 'ideals'. This was true of both camps.

The ideals of capitalism and communism

Ideals of capitalism

One important belief of capitalism is that the main businesses should be privately owned and run by individuals, families or companies, and not be restricted by the state – the free competition of a market economy is the most efficient way to run an economy. The wealth created by companies and wealthy individuals will lead to new jobs and will 'trickle down' to benefit the poorer sections of society.

Supporters of capitalism believe in a liberal parliamentary system, based on indirect democracy or representation, and that individuals should also have political rights, such as free speech, freedom of the press, information, assembly and religion, and the right to protest peacefully.

Ideals of communism

An important communist ideal is the creation of a classless society, based on abundance, which would mean that all have equal chances and opportunities. To achieve this, the most important parts of the economy should be socially owned and controlled (by either the state, local councils or co-operatives), with self-management by employees.

Politics should be wider and more democratic than the capitalist parliamentary system, and be based on a multi-party system with regular elections and **direct democracy**. Organised religions should be tolerated, but their involvement in education and people's lives should be controlled, and the state should actively encourage atheism.

Realities of capitalism

After 1945, many of the ideals of capitalism were met to a greater or lesser extent in most states in the Developed World. However, this was not usually the case in those Developing World countries that had capitalist or market economies. In the latter, there was extensive poverty, disease and even periodic starvation. At times, even much-needed education and health programmes were reduced at the insistence of capitalist banks based in developed capitalist states.

Many Developing World capitalist states were also either dictatorships, with no individual rights (torture of opponents was not unknown), or were corrupt political systems with power in the hands of powerful élites or families. In such states, elections were of little significance.

Furthermore, even in developed capitalist countries during the 1920s and 1930s, governments actively intervened on the side of the employers during industrial disputes, often using the police or the army to defeat strikes. In several capitalist countries – notably Italy and Germany – major capitalist banks, companies and even political parties actively supported the rise and rule of fascist dictatorships, as a way of protecting their financial interests during economic crises (such as the Great Depression) and against increasingly radical workers' trade union and political movements.

Realities of communism

In the Soviet Union, a one-party system had been established as early as 1921, even though this was acknowledged to be a temporary departure from Marxist principles. While there is still fierce historical debate about whether Lenin eventually intended to restore the Soviet multi-party democracy that had existed for several years after the Revolution – between 1917 and 1921 – once Stalin was in control, all other political parties were banned. Only the Communist Party was allowed to exist, and the USSR became a one-party dictatorship in both theory and practice, with Stalin's form of Marxism–Leninism justifying such a system.

direct democracy The right of voters to recall, between elections, any elected official who is felt have broken their promises.

Vladimir Ilyich Lenin (1870–1924) Lenin's real name was Vladimir Ilyich Ulyanov. He joined the Russian Social Democratic Labour Party, a Marxist party, in 1898. He provoked a split in the RSDLP in 1903, and formed the Bolshevik faction. Exiled from Russia until April 1917, he returned and, in November that year, pushed for the Bolsheviks to overthrow the provisional government.

> **Fact**
> While significant steps were taken to provide real improvements in the provision of education, health care and housing, the top leadership enjoyed special perks and privileges, as well as access to luxury goods not available to the bulk of society.

In fact, the Communist Party as a whole was not influential, coming as it did under the control of a small minority at the top of the party. During Stalin's leadership, the party was, in practice, under his control alone.

Moreover, despite the ideals of early communists, industries in the USSR were state-owned and run by bureaucrats, with the citizens and workers having no real say over investment, work rates or priorities. In addition, élite political and economic managers in the USSR had established a range of economic privileges for themselves which were not available to the rest of Soviet society.

Communism and capitalism – similarities and differences

So by 1945 there were marked differences between the ideals and realities of both these ideologies. In addition, both systems accepted that violence was justified at times. Communism embraced the need for revolution, arguing that everyday capitalist inequality resulted in the early and preventable deaths – as well as wasted abilities – of thousands of people across the world. For this reason, the USSR sometimes offered support to revolutionary political movements in the Developing World.

Supporters of capitalism also believed violence was needed, in order to protect societies from revolutions that would result in the confiscation of the wealth and property of rich capitalists. Consequently, the US and the West often intervened in social conflicts around the globe to resist or destroy revolutionary movements – even if this meant giving support to, or installing, undemocratic and even vicious dictatorships.

SOURCE D

The idea of communism was simple and noble – the creation of a society based on the principle of 'from each according to his ability, to each according to his need' rather than a [capitalist] system based on greed and profit ... the vision of society adumbrated by the founders of communism was a far cry from what became known as 'actually existing socialism' as it was in the Soviet Union (1917–91) and China (1949–89). ... Engels has always stressed that a workers' movement and its victory was inconceivable without freedom of the press and assembly. It is, he insisted, 'the air it needs to breathe'.

Ali, T. 2009. The Idea of Communism. *London, UK. Verso. Inside front cover.*

By 1945, the Western allies – who had joined with the Soviet Union in destroying the pre-war fascist regimes – tried hard to emphasise to their citizens, and the rest of the world, the contrasts between the ideals of Western capitalism and communism. However, in point of fact, they tended to ignore the wider global realities of their own system, and to equate the practices of Stalinist 'Marxist–Leninist communism' with the ideals and practices of communism proper.

Meanwhile, in the USSR, the state ignored the real achievements and benefits of capitalism in the West, and instead told its citizens of the sufferings of the workers in capitalist states. It claimed that its own practices were in accordance with the early ideals of Marx. By 1940, Stalin had executed most of the original 'Old Guard' Bolsheviks who could have challenged this, so it was difficult for Marxist dissidents to make their case.

By 1945, the gap between political practices in the West and those in Stalin's Russia was widely visible. Not surprisingly, the realities surrounding these different systems and their ideals were much affected – and complicated – by the start and development of the Cold War. For instance, although Western governments were aware, often through their intelligence services, of the genuine liberalisations taking place in the USSR after Stalin's death in 1953, and especially after Nikita Khrushchev's reforms post-1956, it often suited their purposes to speak and act as if the USSR was still run in the same way it had been under Stalin.

SOURCE E

The tendency to perpetuate 'Stalinism' by backdating it to 1917 and extending it to the end of the Soviet Union, pertains to those 'uses and abuses' of history of which there are many examples.

In this respect, mention should be made of the *Historikerstreit* (the 'historians' controversy) set off by conservative German historians … counting on Western connivance encouraged by the Cold War. They wished us to believe that Hitler's madness could somehow be attributed to Stalin. … The anti-communist indoctrination characteristic of the Cold War permitted this kind of ideological manoeuvre in the West.

Lewin, M. 2005. The Soviet Century. London, UK. Verso. pp. 4–5.

The Cold War and the United Nations

Another aspect of how the Cold War played out in the period 1945–91 is evident in the way in which it affected the operations of the United Nations. During the Cold War, both the main superpowers used their place on the UN Security Council, and their allies in the General Assembly, to block decisions they didn't like, and to protect their allies – even if their allies were in the wrong.

The United Nations had been agreed in the **Atlantic Charter** of 1941 – mainly advocated by Franklin D. Roosevelt of the USA and Winston Churchill of Britain – and was set up after the Second World War to replace the League of Nations, which was seen as being partly responsible for the failure to prevent the outbreak of war in 1939. In 1945, the Allies seemed willing to co-operate with each other to achieve stability, peace and security throughout the world. By establishing the UN, this stability was intended to be achieved through collective security, with peacekeeping to be carried out with the approval of UN member states. Like the League of Nations, the UN had no independent military force.

Fact
Ignoring the genuine liberalisations after the death of Stalin was also the stance taken by the well-known Soviet writer and dissident Alexander Solzhenitsyn. When his book *The Gulag Archipelago* was published, he made no mention of the fact that, following Stalin's death, the Gulag he had known and suffered no longer existed. Instead, he preferred to act and speak as if Stalin's Russia continued to operate in the post-Stalinist years. Such writings were eagerly used by governments in the West during the 1960s and 1970s to justify, to their citizens and the world in general, their opposition to the 'evil empire'.

Atlantic Charter The agreement signed by Roosevelt and Churchill in August 1941, prior to US entry into the Second World War, setting out their aims for the post-war world, and in particular their desire for a more popular and effective organisation to replace the League of Nations. The new organisation – which eventually became the UN – was to defend self-determination for nations and to work towards world peace. In January 1942 this was confirmed by the signing of the United Nations Declaration. In August 1944, a conference at Dumbarton Woods in the USA agreed the structure of the UN.

The UN Charter gave permanent seats on its Security Council to the USA, the USSR, Britain, China and, later, France, but each member of the Security Council could veto the decisions of this body. In the event of a veto, the matter passed to the General Assembly. In reality, the US and the USSR tended to dominate the Security Council, as they were the two most powerful states. With these two states – increasingly at odds with each other after 1945 – on the Security Council, it soon became clear that the UN would find it hard to follow an independent and neutral line in any crises that seemed to threaten peace and security.

As the US and the USSR adopted policies in their respective 'spheres of influence' in Western and Eastern Europe, the UN was sidelined. For example, it was powerless to intervene during the Berlin Blockade and Airlift of 1948–49 (see pages 81–82). One historian, David J. Whittaker, summed up the position of the new UN with these words: 'Europe's collective security relied on the superpowers pulling back from the brink, without any prospect of UN intervention.'

A whole range of different conflicts that the UN attempted to solve via mediation – in order to avoid being completely irrelevant – thus in turn influenced and were influenced by the events and development of the Cold War. By 1950, the USSR increasingly saw the UN as a tool for Western capitalism, evidenced by its refusal to recognise the new communist government of China in 1949. Meanwhile, as early as 1948, US president Harry S. Truman had described the UN as 'a God-given tool' to resist the actions of the USSR and to protect US interests.

Of the many conflicts or crises that involved and affected the UN during the Cold War, a good example is provided by events in the Congo from 1960 to 1964.

The Congo, 1960–64

In 1960, Belgium unexpectedly ended its colonial rule of the Congo, leaving the newly independent country and government totally unprepared for self-rule. Within weeks, the new country's army – the Armée Nationale Congolaise (ANC) – mutinied against the government, headed by the president, Joseph Kasavubu, and the prime minister, **Patrice Lumumba**.

As there was still a large expatriate Belgian community in the Congo, the Belgians sent in their own troops. At the same time – and with encouragement from Belgium, Britain and France – the leader of another political party, CONAKAT, Moise Tshombe, declared the mineral-rich province of Katanga to be independent. The new Congolese government then appealed to the UN for help.

At first, this African crisis did not seem to affect the interests of the two superpowers. When Lumumba approached both the USA and the USSR for help, they referred him to the UN. Despite Britain and France abstaining, the Security Council agreed to send in a UN force – the Opération des Nations Unies au Congo (ONUC).

When this force failed to take serious action against the ANC and the breakaway province of Katanga, Lumumba became convinced that the UN was not prepared to challenge the interests of European imperialist powers. As a result, he appealed again to the Soviet Union for assistance, and received some military equipment from them. He also began to make anti-Western statements. He was dismissed as prime minister by President Kasavubu. At the same time, the UN closed all the country's airports and the main radio station. This caused great difficulties for Lumumba, but helped the various rebel

Patrice Lumumba (1925–61)
Lumumba wanted the Congo to be independent and, in 1958, founded the non-tribal National Congolese Movement (MNC), which campaigned for independence from Belgium. After Belgium suddenly announced its decision to pull out, Lumumba became the Congo's first democratically elected prime minister. He favoured a non-aligned foreign policy, and wanted to address problems of poverty, health and education. This worried the US, and the CIA began to consider various options. Lumumba was brutally murdered on 17 January 1961, following a vicious civil war.

groups. In the UN, the Soviet Union denounced the ONUC as a tool of Western imperialism. In September 1960, Soviet leader Nikita Khrushchev made a strong speech attacking both the UN and its secretary-general.

In mid-September, the ANC carried out a coup and, with Kasavubu's support, expelled all Soviet and Eastern bloc diplomats – an event which only strengthened Soviet fears about Western plots. At first Lumumba sought protection from the UN but, when the UN General Assembly (with Western encouragement) seemed indirectly to acknowledge the new military Congolese government, Lumumba left the UN compound.

What happened next was the subject of intense speculation for many years. However, research in Belgian archives by the Belgian historian Ludo de Witte, as well as recently released CIA documents, show that Lumumba – who had already been the subject of an unsuccessful CIA plot to assassinate him with a tube of poisoned toothpaste – was quickly captured by ANC troops. ONUC refused his appeal for assistance, on direct orders from the UN headquarters in New York.

Fact
Even the British secret service had decided that killing Lumumba was the best 'solution' to the crisis in the Congo.

Instead, Lumumba was publicly humiliated and beaten in front of international journalists and TV cameras, before being handed over to the forces in Katanga. There he was murdered, with the direct involvement of Belgian officers and CIA agents, acting on instructions approved by US president Dwight D. Eisenhower himself, who saw Lumumba as a potential Soviet puppet.

Former Congolese prime minister Patrice Lumumba is captured in December 1960

Fact
The UN tried for some time to bring about a unified Congo, but its actions against the province of Katanga were often limited and unsuccessful. By then, the emergence of the Non-Aligned Movement began to pressure the UN to take tougher action. Eventually, the ONUC forces took control of Katanga, and the Congo was unified once more. In 1964, ONUC forces were withdrawn.

Marshal Tito (1892–1980)
Tito's real name was Josip Broz. He became a leading member of the Yugoslav Communist Party after the First World War and, during the Second World War, he organised partisan resistance against the Axis forces. In 1945, he ignored Stalin's instructions to form a coalition government with non-communist parties and instead established a communist government. His continued differences with Stalin eventually led to Yugoslavia's expulsion from the communist bloc in 1948. From then on, Tito followed a policy of non-alignment. He continued to rule Yugoslavia until his death in 1980.

The crisis in the Congo continued, but after Lumumba's murder the UN was no longer particularly divided about it along Cold War lines. By 1961, both superpowers favoured a unified Congo.

In general, during the 1960s, the UN was able to operate as peacekeeper in areas that were not of vital interest to either of the two superpowers. However, where this was not the case, Cold War divisions often meant that the UN could play no effective part. For example, the UN was not involved in either the Cuban Missile Crisis of 1962, or the growing military conflicts in Vietnam and other states in Indochina.

Throughout the Second Cold War (1979–85), UN influence declined even further. No agreements on peacekeeping missions could be made within the Security Council, as the two superpowers adopted strongly antagonistic Cold War attitudes.

The Non-Aligned Movement and the Developing World

The role of the UN and the actions of the two superpowers were also affected by the emergence of what became known as the Non-Aligned Movement. This was an attempt by various small Developing World states – mostly in Asia and Africa – to remain neutral as the two superpowers began forming alliances.

During the 1950s and 1960s, many former European colonies in Africa and Asia achieved independence, sometimes after wars of liberation against the colonial powers. It was from among these states, struggling with the effects of decolonisation and trying to resist new forms of imperialism, that many members of the Non-Aligned Movement were drawn. Although their anti-imperialist stance was directed against the former European colonial powers at first, the USA's association with these states often meant that anti-imperialism took on a strong anti-American flavour. Despite the fact that the US had mainly opposed the pre-war colonialism and empires of European states such as Britain and France, the US was often seen as following a more modern informal version of colonialism – that of economic imperialism, often known as 'neo-colonialism' or 'dollar imperialism'. This was true especially of the 1950s and 1960s, when the US was trying to create a global pattern of 'spheres of influence' in order to protect its economic and security interests.

The idea of the Non-Aligned Movement was first put forward by **Marshal Tito**, the ruler of communist Yugoslavia, who was resisting pressure from Stalinist Russia. Instead, he tried to avoid allying with either of the two superpowers. In 1954, the Indian prime minister, Jawaharlal Nehru, used the term 'non-aligned' in a speech about Sino–Indian relations. Another of its early leaders was Gamal Abdul Nasser, who became leader of Egypt in 1954. He followed a strongly nationalist and anti-colonial policy, directed towards removing all European influence from Egypt and the rest of the Middle East and North Africa.

The creation of NATO by the US and the West in 1949, and then the formation of the Warsaw Pact by the USSR in 1955, led to a meeting of those states wishing to remain neutral at the Bandung Conference in Indonesia in 1955. Twenty-nine mainly Asian and African countries were represented at this conference. In 1961, at the Belgrade Conference in Yugoslavia, they decided to formally establish the Non-Aligned Movement. Their aims were to resist colonialism and imperialism in all its forms, and to develop Afro–Asian co-operation in order to achieve economic growth. They were also willing to follow Tito's lead on the need to resist the increasing nuclear arms race between the two superpowers.

The members of the Non-Aligned Movement hoped their neutrality would enable them to gain advantages by playing off one superpower against the other.

The establishment of the NAM meant that the UN General Assembly now contained a sizeable group of states prepared to resist the power politics of the USA, the USSR and the former European colonial powers. By the mid 1960s, the number of NAM nations within the UN had grown to 115. This removed a source of power from the USA, while at the same time making the USSR less suspicious of the UN, which it felt had often acted as a rubber-stamp for US foreign-policy objectives. The original NAM group was joined in 1964 by the **Group of 77**, which also tried to influence decisions in the UN.

However, the unity of the NAM began to dissolve. The first sign of this was the Sino–Indian border war of 1962, in which two important NAM members fought each other. From the late 1960s, many leading figures in the NAM either died or were removed from power, while Cuba's membership clearly raised issues of neutrality. Developments – especially in Africa – saw several states beginning to move closer to the Soviet camp. In part this was a result of the USA's policy of containment, which meant it did not want to support the NAM for fear its anti-colonial stance would alienate key Western allies such as Britain. At the same time, the USSR was willing to give economic assistance to radical regimes, while the US increasingly would only give aid to those states that were strongly anti-communist.

In 1979, at the NAM Conference in Havana, Cuba, Fidel Castro, then the chair of NAM, suggested that, for all nationalists, a 'natural alliance' with the USSR made sense. Initially this gained some support, but after Soviet troops were sent into Afghanistan in December of that year, the NAM began to split; many Muslim countries were particularly angered by this Soviet action. During the Second Cold War, the NAM thus began to lose influence; although membership continued to grow, the focus was increasingly on economic rather than political issues.

Aid

The superpowers also vied with each other in trying to help poorer countries by giving them financial and technical aid. The main aim of this was to increase their respective spheres of influence by widening their rival global networks of potential allies, and securing bases in strategically important areas of the world. The USA started from an initial advantage in 1945, as the USSR had no allies at all until it began to establish control over Eastern Europe. However, the victory of the communists in China in 1949 gave the USSR – for a time at least – an ally outside Europe. Under Khrushchev, the Soviet Union began to offer money, technicians, equipment and loans. However, as with the arms and space races (see pages 33–38), such measures were very costly and added to the burdens already being placed on the fragile Soviet economy. Once again, the USSR found it was unable to compete with the much wealthier USA.

Cultural and sporting competition

Apart from international crises, another aspect of the nature of the Cold War was an almost constant competition between the two main superpowers to be the best in cultural and sporting matters. For instance, the CIA funded certain artistic movements so that the freedom of artists in the West could be contrasted to the more restricted and old-fashioned representational art fostered by the Soviet state.

Fact
Inspired by Yugoslavia's successful resistance to Soviet pressure and neutral stance, countries such as India and China were encouraged in the 1960s to avoid being drawn into the bi-polar international relations created by the Cold War. For India in particular, the NAM was a way of countering US support for Pakistan (which was strongly anti-communist), without having to join the USSR in any firm alliance.

Group of 77 Set up on 15 June 1964, this was a loose coalition of developing nations. It was formed after differences within the NAM (including the Sino–Indian War), as some felt that the NAM was moving too close to a pro-Soviet–anti-US stance.

31

Question

What do you understand by the term 'Non-Aligned Movement'?

On the other hand, the USSR poured money into chess, and through most of the Cold War it was able to maintain dominance at least over the chessboard through the achievements of brilliant chess masters such as Mikhail Tal, Mikhail Botvinnik and Anatoly Karpov.

In sport, Khrushchev was the first Soviet leader who encouraged competition with the USA. Starting with the 1956 Olympic Games in Melbourne, Australia, Soviet athletes challenged US domination of the medals table. State funds were made available so that Soviet athletes could spend more time training. At the Olympics in Rome, Italy, in 1960, the Soviet Union won more medals than any other country. This Soviet dominance in sport continued until the end of the 1970s.

Both states made a great deal of fuss when their athletes did well in the Olympic Games, and each liked to beat the other. At times, the sporting politics of the Cold War became even more overt. In 1980, following the Soviet invasion of Afghanistan in December 1979, the USA refused to participate in the Olympic Games due to take place in Moscow. The USSR had spent enormous sums on preparations for the Games, and were annoyed when several of the USA's allies joined the boycott.

Fact

The next Olympics after the boycotted Moscow Games were held in Los Angeles in the USA, in 1984. In a tit-for-tat response, the USSR and some of its allies boycotted those Games. Many people – especially athletes who had trained hard for the preceding four years – were angry that the two superpowers were hijacking international sport to make a political point.

32

Successful Soviet athletes at the Olympic Games in Rome, 1960

The arms race

The decision by the US to drop nuclear bombs on Japan in August 1945 was not only a factor in the start of the Cold War, but it also triggered one of the main aspects of the Cold War. This was the intense arms race – involving both conventional and nuclear weapons – between the two major powers. While the US had a nuclear weapons monopoly between 1945 and 1949, this ended when the USSR successfully tested its first **A-bomb**. The arms race affected the ways in which some international crises were dealt with, as well as affecting the economies of the states involved (especially that of the Soviet Union). This was, in turn, a significant factor in the collapse of the USSR in 1991 and the end of the Cold War.

Nuclear weapons

The first main step in the nuclear arms race, after both sides gained possession of the A-bomb by 1949, was the USA's development of the **H-bomb** in 1952. However, the USSR matched this the following year. The next major development came in 1957, when the USSR launched *Sputnik* – the world's first satellite (see page 35) – and developed long-range inter-continental ballistic missiles (**ICBMs**).

Although the US was also developing such missiles, they withheld this announcement until 1958. At the time, the US publicly claimed there was a missile gap – to the advantage of the USSR – and that the US must therefore rapidly build up its stock of ICBMs. Both Eisenhower and his successor John F. Kennedy knew this was not the case – flights of the USA's U-2 spy planes had shown them the real level of Soviet nuclear weaponry. Nonetheless, the US build-up forced the USSR to try to catch up, with serious long-term consequences for its relatively weaker economy. A particularly significant development came in 1960, when the US announced its possession of submarine-launched ballistic missiles (**SLBMs**). The USSR took until 1968 to follow this new technology but, without the global system of alliances enjoyed by the US, there were few harbours that could service Soviet nuclear submarines.

However, in 1968, the USSR beat the US to another new development – the building of an anti-ballistic missiles (**ABM**) defence system. In 1970, the US took another important step by developing multiple independently targeted re-entry vehicles (**MIRVs**), which greatly increased the chances of avoiding detection by any ABM system and thus of hitting their intended targets. In addition, by 1972, the US had created its own ABM system. In 1975, the Soviet Union developed its own MIRV programme.

During all this time, while there was a massive build-up of nuclear warheads, considerable effort was also put into developing specific strategies for the use of nuclear weapons, despite the fact that early Cold War leaders such as Stalin, Khrushchev and Eisenhower all believed that a nuclear war would be a global catastrophe. However, Eisenhower also insisted that, if attacked, the US would respond with every weapon at its command, rather than attempting to pursue a 'limited nuclear war', as favoured by some of his advisers. Eisenhower's 'massive retaliation' policy was replaced under Kennedy by a more 'flexible response' strategy. This was largely the work of his secretary of defense, Robert McNamara, who came up with 'counterforce' as a more limited way in which to fight a nuclear war, focusing on military but not civilian targets. However, this strategy was seen by the Soviet Union as an attempt by the USA to launch pre-emptive strikes in any international crisis short of war.

A-bomb The atomic bomb was the first type of nuclear weapon, as dropped by the US on Japan in August 1945. At first, these were only deliverable by special strategic bombers.

H-bomb The hydrogen bomb was a thermo-nuclear weapon, much more destructive than the earlier A-bombs. These were eventually deliverable by rocket missiles. The US developed the first H-bomb in 1952; the USSR followed in 1953.

ICBM Land-based inter-continental ballistic missiles were rockets that could deliver nuclear weapons across much greater distances than earlier missiles. They appeared to allow the USSR to 'catch up' in the nuclear arms race, as it could potentially reach any target in the US, thus making up for its lack of allies and bases across the globe. However, Eisenhower and his advisers had wanted the USSR to be the 'first', so they could justify the development of their own ICBM system, which was already well advanced.

SLBM Submarine-launched ballistic missiles were much more mobile and therefore harder to detect than land-based missiles. The USSR was not able to keep as many nuclear submarines at sea as the USA, because it lacked access to naval bases around the world.

ABM Anti-ballistic missile systems were intended to knock out enemy missiles before they reached their target. Although the USSR was the first to develop these, the US followed very quickly, and soon had a big lead in this area.

MIRV Multiple independently targeted re-entry vehicles were missiles with multiple warheads, each one capable of being directed to a different target. To a large extent, they reduced the effectiveness of any anti-ballistic missile system.

Fact

Pershing and Cruise missiles were 'new generation' nuclear weapons that were much faster, and harder to detect – especially the Cruise missiles, which could be launched from mobile missile carriers. Pershing IIs were based in West Germany, while Cruise missiles were placed in several West European states, including Britain.

Fact

The US SDI system was designed to make it impossible for the USSR to respond to any US nuclear strike, because any Soviet missiles fired in retaliation would be destroyed by SDI missiles before reaching the USA.

While there was a build-up of nuclear warheads, effort was also put into developing strategies for the use of nuclear weapons, despite the fact that leaders believed that a nuclear war would be a global catastrophe.

This strategy did not survive the Cuban Missile Crisis of 1962 (see pages 138–141). It was replaced by Mutually Assured Destruction (MAD), aimed at civilian and military targets to cause maximum casualties and destruction – the idea being that the risk of such a war would cause both sides to avoid any future crisis getting out of control. In many ways, this was a reversion to Eisenhower's idea of 'massive retaliation'.

After 1962, both sides came to accept that this was the best way of avoiding nuclear war, and in 1963 a hotline was set up to facilitate direct communication between the Kremlin and the White House. One result of such mutual fears was the 1972 Anti-Ballistic Missiles Treaty, which banned defences against ICBMs to ensure that the 'logic' of MAD remained. In the same year, the Strategic Arms Limitation Interim Agreement tried to restrict the number of land- and sea-based ballistic missiles.

This mutual stalemate was broken by president Ronald Reagan during the Second Cold War in the 1980s, when the US spurred on the nuclear arms race by developing the stealth bomber, the neutron bomb, and extremely accurate 'first strike' missiles (such as Pershing II and Cruise, first deployed in Europe in 1983). The US also announced its intention to develop the Strategic Defense Initiative (SDI) – better known as 'Star Wars'. This was to be a missile system based in space to intercept and destroy enemy missiles. Both the US and the USSR knew that the Soviet economy would not be able to withstand the costs of trying to match this new nuclear technology.

Conventional weapons

While the most obvious feature of the Cold War arms race was the stockpiling of nuclear warheads and new types of weapons-delivery systems, conventional weapons also played a part. For most of the duration of the Cold War, the USSR had a huge superiority in Europe in relation to NATO in terms of numbers of troops and tanks (though not as regards a straight Warsaw Pact v. NATO comparison on a global scale).

Apart from the fact that the USSR was a European state, however, a large proportion of its conventional forces was in fact deployed along the borders on its eastern front with China, which, from the 1960s and especially during the 1970s, was another potential enemy. In 1981, the USSR felt it necessary to deploy 44 divisions on its border with China, compared to 31 divisions facing NATO in the west. In addition, although the USSR had superior numbers, the qualitative advantage in terms of both training and equipment lay with NATO. For instance, the USSR's greater number of tanks was matched by NATO's vast arsenal of sophisticated anti-tank guided missiles. This Soviet superiority in tanks was used to justify the USA's development of the neutron bomb. Yet even before then, NATO commanders were confident that they could deal successfully with any Soviet/Warsaw Pact offensive in Europe.

As regards air-force capacities, the USSR's main lead was in intercepter fighters – an essentially defensive aspect – whereas NATO had a big lead in fighter ground-attack aircraft. Finally, while the USSR greatly developed its navy during the 1960s and 1970s, and thus managed to take the numerical lead over NATO, the USA developed fewer but larger and more sophisticated ships, especially aircraft carriers. It also had a much more extensive global network of friendly ports. The USSR only had six major naval bases, all in the Soviet Union. While most attention was always focused on nuclear weapons, in fact the bulk of Cold War military spending went on conventional forces and weapons.

The space race

From the late 1950s, the Cold War also manifested itself in a race between the USSR and the USA to gain a lead in a new area of scientific endeavour and exploration – space. Although this was mainly linked to military developments, such as rockets to launch nuclear warheads, there was also an important element of scientific rivalry. Each side was determined to show that its social and economic system was superior – the best system would, it was argued, inevitably win the race. Khrushchev was determined that the USSR should win this space race, and at first the USSR was able to score a series of successes.

SOURCE F

The *Sputniks* prove that socialism has won the competition between the socialist and capitalist countries. The economy, science, culture and the creative genius of people in all spheres of life develop better and faster under socialism.

Khrushchev, speaking about the success of the Soviet Union in 1957. Quoted in Chandler, M. and Wright, J. 1999. Modern World History. Oxford, UK. Heinemann. p. 242.

The first Soviet satellite Sputnik – the first step in the space race

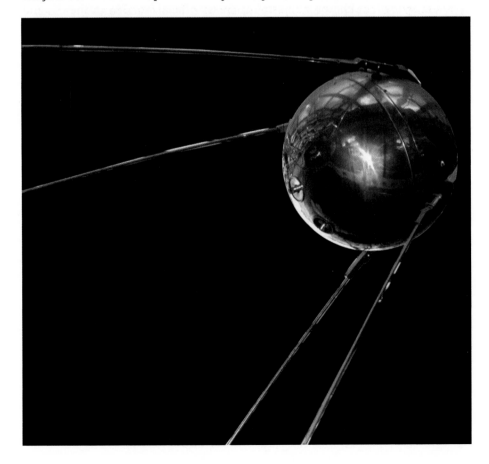

In 1957, the USSR launched *Sputnik*, the world's first satellite, and also sent the first animal into space (a dog called Laika). An even more significant first was achieved in 1961 – Yuri Gagarin became the first man in space when he went into orbit around Earth.

As in the sporting rivalry, the USSR managed to achieve dominance in the initial stages of the space race by spending vast amounts of money. However, these Soviet successes spurred President Kennedy to pour government money into a US space programme. During the 1960s and 1970s, the USA – with a much larger national 'pot' than the USSR – quickly caught up and then overtook the Soviet Union. In 1969, the USA sent the first men to the Moon. Soviet attempts to keep up in the space race played a major role in ruining the weaker Soviet economy. This contributed to the eventual collapse of the USSR and the end of the Cold War. Some people have speculated about what more might have been achieved in this arena if the two powers had co-operated instead of competing against each other.

Spies and lies

One feature of the Cold War that entered the consciousness of many people in both East and West was spying: Ian Fleming's James Bond became one of the best-known fictional characters during the Cold War period. In the real world, the activities of the CIA and the KGB often hit the headlines, either as a result of CIA-sponsored coups to overthrow radical governments in the Developing World, or KGB assassinations of agents and double-agents.

In September 1986, Nicholas Daniloff, an American journalist working in Russia, was arrested and accused of spying for the USA. In retaliation, the USA arrested Gennadi Zakharov, a Russian embassy official working in the US, and accused him of spying. The US then used the dispute as an excuse to threaten to call off a special summit meeting on defence, which was due to take place later that year between Sovier premier Mikhail Gorbachev and US president Ronald Reagan.

Both sides constantly spied on each other, despite public denials of such activity. At other times, they decided to make political points by expelling or even arresting spies – or alleged spies – working for the other side.

In addition, relentless propaganda campaigns were waged by governments and the media in both the West and the East, each portraying the opposing side in the worst possible light while presenting themselves as paragons of virtue. Citizens on both sides of the Iron Curtain were frequently lied to, and many of their governments' actions – assassinations, sabotage, support for terrorists – were kept secret for many years. However, as more documents and memoirs become available for historians to study, it is clear that neither side was 'squeaky clean' in the actions they took during the Cold War.

The general public and its fears

Another aspect of the nature of the Cold War was the fear felt by many ordinary citizens in both East and West. Many believed that the Cold War and its nuclear arms race would lead to a Third World War between the USA and the USSR, in the course of which the whole of humanity would be wiped out.

Fact

Real-life spies and spy-masters (as opposed to fictional ones like James Bond and 'M', or John le Carré's George Smiley) hit the headlines from time to time. Most notorious, perhaps, were the British MI5 spies Philby, Burgess and Maclean, who were later discovered to be Soviet agents. In the USA, during the era of the Red Scare and McCarthyism, some of those found guilty of being Soviet spies were executed, including Julius and Ethel Rosenberg in 1953.

Many people soon became aware of the dreadful destruction caused by the atomic bombs dropped on the Japanese cities of Hiroshima and Nagasaki in August 1945. In Hiroshima, almost everyone within a 3-km (2-mile) radius of where the bomb dropped was killed, and all buildings were destroyed by the heat and fire. For months afterwards, people who wore spectacles were removing fragments of shattered glass from their eyes. In the outskirts of the city, some saw thousands of people running away from the blast and thought they were African-Americans, because their skin had been blackened by the heat. Up to 8 km (5 miles) away, buildings were destroyed by a blast of hot air travelling at 800 km/h (500 mph). For years afterwards, people died from radiation sickness caused by the bomb, and many years later babies were still being born with deformities as a result of that single bomb. Soon, nuclear warheads had been developed that were a thousand times more powerful than those dropped on Hiroshima and Nagasaki.

In an attempt to alleviate the fears such developments generated amongst the civilian population, many governments began to draw up and publicise civil defence programmes to show people how to protect themselves should a nuclear attack occur.

A British government pamphlet entitled 'Protect & Survive' showed people what to do in the event of a nuclear attack

Fact

At the height of the Cuban Missile Crisis in 1962, many school students in the West listened anxiously to transistor radios brought into schools (against the rules!), to hear if the Third World War was about to start.

Question

Why were the fears of nuclear war heightened during the late 1970s and the 1980s?

This often involved using internal doors removed once the warning of an attack had been issued, or hiding under beds and using rubbish bags. In addition, people were urged in the pamphlet referred to on page 37 to take the following items into their home-made shelter: 16 litres (3.5 gallons) of drinking water per person, tinned food, a portable radio, warm clothing, blankets and plastic bags, a clock, toys and magazines. Many people were not convinced these methods would offer much protection from a nuclear attack.

Public fears stimulated the emergence and growth of various anti-nuclear and peace movements, including the Campaign for Nuclear Disarmament (CND) in Britain. Formed in 1957, and officially launched the following year, CND soon became Europe's biggest single-issue peace movement, and organised annual marches at Easter from Trafalgar Square in London to the Atomic Weapons Research Establishment near Aldermaston. Over 150,000 people took part in

The Greenham Common Women's Peace Camp, Berkshire, UK, established in 1981 to protest against the presence of US first-strike Cruise nuclear missiles at RAF Greenham Common

the 1961 and 1962 marches. Its members included many well-known writers, artists, scientists and academics, including Bertrand Russell. The organisation argued for the unconditional renunciation of all nuclear weapons.

Such movements appeared in most of the main Western states, including the USA. US folk singer Bob Dylan wrote in his song 'Masters of War' – referring, in part, to the nuclear arms race and the Cold War – of the fear the nuclear threat instilled in the general public. This included the fear of bringing children into a world where the risk of a nuclear Third World War seemed to be a possibility.

Such movements also appeared in the Eastern bloc, but these were often 'sponsored' by the state. While groups such as CND declined in the 1960s and 1970s, there was a resurgence in the 1980s. This was a result of concerns over US decisions to deploy 'first strike' nuclear weapons in Western Europe. US Cruise and Pershing missiles in particular were seen as dangerously escalating the nuclear arms race. As a result, CND membership grew to over 100,000 by 1984, and public support for unilateral nuclear disarmament increased. In 1981, over 250,000 people joined an anti-nuclear demonstration in London, while in October 1983, over 3 million people took part in simultaneous demonstrations across Europe – including 300,000 in London.

The growth of CND led to the creation of various anti-CND organisations, such as Peace Through NATO, which often claimed that CND's leaders were linked to the USSR. There was also an increase in state surveillance of CND and its supporters. The extent of this was revealed in 1985, when Cathy Massiter, an MI5 officer who had been responsible for monitoring the CND between 1981 and 1983, resigned and made MI5's activities public.

> **Many people believed that the Cold War and its nuclear arms race would lead to a Third World War between the USA and the USSR, in the course of which the whole of humanity would be wiped out.**

Chapter summary

You should now have a sound overall understanding of what is meant by the term 'Cold War', and an awareness of its general nature, along with an appreciation of some of the differences amongst historians about the nature of the Cold War and even its timescale. You should also have an understanding of the main features of the Cold War, and how they manifested themselves in various aspects of 20th-century history.

End of chapter activities

Historical debate

Read Source E (page 27) again. Moshe Lewin raises several issues about the writing of history during the Cold War. Try to find more details about the particular controversy he mentions. Does this mean any objective historical writing is impossible while the events of a particular period are still taking place?

1 Compile tables to illustrate the relative strengths of the two sides at different periods of the Cold War.
2 Produce a chart briefly summarising the eight theories about the essential nature of the Cold War. Then try to find the names of specific historians associated with each theory.
3 Find out about the main similarities and differences between the ideas of Marx, Lenin and Stalin concerning the state under communism.
4 Research and make some brief notes on the ideals behind, and the structure of, the United Nations.
5 Draw a timeline to show all the main developments in nuclear weapons between 1945 and 1991.
6 Carry out your own research on the UN during the Cold War. Then make some brief notes on the following crises:

* the Korean War, 1950–53
* the Suez Crisis, 1956
* Hungary, 1956
* the Middle East, 1967–82
* Africa in the 1970s and 1980s.

Discussion point

After considering the various activities of the UN in relation to the crises mentioned in this chapter, do you think the UN always played a neutral role? Make sure you have specific examples to support your points.

Paper 1 exam practice

Question

What message is suggested by Source A opposite about the commitment to democracy in both the USSR and the West in the years after the death of Stalin in 1953?
[2 marks]

Skill

Comprehension of a source

SOURCE A

The new version of an extensive criminal code, and the strengthening of legal institutions [in the Soviet Union after 1953] afforded a marked contrast with the past, even if the overall framework remained undemocratic. …

A realistic approach, which does not shy away from unpalatable facts, is bound to admit that democracies which achieve the status of great powers do not always respect rights and are not always very democratic. … Historical realities do not necessarily correspond to ideals or propaganda claims. The West knows perfectly well whose human rights are to be promoted and whose can be neglected or even curtailed. Ardour for democratic freedoms burns or dims according to global strategic considerations.

Lewin, M. 2005. The Soviet Century. London, UK. Verso. pp. 200–201.

Theory of knowledge

Science and society

Some scientists claim that they simply discover and explain things, and that science has no moral role to play in society. Any bad uses that result from their discoveries are the fault of society as a whole. Given what happened in Hiroshima and Nagasaki, should scientists have kept the discovery of how to split the atom and create nuclear weapons secret from politicians?

Examiner's tips

Comprehension questions are the most straightforward questions you will face in Paper 1. They simply require you to understand a source *and* extract two or three relevant points that relate to the particular question.

As only 2 marks are available for this question, make sure you don't waste valuable exam time that should be spent on the higher-scoring questions by writing a long answer here. All that's needed are a couple of short sentences, giving the necessary information to show you have understood the message of the source. Basically, try to give one piece of information for each of the marks available for the question.

Common mistakes

When asked to show your comprehension/understanding of a particular source, make sure you don't comment on the *wrong* source! Mistakes like this are made every year. Remember, every mark is important for your final grade.

Simplified markscheme

For **each item of relevant/correct information** identified, award **1 mark** – up to a **maximum of 2 marks.**

Student answer

Source A shows that, although the legal changes made in the Soviet Union after 1953 were an improvement on what had existed before, the overall set-up in the USSR was still basically undemocratic.

Examiner's comments

The candidate has selected **one** relevant and explicit piece of information from the source and has clearly understood the point being made in relation to democracy in the Soviet Union. This is enough to gain 1 mark.

However, as no point/information relating to the West's record on democracy has been identified, this candidate fails to gain the other mark available.

Activity

Look again at Source A and the student answer on page 41. Now try to identify *one* other piece of information from the source, and make an overall comment about the source's message. This will allow you to obtain the other mark available for this question.

Summary activity

Copy the spider diagram below and, using the information from this chapter and any other materials available, make brief notes under the relevant headings. For the different theories about the nature of the Cold War, try to mention specific historians.

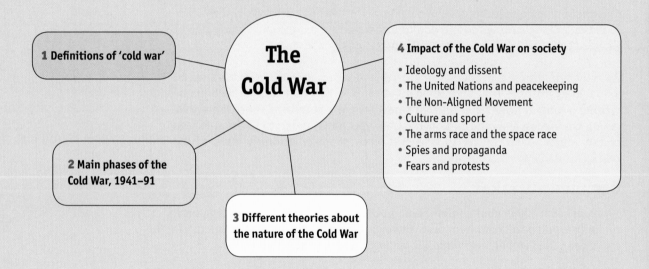

The Cold War

1 Definitions of 'cold war'

2 Main phases of the Cold War, 1941–91

3 Different theories about the nature of the Cold War

4 Impact of the Cold War on society
- Ideology and dissent
- The United Nations and peacekeeping
- The Non-Aligned Movement
- Culture and sport
- The arms race and the space race
- Spies and propaganda
- Fears and protests

Practice Paper 2 questions

1 Assess the effects of the Cold War on the work of the United Nations.
2 In what ways, and for what reasons, did differing ideologies play a part in the Cold War?
3 Explain and evaluate the impact of the Cold War on developing countries.
4 'The Cold War had little impact on the lives of ordinary people in the Western bloc.' To what extent do you agree with this statement?
5 Analyse the role of the nuclear arms race in the origin and development of the Cold War.

Further reading

Try reading the relevant chapters/sections of the following books:

Gaddis, John Lewis. 1972. *The United States and the Origins of the Cold War, 1941–1947*. Columbia, USA. Columbia University Press.

Crockatt, Richard. 1995. *The Fifty Years War*. London, UK. Routledge.

MacQueen, Norrie. 1999. *The United Nations Since 1945: Peacekeeping and the Cold War*. London, UK. Longman.

Walker, Martin. 1994. *The Cold War*. London, UK. Fourth Estate.

Whittaker, David J. 1997. *United Nations in the Contemporary World*. London, UK. Routledge.

Young, John W. and Kent, John. 2004. *International Relations Since 1945: a Global History*. Oxford, UK. Oxford University Press.

3 Origins of the Cold War

Timeline

1917 Nov: Bolshevik (Communist) Revolution takes place in Russia

1918 Jan: Woodrow Wilson delivers his 'Fourteen Points' speech

1919 Mar: Communist International (Comintern) founded

1941 Jun: Nazi Germany invades the Soviet Union

Aug: Atlantic Charter issued

Dec: Japan attacks the USA

1942 Jan: Declaration of the United Nations

1943 Nov: Tehran Conference

1944 Jul: Bretton Woods Agreement reached

1945 Feb: Yalta Conference takes place

Apr: President Roosevelt dies and is replaced by vice-president Truman

May: Red Army occupies Berlin

Jul: Potsdam Conference takes place

Aug: US drops atomic bombs on Hiroshima and Nagasaki

Sep: USA ends Lend-Lease to USSR

Dec: Council of Foreign Ministers meets in Moscow

Introduction

Having examined different aspects of the nature of the Cold War in Chapter 2, it is now time to consider more specifically how it came to start. Establishing the precise origins of the Cold War can be difficult, as different historians emphasise different events and actions as the key reasons for its evolution.

Many – if not most – historians focus on disagreements between the Allies during the closing stages of the Second World War, and stress the importance of the events of 1946–48. They argue that, before this period, the Cold War was not inevitable. Instead, it arose either because of the actions, attitudes and mistakes of leaders such as Harry S. Truman and Joseph Stalin, or because both the main powers after 1945 were attempting to create their own empires for economic or security reasons. Other historians stress the incompatibility of the various security concerns of the USA and the USSR; the long-term vulnerability felt by Soviet statesmen given Russia's past experiences; and the pressure of big business lobbies in the USA to maintain a large defence budget in peacetime, which required a real or a created 'enemy'.

On the other hand, a minority of historians trace the origins of the Cold War back to the tensions between the Allies in the period 1941–45. Some go even further back, to November 1917 when the Bolshevik Revolution took place in Russia, and the decision by the US in 1918 to intervene against the Bolshevik government in the Russian Civil War. From 1917 onwards, until the final collapse of the USSR in 1991, this fundamental and underlying conflict continued even though there were periods of improved relations and sometimes even co-operation. Such an explanation, favoured by historians such as Fred Halliday and R. C. Nation, sees the Cold War that followed Allied co-operation during the Second World War as just another manifestation of this 'Great Contest'. That is, one element of a bigger web of international relations, which alternated between isolation, ideological confrontation and coexistence.

Key questions

- What were the origins of the Cold War?
- Why did the Cold War begin?
- Who was to blame for the Cold War?

Overview

- Distrust between the capitalist West and the communist Soviet Union had been a feature of international politics since the Bolshevik Revolution of 1917. Both sides were mutually suspicious, and had very different views of the world.
- When Germany invaded the Soviet Union in 1941, these differences had been put aside. Both sides had co-operated in a Grand Alliance against the common threat of Nazi Germany.
- Signs of strain soon began to emerge, however. In 1943, at the Tehran Conference, Stalin expressed concern about the delay in opening a second front in the west, and there were disagreements over the post-war features of Germany and Poland.
- In 1945, in the closing stages of the Second World War, these differences deepened at the Yalta and Potsdam Conferences, especially when Truman became president of the USA following Roosevelt's death.
- Tensions over Germany – and the growing Soviet domination of Eastern Europe – heightened after the US dropped atomic bombs on Japan and refused to share the technology with the USSR.

What were the origins of the Cold War? (Long-term causes, 1917–41)

As discussed in Chapter 2, the term 'Cold War' is often used to describe the antagonism between the United States and the West on one side, and the Soviet Union and the East on the other, during most or all of the period 1945–91. This conflict existed both in Europe and in other regions of the world, including the Middle East, Asia, the Americas and Africa.

The origins of this 46-year period of international relations – which has come to be called the Cold War – can conveniently be divided into long-term and short-term causes. The long-term causes have their roots in the period 1917–41; the short-term causes can be found in the years 1941–45.

Although most historians argue that the events of the closing stages of the Second World War are central to the origins of the Cold War, some emphasise the view that the rivalry and hostility between the US/West and the Soviet Union arose from the **Bolshevik** Revolution of November 1917. This event brought to power the Bolshevik Party under the leadership of Vladimir Lenin and Leon Trotsky, and resulted in the emergence of what was arguably the world's first workers' state based on Marxist ideology. According to Howard Roffman, the Cold War proceeded 'from the very moment the Bolsheviks triumphed in Russia in 1917'.

Isaac Deutscher saw the events of 1917 as the start of what he called the '**Great Contest**' between the conflicting ideologies of capitalism and communism, illustrated by the markedly different global outlooks and aims of US president Woodrow Wilson and Lenin at the end of the First World War. The objectives of these leaders were set against a background of fear or hope concerning the 'spectre of communism' mentioned by Karl Marx and Friedrich Engels in their *Communist Manifesto* of 1848.

The fear felt by wealthy capitalists outside Russia was intensified by the outbreak of (short-lived) revolutions in Germany and Hungary. Consequently, Wilson, along with the French and British prime ministers Georges Clemenceau and David Lloyd George, tried to isolate the new Soviet Republic (the Soviet Union)

Bolsheviks The more revolutionary element of the Russian Social Democratic Labour Party (a Marxist party). Led by Lenin – later joined by Trotsky – they took power in Russia in November 1917. The Bolsheviks later changed their name to the Russian Communist Party, and worked hard to aid and encourage socialist revolutions in other countries, especially in more advanced capitalist countries such as Germany. After Lenin's death in 1924, Stalin was able to establish himself as dictator of both the party and the state.

Great Contest By this term, Deutscher meant the global conflict between the two rival social systems of capitalism and socialism. According to him, this began as soon as the Bolsheviks came to power after the November 1917 Revolution.

45

economically and diplomatically via a 'cordon sanitaire'. Originally a term for a barrier to prevent the spread of disease, this came to mean a chain of 'buffer' states used to isolate a potentially hostile nation.

According to Deutscher, an intense antagonism between these two fundamentally opposed social and economic systems – one headed by the USA and the other by the Soviet Union – thus broke out immediately after 1917. Each side feared the other. Western capitalist states were horrified by the prospect of the spread of revolution elsewhere, especially to economically significant states such as Germany. In turn, the new USSR feared imminent invasion by the West (in fact, the first attempts at this after the 1917 Revolution took place in the period 1918–21).

However, this argument is complicated by the fact that the relationship between the USSR and the West before 1941 was not always one of open antagonism. Consequently, it is possible to divide the period 1917–41 into two different periods: 1917–28, when the hostility was almost constant; and 1929–41, when relations were more variable.

Question

How might scenes such as those in this photograph have contributed to the long-term origins of the Cold War?

A communist rally in Germany, 1918; such events caused governments to fear the spread of communism across Europe

46

The 'Great Contest', 1917–28

Impact of the Bolshevik Revolution, November 1917

The Bolshevik Revolution had a great impact on international relations, and thus on the foreign policies of the most important states. Deutscher focused in particular on the essential motives and long-term aspirations of the USSR and other states, which lay behind foreign-policy decisions during the Cold War of 1945–91. These, he argued, were mainly the result of the states' different economic and social systems.

Thus, for Marxist historians such as Deutscher, the foreign policy of any state was usually intended to protect and further the economic interests of the dominant social and economic classes. States with different dominant classes or élites were bound to come into conflict at some point.

Question

What do you understand by the term 'Great Contest'?

SOURCE A

The foreign policy of any government, especially of the Soviet Government, is a prolongation of its domestic policy. This is all too forgotten in a period of 'summit' meetings, when the public is led to believe that three or four Big Men solve, or fail to solve, the world's predicaments according to whether they have or do not have the wisdom, good will, or the magic wand needed to do their task.

Halliday, F. (ed.). 1970. Isaac Deutscher: Russia, China and the West, 1953–1966. Oxford, UK. Oxford University Press. p. xiii.

SOURCE B

If America is not to have free enterprise [capitalist market economy], then she can have freedom of no sort whatever. ... Our industries have expanded to such a point that they will burst their jackets if they cannot find a free outlet to the markets of the world. ... Our domestic markets no longer suffice. We need foreign markets.

Comments made by Woodrow Wilson in 1912. Quoted in Williams, W. A. 1972. The Tragedy of American Diplomacy. London, UK. Norton. p. 58.

Activity

Study Sources A and B carefully. How, and to what extent, do they support Deutscher's claim that the foreign policies of states are linked to their domestic social and economic systems? Do you think this is therefore a sufficient explanation for the start of the Cold War?

Early conflicts, 1918–21

The rivalry between the two social systems of capitalism and socialism/communism had many facets – economic, ideological, territorial and military. Such long-term explanations of the origins of the Cold War see the capitalist system as facing a direct challenge to its interests and values, as a result of the revolutionary Soviet Republic's attempts to create a collectivist socialist economy within its borders. This was completely opposed to capitalism, which was based on private ownership, a market economy and individualism.

Furthermore, throughout 1917 the first leaders of Soviet Russia, Lenin and Trotsky, had openly called for revolution in Europe (initially to end the First World War). They showed their calls were serious in 1919 when they formed the Communist International, usually known as Comintern, to stimulate and aid world revolution. Capitalist companies and states were understandably suspicious and even fearful of this new revolutionary government.

Consequently, from 1918 to 1921 the new Soviet state faced foreign military intervention in the Russian Civil War. Armies from the US, Britain, France and Japan gave supplies and assistance to the opponents of the Bolsheviks. The Bolsheviks saw this as a deliberate capitalist attempt to destroy their revolutionary socialist experiment.

Though the Bolsheviks eventually emerged victorious from the civil war, the United States (among others) refused to recognise the Soviet government. In 1918, Woodrow Wilson had already begun the USA's attempt to replace the old European state system with a new international order, under US hegemony, to make the world 'safe for democracy'. By 'democracy' Wilson meant an international liberal capitalism, based on free market economics, and individualism. The first concrete evidence of this had been his **Fourteen Points**, issued in January 1918.

> ### SOURCE C
>
> Many scholars trace US–Soviet or Western–Soviet rivalry back to the Russian Revolution. They stress the part played by the ideological antagonism between Wilson's and Lenin's views of the future of the world as well as their different political interests in leading to conflict.
>
> Sewell, M. 2002. The Cold War. *Cambridge, UK. Cambridge University Press.* p. 16.

Fourteen Points Wilson's ideas for a new political and diplomatic settlement in Europe and beyond once the First World War was over. They were announced on 8 January 1918, two months after Lenin's call for world proletarian revolution. Though calling for open diplomacy, general disarmament, free trade and self-determination for national groups, the Fourteen Points were premised on the idea of the US taking a leading role in world affairs, as happened in the Paris Peace Conference. The US decision to intervene against the Bolshevik government in the Russian Civil War was another source of Soviet–American hostility.

In 1920–21, Poland (backed by Britain and France) attacked and invaded Russia. The resultant Treaty of Riga (1921) saw Russia lose significant areas of land to Poland along the Soviet–Polish border.

Soviet weakness and isolation in the 1920s

The relative general economic backwardness of Russia – inherited from its tsarist days – and the impacts of involvement in the First World War, the revolution of 1917, the civil war and foreign intervention, and then the Polish invasion, all combined to weaken the Soviet Union. In addition, the new Soviet Republic remained isolated after the crushing of various attempts at socialist revolutions elsewhere in Europe by 1923. In addition, the Treaty of Brest-Litovsk (1918), imposed by Germany and later confirmed by the West, had deprived it of much valuable industrial and agricultural territory.

The earlier military attacks by the West on the Soviet Republic were replaced after 1921 by economic embargoes and bans on trade, which restricted attempts by the Bolsheviks to rebuild the Russian economy. Furthermore, the Bolshevik government was excluded from the peace settlements and 1920s diplomacy.

How real was the 'threat' of Soviet communism before 1928?

Some of Stalin's economic policies from the late 1920s, especially in agriculture, also had a negative effect on the relative strength of the Soviet Union. Thus, the 'Great Contest' can be seen as very much a one-sided contest, given that the USA – unlike Russia – had emerged economically and militarily strengthened from the First World War. Consequently, for most of the 1920s, Soviet communism was arguably no serious rival to world capitalism.

Antagonism and co-operation, 1929–41

According to the historian R. C. Nation, the result of the Bolshevik Revolution was a complex and changing relationship between the Soviet state and the West, combining ideological denunciation, isolation, coexistence, and occasionally co-operation. Both the major protagonists in the Cold War thus had a long history of fear and mistrust, whether it was Soviet fears of Western intentions to invade again at a later date, or US/Western determination to protect their global economic interests against the prospect of socialist revolutions in other, possibly more economically significant, countries.

Another aspect of developments in international relationships between the USSR and the USA/West before the Second World War, which prefigured later developments in the Cold War, was the way in which state interests usually took precedence over commitments to their respective ideologies. Certainly, from Stalin's rise to power in the USSR in 1929, the main Soviet concerns were domestic economic and political policies. In addition, Stalin's commitment to 'world revolution' was very much subordinate to his desire to ensure the security of the USSR by building 'Socialism in One Country' – a policy that had never even been voiced while Lenin was alive.

At the same time, the onset and impact of the Great Depression in the USA and the rest of the capitalist world meant that, for many in the West, the 'Great Contest' was of less importance than economic survival.

From 1933, the threat of European expansion from Nazi Germany, the growing power of Japan in the Pacific, and the possibility of another world war all contributed to the tensions between the USSR and the West being seen by many politicians as of lesser importance – at least for a time. Certainly, after Hitler came to power in Germany in 1933, relations between the USA and the USSR began to improve. The US at last gave official recognition to the USSR in 1933, and in 1934 Stalin's Soviet Union became a member of the League of Nations. However, this improved relationship was fragile – for instance, between 1935 and 1938, the Great Purge and the Great Terror in the USSR strengthened anti-Soviet attitudes in the USA (see the section on the Riga Axioms, pages 50–51).

Fact
In the words of the British politician Winston Churchill – a determined anti-communist – economic embargoes and trade bans were intended to 'strangle infant Bolshevism in its cradle'.

49

The 'Great Contest' can be seen as very much a one-sided contest, given that the USA – unlike Russia – had emerged economically and militarily strengthened from the First World War.

Munich Agreement An agreement established in September 1938 between Nazi Germany, Britain and France. The terms of the agreement stated that Germany should be allowed to have the Sudetenland, which belonged to Czechoslovakia but was inhabited by large numbers of German speakers who had been part of the Austro-Hungarian Empire before 1919. Czechoslovakia was not invited to the conference. Nor was the Soviet Union, which had told Britain it would be prepared to send troops to defend Czechoslovakia, if Britain and France also stood up to Hitler.

George Kennan (1904–2005) Kennan, a US diplomat, worked at the Riga centre of the US Division of Russian Affairs in the 1920s, prior to Roosevelt's recognition of the USSR in 1933. Kennan's advice on policy options – based on his belief that the Soviet Union was intent on world domination – became known as the Riga Axioms. In 1946, his 'Long Telegram' (see pages 70–71) formed the basis of the USA's Cold War policy of containment of the Soviet 'threat'.

Ideology and *realpolitik*

Realpolitik refers to politics and foreign diplomacy based on realities and strategic or material needs, rather than on political principles, ideology or morals. This might entail being prepared to do deals with enemies in order to gain some short-term advantage. One example of such *realpolitik* had occurred in 1922, when the USSR signed the Rapallo Treaty with Weimar Germany. Another example of this approach was the Nazi–Soviet Non-Aggression Pact of August 1939. In Cold War terms, even under Lenin, the Soviet Union had been prepared to do deals with capitalist countries in order to develop its economy.

However, the placing of Soviet interests above those of ideology and world revolution became much more marked under Stalin, who had seized control of the USSR by 1929. Under his leadership, the theory of 'Socialism in One Country' led to Comintern increasingly becoming almost a wing of the Soviet Foreign Ministry. Between 1933 and 1939, the Soviet Union became more willing to work with capitalist states and parties in popular fronts against fascism and Nazism. In 1939, when an alliance with the major capitalist states against Nazi threats failed to emerge, Stalin decided to sign a non-aggression pact with Hitler – whose fascism made him Stalin's sworn 'class enemy'. By doing this, he hoped to buy time and gain (or, in the case of Poland, regain) territory to build up Soviet defences against the expected German invasion.

Before 1939, and despite their frequent public speeches about the superiority of liberal parliamentary democracy, the USA and several other Western states were prepared to support right-wing dictatorial regimes and groups in order to ensure bulwarks against the possibility of communist revolution. For example, both Britain and France gave political and military backing to Jozef Pilsudski's undemocratic and anti-Semitic regime in Poland, and refused – until too late – to accept Stalin's repeated offers after 1933 of an alliance against the threat posed by Nazi Germany. During the Spanish Civil War (1936), many US companies (with the tacit approval of the US government) gave significant economic assistance to Francisco Franco's semi-fascist nationalist movement in Spain.

This *realpolitik* approach to foreign affairs continued after war broke out in Europe in 1939. Stalin remained neutral until the German invasion of the USSR in 1941. After this, both he and the leaders of the USA and Britain were prepared to bury their ideological differences to unite in a Grand Alliance against what was seen as a greater threat. This was very much a 'marriage of convenience', however. Churchill never lost his early hatred of communism, and from the outset, Stalin's suspicions – strong since the **Munich Agreement** – persisted over the West's motives. In particular, Stalin increasingly came to believe that the West was prepared to sacrifice any number of Russian lives in the fight against Hitler. Both the USA and Britain were determined to protect their global economic investments and interests from the threat of revolution.

The Riga Axioms

Stalin's Great Purge in the USSR, however, had had the effect of strengthening hardline attitudes in the US against the USSR. Significantly, the US had set up the Division of Russian Affairs (DRA), which later was responsible for the important Riga Axioms. This is the name given to the views and policies of the US diplomatic experts based in the Latvian capital, Riga, who worked for the DRA during the 1920s to discover Soviet foreign-policy objectives. Latvia provided a haven for Russian exiles opposed to the Soviet government. Their views greatly influenced those who worked in the DRA – including **George Kennan**, author of the 'Long Telegram' (1946) – to regard Soviet aims as threatening world revolution. These opinions helped shape US policy towards the Soviet Union into the 1930s and 1940s.

The DRA was headed by Charles Bohlen and George Kennan, and was much influenced by 'White' Russian exiles opposed to the Bolsheviks, who tended to stress the world revolution aims of the new Soviet state. The Riga Axioms assumed real influence after 1945, when the legacy of the Russian Revolution of 1917 began once more to have a significant impact on international relations.

Co-operation and the Second World War

Initially, in the period 1939–41, the views of US 'hardliners' such as Kennan and the Riga Axiomists seemed confirmed by the Nazi–Soviet Non-Aggression Pact. This agreement was made between Nazi Germany and the USSR in August 1939. Following the Munich Conference in September 1938, Stalin had continued to urge Britain and France to join the USSR in taking military steps to stop Hitler's aggressive foreign policy. After repeated rejections, Stalin decided to accept German proposals for a non-aggression pact, in order to buy time for the USSR to prepare for the strong possibility of German attack. This pact – which was supposed to last ten years – did not make the two countries allies.

The hardline opinions were supported by others, such as Robert Taft and, especially, the US ambassador in London, Joseph Kennedy, who had supported the British foreign policy of appeasing Nazi Germany rather than allying with the Soviet Union.

However, they were opposed by Joseph Davies, the US ambassador in Moscow during 1937–38. Davies believed that the USSR was genuinely interested in co-operation in order to stabilise Europe against Nazi aggression. US president **Franklin D. Roosevelt** believed Nazi Germany to be more expansionist than the USSR. He believed that a weakened post-war Soviet Union could be persuaded to drop the idea of world communism, in return for security guarantees and help in economic reconstruction; the latter would also help the US economy. Roosevelt initially felt this was preferable to the continued existence of world blocs, an arms race, and the threat of future wars. There is evidence that his attitude towards the demands of the USSR began to harden during the last months of his life.

However, the foreign-policy developments of the 1930s, following Hitler's rise to power in 1933, played a big role in making the USSR and the states opposed to communism mutually suspicious. Stalin saw the refusal of Britain and France to join an anti-Nazi alliance, appeasement and the Munich Agreement as encouragement for Nazi Germany to attack the USSR. The West saw the dismemberment of Poland following the Nazi–Soviet Non-Aggression Pact, the war against Finland and then the annexations of the Baltic states as evidence of Soviet expansionism. These mutual suspicions remained even after the formation of the Grand Alliance.

Franklin D. Roosevelt (1882–1945) Roosevelt became a Democrat state senator in 1910, then governor of New York and, in 1933, president of the USA at the height of the Great Depression. He introduced the New Deal to cope with these problems, and went on to win the presidential elections in 1936, 1940 and 1944. He was opposed to fascism and was prepared to make some concessions to allay Stalin's security fears after the Second World War. He died after the Yalta Conference in February 1945, and was succeeded by his vice-president, Harry S. Truman.

The Grand Alliance

When the USSR was attacked by Germany in June 1941, and then the US by Japan in December of the same year, the USA and Britain soon joined with the Soviet Union in a Grand Alliance, as they now saw Hitler as a more serious and immediate threat than Stalin. One result was that the USA began to send military supplies to the USSR under the Lend-Lease scheme.

The outbreak of the Second World War seemed temporarily to end the US/West v. USSR rivalry, but new problems soon emerged within the Grand Alliance, and combined with the earlier misgivings. Some of these new problems included Soviet restrictions on Allied service personnel operating on Soviet territory, and what Stalin considered inadequate Allied aid, given that

Question

Why might the unity shown in this cartoon not be a true reflection of the relationships between the members of the Grand Alliance?

This Soviet cartoon from 1942 celebrates the victories of the wartime Allies

52

most **Axis** forces were committed to the East. He came to suspect, given the massive Soviet casualties, that the USA and Britain were prepared to fight Nazism 'down to the last Russian'. At times, Stalin even feared his allies would make a compromise peace with Hitler, then launch a joint attack against the USSR.

SOURCE D

The condominium of the 'Big Three' was toppling even before it had taken solid shape. It would be futile to try to establish which of the Allies made the first decisive move away from it. Through the labyrinth of conflicting versions and recriminations it is hardly possible to trace the first 'broken pledge'. The pledges of the Allies had, anyhow, been so vague and contained so many loopholes that by reference to the text each side could justify its conduct. The point is that the fundamental cleavage between the Allies could not but lead the one side, or the other, or both, to abandon mutual commitments. In this 'mariage de convenance' [marriage of convenience] the thought of the inevitability of divorce had been in the back of the mind of each partner from the beginning; and almost from the beginning each side had to think about the advantages it would secure and the disadvantages from which it would suffer at the moment of the divorce.

Deutscher, I. 1969. Stalin. Quoted in Rayner, E. G. 1992. The Cold War. London, UK. Hodder Murray. p. 9.

Why did the Cold War begin? (Short-term causes, 1942–45)

The second front

From 1942 onwards, Stalin began to press the USA and Britain to open up a second front in Western Europe to take pressure off the Soviet Union, which was facing the bulk of Hitler's armies. In 1943, the US and Britain decided to invade Italy first. The repeated delays made Stalin suspicious about his allies' motives. In particular, he felt they were stalling on purpose to ensure the USSR was seriously weakened. In all, about 80% of all Axis military resources were thrown against the Soviet Union. By the time a second front was finally opened up in June 1944, there were 228 Axis divisions on the eastern front, compared to 61 divisions in Western Europe.

There were also Soviet concerns over Roosevelt's foreign policy, which he said was based on 'democracy and economic freedom'. The USSR remained suspicious, viewing Roosevelt's **Open Door** policy – based on 'free' world trade and 'equal' access to raw materials – as being designed to benefit more economically advanced countries, especially the USA.

Axis The Axis powers were the countries that opposed the Allies during the Second World War. The three main Axis powers were Germany, Japan and Italy. Often known as the Rome-Berlin-Tokyo Axis, these three nations signed the Tripartite Pact in 1940. Bulgaria, Hungary, Romania, Yugoslavia, Slovakia and Finland were also members of this group.

Open Door This was the US policy of demanding 'equal opportunity' in all foreign markets, via the establishment of free trade. In 1898, John Hay was appointed secretary of state, and began to work on the Open Door policy, announcing two Open Door Notes in 1899. It became a central US policy, influencing, for example, the Marshall Plan of 1947. The policy tended to equate US interests with what was good for the rest of the world. However, because the US was by far the most advanced economic power, such a policy of 'equal opportunity' was much more likely to lead to increased US global domination than to any 'mutual benefits' – especially for the relatively backward and weakened Soviet Union.

Questions

What were the Soviet suspicions over the opening of a second front in Western Europe? Do you think they were justified?

53

SOURCE E

Stalin's postwar goals were security for himself, his regime, his country, and his ideology, in precisely that order. He sought to make sure that ... no external threats would ever again place his country at risk. The interests of communists elsewhere in the world, admirable though those might be, would never outweigh the priorities of the Soviet state as he had determined them.

Gaddis, J. L. 2005. The Cold War. London, UK. Penguin. p. 11.

The Tehran Conference, November 1943

As the war was continuing, the Big Three managed to maintain the alliance when they met at Tehran in November 1943. There was initial outline agreement that the Soviet Union (invaded three times via Poland since 1900) could restore its 1918 border with Poland, while Poland's western border would move further west, at Germany's expense. There was also agreement that no central European alliance would be allowed against the Soviet Union. These two points seemed to remove some of Stalin's main security concerns, though Churchill and Roosevelt were not in total agreement on these issues. Then, on 6 June 1944, the second front for which Stalin had long been pressing was finally opened up, with the start of the D-Day operations.

The 'Percentages Agreement', 1944

Following the Tehran agreements and the D-Day invasions, Churchill and Stalin met in Moscow in October 1944. They made the informal 'Percentages Agreement' concerning influence in south-eastern and eastern Europe. Although Roosevelt was not present, he was briefed afterwards and made no objections. Poland was not mentioned in these briefings.

The quest for security in 1944–45

The term 'superpower' was used during the war to refer to the three main members of the Grand Alliance. However, even before 1945, it was clear that the USA was by far the most powerful of the three, both economically and militarily. This was reinforced when the US unleashed its new secret super-weapon against Japan in August 1945, and decided to exclude the USSR from the technology. Many historians see this decision as key to the start of the Cold War, but the point is still hotly debated.

Both the Soviet Union and the United States claimed they were searching for security after 1945, but each defined this in a different way. In 1945, the USSR was clearly a regional power in Europe, and security meant 'friendly' states on its borders and economic reconstruction. The latter would come in part via compensation from Germany and the other nations that had wrought such destruction on Soviet territory after 1941. However, by 1945, the USA was a global rather than a regional superpower, with much greater economic and military power. For the US, security meant primarily the entire world being open to the 'free' exchange of goods, money and people. In particular, according to W. A. Williams, the USA had a 'vast preponderance of actual and potential power'

Fact

At the Moscow Conference in October 1944, Churchill and Stalin made an outline agreement – the 'Percentages Agreement' – about 'spheres of influence'. The percentage ratios for Britain and the USSR respectively in the east European states was to be:

Romania	10:90
Greece	90:10
Bulgaria	25:75
Hungary	25:75
Yugoslavia	50:50

As the Cold War began, it soon became clear that Stalin intended to impose Soviet political control (and Soviet-style economic and social systems) on those countries in the Soviet 'sphere'.

Question

What was the 'Percentages Agreement'?

in relation to the USSR from 1944 until at least 1962. This actual and relative inferiority of power played heavily on the minds of Stalin and other Soviet leaders during the Allied conferences and negotiations about post-war Europe.

Breakdown of the Grand Alliance, 1944–45

The tensions that finally led to the breakdown of the Grand Alliance and the start of the Cold War began to emerge more sharply at the 1945 Big Three Conferences, held at Yalta in February and at Potsdam in July. There were four main areas of disagreement between the Allies: Germany; Poland and Eastern Europe in general; economic reconstruction; and nuclear weapons.

Germany

The war against Germany and Japan was ongoing when the Allies met at Yalta in February 1945, but the Second World War was nearly over as far as Europe was concerned. The problems that had emerged at Tehran – especially those concerning Poland and the fate of the Eastern European countries – now clearly had to be resolved. At the conference it was agreed, quite amicably, to temporarily divide Germany into four zones of occupation, with outline agreement on compensation (reparations) for the damage done by Nazi Germany, especially to the USSR. Despite wanting huge reparations from Germany, Stalin was against the idea of splitting Germany permanently into two. He hoped reparations would both weaken Germany sufficiently to prevent it becoming a future threat (something that the French also wanted), and allow the USSR to rebuild following the destruction suffered at the hands of the German armed forces. Even as late as 1952, Stalin appears to have opted for a reunited Germany over which the USSR had some influence, but not control.

Poland and Eastern Europe

Poland proved more difficult. Eventually, it was agreed at Yalta that the USSR's demands over Poland's eastern borders would be met, and that Poland would receive territorial compensation from Germany up to the Oder-Neisse rivers.

Stalin believed the Allies had accepted the Lublin (mainly communist, or sympathetic to the Soviet Union) provisional government for Poland, with a few 'London' Poles to be added. However, Churchill remained deeply suspicious about Stalin's intentions, and by 1945 had returned to his earlier strong anti-communism. In fact, Roosevelt – by now seriously ill – also began to have doubts about Stalin's intentions to carry out all aspects of the Yalta agreements.

Fact
It is important to note that tentative agreements were reached during 1944–45. While Stalin clearly did not want to allow the Soviet Union to be so vulnerable to attack in the future, he seems to have hoped that co-operation with Britain and the USA would continue after the war.

Question

Can you identify and explain the main reasons for the disintegration of the Grand Alliance?

SOURCE F

Even after the defeat of Germany, the danger of war/invasion will continue to exist. Germany is a great state with large industry … it shall never accept its defeat and will continue to be dangerous. … The crisis of capitalism today is … favourable for the victory of socialism in Europe. But we have to forget the idea that [this] could be realised only through Soviet rule. It could be presented by some other political systems – for example by a democracy, a parliamentary republic.

Comments made by Stalin on 28 January 1945, to a delegation sent by Tito on the eve of Yalta. Quoted in Roberts, G. 2006. Stalin's Wars. *New Haven & London. Yale University Press. p. 236.*

Harry S. Truman (1884–1972)
Truman became a leading Democratic politician, and was Roosevelt's vice-president following the 1944 election. He had little experience of foreign affairs, but became president in 1945, following Roosevelt's death. It was Truman who authorised the use of atomic weapons against Japan, and he was responsible for the Truman Doctrine and the Marshall Plan, all of which were key factors in the early years of the Cold War.

Truman's impact

Roosevelt died in April 1945, and the more optimistic 'Yalta Axioms' soon faded, as vice-president **Harry S. Truman** took a more hardline approach to the Soviet Union.

SOURCE G

After only eleven days in power Harry Truman made his decision to lay down the law to an ally which had contributed more in blood and agony than we had – and about Poland, an area through which Russia had been invaded three times since 1914. The basis for the Cold War was laid on 23 April in the scourging which Truman administered to Molotov [the Soviet foreign minister], giving notice that in areas of the most vital concern to Russia our wishes must be obeyed.

Extract from Fleming, D. F. 1961. The Cold War and its Origins, 1917–1960. Quoted in McAleavy, T. 1996. Modern World History. Cambridge, UK. Cambridge University Press. p. 102.

Truman refused to listen to Vyacheslav Molotov's explanations about why the free elections in Poland promised at Yalta had not taken place. Molotov complained that 'I have never been talked to like that before in my life'. Truman's response was: 'Carry out your agreements and you won't get talked to like that.'

The Riga Axioms, put to one side during the war against Germany, now increasingly came to dominate US foreign policy. Nonetheless, the Potsdam Conference also saw a final acceptance of Soviet plans for Poland.

SOURCE H

Poland has borders with the Soviet Union, but does not have any with Great Britain and the USA. I do not know whether a democratic government has been established in Greece, or whether the Belgian government is genuinely democratic. The Soviet Union was not consulted when these governments were being formed. We did not claim the right to interfere in those matters, because we realise how important Belgium and Greece are to the security of Great Britain.

An extract from a note sent by Stalin to Truman and Churchill in April 1945, stressing the importance of Poland to Soviet security. Poland was one of the main issues dividing the Allies at the two conferences held in 1945. Quoted in Walsh, B. 2001. Modern World History. London, UK. John Murray. p. 322.

Clement Attlee, Harry S. Truman and Joseph Stalin (front row, left to right) at the Potsdam Conference, July 1945

Question

What changes in leadership had taken place since the earlier Conference at Yalta?

The issue of Poland was complex: Stalin saw it as a life and death question for the Soviet state, while Churchill saw it as a matter of honour. Yet at Yalta, Roosevelt had backed away from a Soviet 'sphere of influence' in Eastern Europe. Stalin felt such a sphere – which he believed had been decided in essence in the Moscow 'Percentages Agreement' in October 1944 – was essential for Soviet security. He was worried by the new US call for an 'Open Door' policy, and the suggestion that there should be no formal spheres of influence.

Roosevelt, who had kept the earlier agreements with Stalin about Eastern Europe secret from the US public, suggested that the planned United Nations organisation should make decisions about these issues after the war was over.

These shifts persuaded Stalin to begin taking practical measures to ensure Soviet security interests in Eastern Europe. When the Soviet Union failed to honour the Yalta agreement on free elections in Poland, US suspicions about Soviet motives increased.

Fact

After Germany surrendered in May 1945, there is evidence that the Western Allies may have supported anti-communist German troops, who killed 35,000 Soviet soldiers between May and December 1945 alone. There is even some evidence that British agents co-operated with German troops before the war ended. These insurgents, relying heavily on British weapons, continued the struggle for years.

Activity

Do the figures in this diagram justify Soviet demands for reparations from Germany? Try to find out about US losses during the war.

Economic reconstruction

Between 1941 and 1945, the Soviet Union suffered staggering losses, whereas the USA was the only power to emerge richer from the war. According to some estimates, by 1945, 25% of the USSR's pre-war capital stock had been destroyed. It was even worse in those western regions of the USSR that had been occupied by Axis forces – there, the figure was 66% and population losses are estimated at an incredible 25%. As the Axis forces retreated in 1944–45, they carried out a systematic destruction. Hardly a mine, factory or collective farm remained intact. In addition, over 1700 towns and over 70,000 villages were razed to the ground. One result of this deliberate destruction was that over 2.5 million civilians were living in makeshift underground hovels. By May 1945, the Soviet economy was in turmoil, while the Soviet people were traumatised.

In view of the dreadful destruction suffered by the USSR, Stalin saw economic reconstruction as a priority. However, as already noted, once Truman became US president, friction increased and the US became more determined to contain Soviet power whenever possible.

Soviet losses incurred during the campaign on the Eastern Front during the Second World War

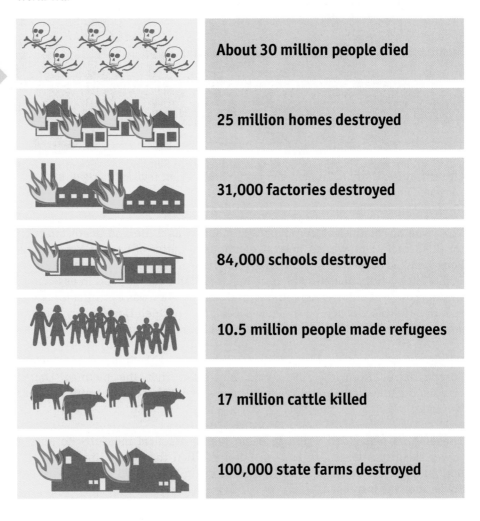

About 30 million people died

25 million homes destroyed

31,000 factories destroyed

84,000 schools destroyed

10.5 million people made refugees

17 million cattle killed

100,000 state farms destroyed

At the Potsdam Conference in July 1945, Truman said the US would only agree to the Soviet Union having reparations from the eastern zone of Germany – which was mainly agricultural and therefore poorer – along with 25% of the machinery from the three western zones, if the USSR sent in return 60% of the value of goods received from the West, in the form of goods and raw materials (especially coal).

SOURCE 1

Disproportionate losses during the war may well have entitled the Soviet Union to disproportionate postwar gains, but they had also robbed that country of the power required to secure those benefits unilaterally. The U.S.S.R. needed peace, economic assistance, and the diplomatic acquiescence of its former allies. … He [Stalin] therefore *wanted* neither a hot war nor a cold war. Whether he would be skilful enough to avoid these alternatives, however, was quite a different matter.

Gaddis, J. L. 2005. The Cold War. *London, UK. Penguin. pp. 11–12.*

Questions

What does this photograph suggest about conditions in the USSR after the Second World War? How might this have contributed to tensions between the Allies?

Russian refugees return to their devastated home town in 1944; the destruction wrought on the USSR during the war made it vulnerable in Stalin's eyes

In 1944, Stalin had made a provisional agreement at the Bretton Woods Conference to join the World Bank and the International Monetary Fund. The promise of a US loan overcame his reservations about growing US influence in Europe. But when the USSR asked for a $6 billion loan in January 1945, the US imposed conditions, especially on opening Eastern European markets to US capital. The USSR saw this as 'dollar diplomacy', which it could not accept. Thus Stalin placed more emphasis on reparations from Germany – at Yalta, it had been agreed that $10 billion would be a starting point for negotiation. A further Soviet request, in August 1945, for a loan of $1000 billion was 'lost' by the US State Department. Consequently, the USSR allowed the December 1945 deadline for membership of the World Bank and the IMF to pass without signing up. Instead, the Soviet Union decided to increase reparations from its own sphere of influence, which necessitated increased Soviet control of Eastern Europe.

The US atomic bomb

The apparent, though partial, agreements reached over Germany, Poland and reparations were further undermined in August 1945, when the US unleashed the world's first atomic bombs on Hiroshima and Nagasaki. More significant than the bomb itself was the USA's refusal to share the technology with its Soviet ally.

At the Yalta Conference, Roosevelt had secured a promise from Stalin to enter the war against Japan once Germany was defeated. However, Truman and his secretary of state, James Byrnes, saw the A-bomb as a way of ending the war against Japan without Soviet participation. This would prevent any Soviet demands for influence in Asia, which was seen as vital to US economic interests. The Potsdam Conference was delayed until 16 July, partly so that Truman could await the results of US atomic tests.

Significantly for the later development of the Cold War, the USA's long-term global aims increasingly conflicted with the USSR's regional objectives. From the outset, Stalin interpreted the refusal to share nuclear technology as a demonstration of US power to a seriously weakened USSR.

Fact
Although the USSR was without its own atomic bomb until 1949, this did not overly affect Soviet policy in Eastern Europe. For instance, US opposition did not force Stalin to reorganise the governments of Romania and Bulgaria.

Fact
The secret development of nuclear weapons was opposed by the US secretary of war, Henry Stimson, who argued that the Soviet Union should be offered an atomic partnership if some concessions on Eastern Europe were made.

SOURCE J

With the strategic location of airfields from the Philippines to Alaska, on the coast of Asia, from Alaska to the Azores in the South Atlantic [sic], we can drop, at a moment's notice, atomic bombs on any spot on the world's surface and return to our base. ... With vision and guts and plenty of atomic bombs, ultra-modern planes and strategically-located airbases the United States can outlaw wars of aggression. ...

The world organisation which I am thinking of is one designed to stop war with the atomic bomb in the hands of the United States as the club behind the door, to be used only when a bandit nation goes berserk.

Extract from a speech made on 28 November 1945 by Senator Edwin Johnson to the US Senate. Quoted in Rayner, E. G. 1992. The Cold War. London, UK. Hodder Murray. p. 12.

This interpretation of the impact of the US refusal to share nuclear weapons technology with the USSR is supported by the revisionist historian Gar Alperovitz. He argues that possession of the nuclear bomb was seen by Truman and his advisers as a 'negotiating tool' to force the USSR to accept its plans for post-war Europe and the world. Stalin was very concerned about this nuclear monopoly, and quickly authorised the development of a Soviet bomb.

Nonetheless, from mid 1944, as Soviet forces took back Soviet territory previously occupied by German forces, Stalin became increasingly aware of how damaged and weakened the Soviet Union was. In all, about 30 million Soviet citizens had died in the war (almost 10 million of them soldiers) – about 20% of the pre-war population. By the end of the war, the Red Army was about 11 million strong, but US forces totalled almost 12 million. Because of the need for rapid economic reconstruction, money had to be shifted from defence to industry. According to Khrushchev, by 1948 the Red Army had been rapidly demobilised, and numbered fewer than 3 million troops.

The more contentious issues at Potsdam were postponed, on the understanding that regular meetings of the Council of Foreign Ministers would deal with them. Throughout September and October 1945, Molotov would not agree to widening the base of the governments of Hungary, Romania and Bulgaria, and Byrnes seemed prepared to make concessions on this in order to secure a wider agreement. However, this was blocked by **John Foster Dulles**, a leading Republican who supported the Riga Axioms.

When the council met again in Moscow in December 1945, the Soviet Union agreed to include two non-communists in the Romanian and Bulgarian governments, in return for US recognition of these states. However, Byrnes was already having doubts as, before the December meeting, he had received the Etheridge Report (commissioned by him), which had been very critical of the USSR's 'imperialist' policies in Romania and Bulgaria. In particular, the report concluded that to concede a 'limited Soviet sphere of influence at the present time would be to invite its extension in the future'. At first Byrnes delayed showing the report to Truman. When Truman did see it on 2 January 1946, he was angry at the concessions made over Romania and Bulgaria, despite the fact that the US had insisted on imposing its own agenda on Japan, which it saw as being within its sphere of influence. The president instructed Byrnes to take a hard line with the Soviets in all future discussions – for instance over Iran.

Who was to blame for the Cold War?

There is considerable historical debate about how and why the Cold War began, and about which individuals and states were most to blame.

Orthodox view

Immediately after the Second World War, the orthodox view (held by academics such as William Hardy McNeill and Herbert Feis) argued that the Cold War resulted from Soviet ideology which, based on Marxism–Leninism, was ultimately aimed at destabilising capitalist states in order to spread world revolution. Hence the Soviet Union was depicted as an expansionist state, with ambitions reaching beyond control of Eastern Europe. As a result, the US and the West had no choice but to take a hard line and seek to contain the 'communist threat'. The responsibility for the Cold War thus rested, according to this theory, with the Soviet Union's aggressive expansionist policies, which were attempting to impose a *Pax Sovietica* on Europe and, ultimately, the world.

John Foster Dulles (1888–1959) Dulles was an important Republican politician in the USA. He held various diplomatic and advisory posts before and during the Second World War. He was strongly opposed to any concessions to the Soviet Union at the end of the war, and was a supporter of the Riga Axioms. He later became secretary of state (1953–59) and was a major influence on US foreign policy during the Cold War. He was an anchor of 'massive retaliation' and became known as one of the 'Cold War Warriors'.

61

Question

What were the main areas of disagreement at the 1945 conferences of Yalta and Potsdam?

Fact

The orthodox view saw Soviet diplomacy as being based on obtaining any advantage possible, without intending to honour any negotiated compromises. Thus, any co-operation with the Soviet Union was impossible.

Revisionist view

However, by the late 1950s, a new explanation was emerging – the revisionist interpretation. This argued that the USA, not the USSR, was responsible for the start of the Cold War. According to this view, the USSR has consistently followed a foreign policy of 'conservative defencism', both in Europe and the Developing World. Historians such as W. A. Williams argued that by 1945 the Soviet Union was too weak in economic and human terms to pose any global expansionist threat. Such historians claimed that, under Stalin, the Soviet Union had concentrated on internal political and economic policies, and had done little in practical terms to aid revolutionary outbreaks, despite public rhetoric that still proclaimed commitment to world revolution. The Soviet goals of security along its western frontiers and of obtaining reparations did not, initially, mean the USSR was planning to impose Soviet control and communist reorganisation on the countries of Eastern Europe.

According to these revisionists, the Soviet Union was pushed into establishing tighter control in Eastern Europe by US actions, which were aimed at establishing a 'new world order' based on US domination – a *Pax Americana*. Given that US gross national product (GNP) had more than doubled during the Second World War, the country's Open Door policy was one deliberately designed to establish US economic power in the post-war world. In particular, revisionists argued that the US entered the Second World War mainly for *economic* reasons: the German and Japanese economies were challenging US attempts to increase its share of the world economy.

US attempts to do the same in relation to Europe – coupled with the US nuclear monopoly and its anti-communist stance under Truman – are therefore seen as pushing the USSR into stronger measures in Eastern Europe. Revisionist historians argued that, in 1945, the Soviet Union (because of its limited goals and economic weakness) was willing to co-operate and negotiate, as shown by its attempts to stifle the activities of communist parties in the western sphere of influence. For instance, the communist parties in France and Italy – popular because of their roles in resistance to the German occupiers – were instructed by Stalin to join post-war coalition governments to help capitalist restoration. In addition, no significant Soviet help was given to the communist movements fighting in Yugoslavia and Greece. The Soviet 'menace' was thus created by the US in order to justify its own global domination policies.

Post-revisionist view

A third interpretation, known as post-revisionism, has also been put forward. There are a number of distinctive strands within this view, but all try to avoid putting the blame on just one of the superpowers.

One argument is that the Cold War developed through misunderstandings, in particular the confusion arising when Truman replaced Roosevelt as president. Roosevelt had believed it was possible to co-operate with the Soviet Union in the post-war world, and had avoided taking a tough line during the war itself, especially as the USSR's help would be needed to defeat Japan. However, many of Roosevelt's advisers – especially William Averell Harriman (US ambassador in the USSR since 1943) and General John Deane (head of the US military mission in Moscow) – wanted him to take a tougher line on spheres

Fact

The desire for global economic dominance was even seen in operation against the USA's other Western ally, Britain. During the war, the US pushed hard to undermine the sterling area and the imperial preference system. After the war, the US loan granted in November 1945 forced Britain to accept the Open Door policy, which allowed US firms to compete in Britain's traditional pre-war markets. The US quickly replaced Britain in Latin America and began to challenge British oil interests in the Middle East.

of influence. This was in opposition to Kennan, who took the view that agreeing to such rival spheres was inevitable.

When Roosevelt died, Truman (who had had little to do with US foreign policy until then) followed the advice of those officials, believing he was continuing Roosevelt's foreign policy. However, he wasn't – and the abrupt change only deepened Soviet suspicions. Byrnes, Truman's secretary of state, was also inexperienced in foreign affairs. At first he went along with trying to reach an agreement with Moscow, believing that the Soviet need for vast loans for economic reconstruction would lead Stalin to make concessions. However, the economic control mechanisms insisted on by the US eventually led the Soviet Union to break off negotiations.

The role of individuals

Some historians have concentrated on the role of individuals in the outbreak of the Cold War – for instance, how Stalin chose to ignore Maxim Litvinov's more moderate advice and instead to take the harder line advocated by others. Revisionist historians such as Williams believed Truman and his advisers bore significant responsibility by ignoring the long-standing security concerns of the Soviet Union. In particular, Truman's decision to use the USA's economic and military superiority after 1945 to push the traditional Open Door policy was seen as a major contributing factor to the outbreak of the Cold War.

Orthodox historians – and others – have tended to place most of the blame on Stalin. The views of some historians, including John Lewis Gaddis, have altered slightly since the end of the Cold War. In his 1998 book, *We Know Now: Rethinking the Cold War*, Gaddis certainly saw Stalin's attitudes and actions as being particularly significant: '… as long as Stalin was running the Soviet Union, a Cold War was unavoidable' (p. 292). However, he also expressed a somewhat contradictory view in his 2005 book, *The Cold War*: 'Stalin fell into the trap the Marshall Plan laid for him, which was to get *him* to build the wall that would divide Europe' (p. 32).

Chapter summary

You should now have a sound overall understanding of the main long- and short-term factors contributing to the origins of the Cold War in the period up to 1946, and of the different historical explanations put forward. You should also be able to comment on the main aspects of these causes and to assess their relative importance.

> **Historical debate**
>
> 'Power games and personal ambitions are part of history. They also exert strong pressure for history to be written in such a way as to serve interests and causes.'
> Lewin, M. 2005. *The Soviet Century*. London, UK. Verso. Introduction.
>
> Since the end of the Cold War, debate about the origins of, and responsibility for, the start of the Cold War has continued. In addition to the earlier 'orthodox/revisionist/post-revisionist debates, other approaches have emerged. To what extent do you think the quotation above explains the emergence of different historical interpretations concerning the Cold War?

> **Fact**
> The Bretton Woods Agreement of 1944, which set up the International Monetary Fund and the World Bank, had been seen as a way of meeting such loans. As late as 1945, Molotov was advising Stalin of the valuable economic benefits membership of these organisations could bring to the Soviet Union.

> **Question**
> What are the main points of the three major historical explanations for the start of the Cold War?

End of chapter activities

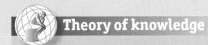

Theory of knowledge

Historical explanations and 'theories of history'

Historians don't just *describe* the events of the past, they are usually much more concerned with *explaining why* those things happened. There is a *range* of possible factors behind the start of the Cold War. However, historians try to identify the *most important or key* factor. This involves making choices and judgements about what kind of factors they consider most important. Rather than getting tied up with applying labels to historians (such as 'orthodox' or 'revisionist'), try to evaluate the findings of different historians on the basis of their methods and selections of evidence.

1 See what you can find out about the historian Isaac Deutscher and his theory about the 'Great Contest'. How would *you* assess his theory?

2 Look again at Source A on page 47. Try to find out what other revolutionary outbreaks occurred in the period immediately following the end of the First World War. How did the US and the major European states react to these outbreaks?

3 Carry out some research on the opening of the second front in Western Europe. Then create a chart showing how US and British reasons for the delay *were* and *were not* valid.

4 Do some further reading on Stalin's concerns and actions relating to Poland immediately after 1945. Then produce two short arguments – one to show how his actions were justifiable, and one to show they were not.

5 Find out more about, and make notes on, how different historians have dealt with Truman's role in 1945 as regards the emerging Cold War.

Discussion points

- Could the Cold War have been prevented if the West had stuck to its earlier agreement to support the Soviet Union's demands for reparations from Germany? Work in pairs, with one person taking one side of the argument, and the other the opposing view.
- Working in pairs, research the extent to which Soviet concerns about the reasons for the delayed second front in the West were valid. Then present your views – for and against – to your class.

Paper 1 exam practice

Question

According to Source A opposite, in what ways were the foreign-policy objectives and actions of the USA and the USSR similar immediately after the end of the Second World War in 1945?
[2 marks]

Skill

Comprehension of a source

SOURCE A

More aware than anyone else of their own weaknesses in the event of a conflict with the United States, the Russians pursued a conservative and cautious line wherever they could find local non-Communist groups willing to abjure the traditional diplomacy of the [anti-Soviet] cordon sanitaire and anti-Bolshevism. … They showed neither more nor less respect for an unborn functional democracy in Eastern Europe than the Americans and British evidenced in Italy, Greece or Belgium. For neither the Americans, British nor Russians were willing to permit democracy to run its course anywhere in Europe at the cost of damaging their vital strategic and economic interests. … The Russians had no intention of Bolshevising Eastern Europe in 1945 if … they could find alternatives.

Extract from Kolko, G. 1969. The Politics of War. Quoted in Rayner, E. G. 1992. The Cold War. London, UK. Hodder Murray. p. 8.

Examiner's tips

Comprehension questions are the most straightforward questions you will face in Paper 1 – they simply require you to understand a source **and** extract two or three relevant points that relate to the particular question.

As only 2 marks are available for this question, make sure you don't waste valuable exam time that should be spent on the higher-scoring questions by writing a long answer here. All that's needed are a couple of short sentences, giving the necessary information to show you've understood the source. Try to give one piece of information for each of the marks available for the question.

Common mistakes

When asked to show your comprehension/understanding of a particular source, make sure you don't comment on the **wrong** source! Mistakes like this are made every year. Remember, every mark is important for your final grade.

Simplified markscheme

For **each item of relevant/correct information** identified, award **1 mark** – up to a **maximum of 2 marks.**

Student answer

> Source A shows that the foreign policies of both the USA and the Soviet Union were based on defending their 'vital strategic and economic interests' after the Second World War.

Examiner's comments

The candidate has selected **one** relevant and explicit piece of information from the source – this is enough to gain 1 mark. However, as no other reason/information has been identified, this candidate fails to gain the other mark available.

Activity

Look again at the source and the student answer above. Now try to identify **one** other piece of information from the source, and so obtain the other mark available for this question.

Summary activity

Copy the diagram below and, using the information from this chapter and any other materials available, make brief notes under the relevant headings.

1 Long-term origins of the Cold War, 1917–41

- The Great Contest, 1917–28
- Antagonism and co-operation, 1929–41

Origins, causes and theories of the Cold War

3 How responsibility for the Cold War has been explained

- Orthodox theories
- Revisionist theories
- Post-revisionist theories

2 Short-term causes of the Cold War, 1941–45

- Second front
- Tehran Conference
- Percentages Agreement
- Quest for security
- Breakdown of the Grand Alliance

Practice Paper 2 questions

1 Assess the part played by differing ideologies in the origin of the Cold War.

2 In what ways, and for what reasons, did the question of Poland contribute to the origin and development of the Cold War?

3 Explain why the members of the wartime Grand Alliance began to have serious differences in 1945.

4 'Truman's attitudes and actions were more important than those of Stalin in the origins of the Cold War.' To what extent do you agree with this statement about the Cold War?

5 Analyse the role of Soviet demands for reparations from post-war Germany in the origin and development of the Cold War.

Further reading

Try reading the relevant chapters/sections of the following books:

Gaddis, John Lewis. 1972. *The United States and the Origins of the Cold War, 1941–1947*. New York, USA. Columbia University Press.

McCauley, Martin. 1998. *The Origins of the Cold War, 1941–1949*, London, UK. Longman.

LaFeber, Walter. 1985. *America, Russia and the Cold War 1945–84*. New York, USA. McGraw-Hill.

Nation, R. Craig. 1992. *Black Earth, Red Star: A History of Soviet Security Policy, 1917–91*. New York, USA. Cornell University Press.

Larson, Deborah Welch. 1997. *Anatomy of Mistrust: US-Soviet Relations During the Cold War*. New York, USA. Cornell University Press.

Kennedy-Pipe, Caroline. *Stalin's Cold War: Soviet Strategies in Europe, 1943–56*. Manchester, UK. Manchester University Press.

4 The First Cold War (1946–53)

Introduction

As we explored in Chapters 2 and 3, historians have found it difficult to establish a precise date on which they can all agree for the start of the Cold War. However, many see events in early 1946, such as Churchill's famous 'Iron Curtain' speech on 5 March 1946, as a good point at which to begin the history of the Cold War proper. By then, the various long-term goals and objectives of the Allies were leading to the emergence of several short-term differences. By the mid 1950s, two rival power blocs had emerged and consolidated – one led by the USA, the other by the Soviet Union.

While the origins and the very early stages of the First Cold War were clearly in Europe, the struggle that emerged after 1945 between the two main powers very quickly spilled over into other regions of the world. In the early period it took place mainly in Asia but, as later chapters will show, it soon affected Africa and the Americas too.

Question

What do you think is the message of this cartoon?

This chapter is divided into two units, which deal with the main aspects of the early stages of the Cold War (1946–53) in Europe and in Asia respectively. During this period there were several actions, reactions and counter-actions by the former Allies. In particular, this chapter will examine the origins of, and the reasons for, the US policy of containment, the problems surrounding the question of Germany, the establishment of NATO in the West, and the corresponding actions and reactions of the USSR – including the increasing control of Eastern Europe.

These developments mostly played out in Europe which, by 1949, had become divided into two rival spheres of influence. However, after 1949 and the victorious Communist Revolution in China, Cold War tensions spread to Asia. The main impact of this revolution was that it led to the development of a new international relations system. From this point on, the Cold War changed from being essentially a US–European conflict to being increasingly a global struggle between two rival economic, social, ideological and military systems. This struggle began to affect other parts of the world, most immediately evidenced by the outbreak of a conventional 'hot' war in Korea in 1950. The global impact of the Cold War spread, and was often characterised by regional civil wars and conflicts, in which the two main powers supported opposing sides. Communist China also began to emerge as a major player in the Cold War.

A French cartoon that appeared in 1950, giving a Western view of Stalin's takeover of Eastern Europe and the possible threat from communism

1 Developments in Europe

Key questions

- How far was 1946 a turning point?
- How important were the Truman Doctrine and the Marshall Plan?
- What were the main points of tension in Europe from 1947 to 1949?
- How did the First Cold War develop in Europe from 1949 to 1953?

Overview

- Continued disagreements during 1946 began an East–West hostility, symbolised by Churchill's 'Iron Curtain' speech in March 1946.
- Economic crisis in Europe, communist electoral successes in Italy and France, and the Greek Civil War saw the US respond in 1947 with the Truman Doctrine and the policy of 'containment'. This was followed by Marshall Aid. Soon, the term Cold War was being widely used.
- Growing Soviet power in Eastern Europe, the Brussels Treaty Organisation formed by Western European states, and the merger of the West's zones in Germany, resulted in a near-complete breakdown of relations in 1948. The Soviet response was the Berlin Blockade, which was met by the West's Berlin Airlift.
- In 1949, NATO was set up initially at the request of states in Western Europe, but soon became increasingly dominated by the US. Though the Berlin Blockade ended in May, Cold War tensions increased when the USSR exploded its first atomic bomb. At the end of 1949, Germany was divided into two separate states.
- From 1949, with the communist victory in China and the start of the Korean War the following year, Cold War tensions shifted mainly to Asia (see Unit 2, page 88). In Europe, the Cold War was heightened by the US exploding its first H-bomb.
- However, a 'thaw' in Cold War tensions began to emerge after Stalin's death in March 1953, despite the USSR exploding its first H-bomb shortly after. The new Soviet leadership soon announced a willingness to negotiate over Cold War problems, as did both Eisenhower and Churchill.

Timeline

1946 Feb: Kennan's 'Long Telegram'

Mar: Churchill delivers 'Iron Curtain' speech

Jul–Oct: Paris Peace Conference held

Oct: communists win elections in Bulgaria

Nov: rigged elections in Romania result in communist victory

1947 Jan: communists rig elections in Poland

Mar: Truman Doctrine (containment) announced

May: Britain and US merge German zones to form Bizonia

Jun: Marshall Plan announced

Aug: communists win elections in Hungary

Sep: Cominform set up; Zhdanov gives 'Two Camps' speech

1948 Feb–Mar: communist coup in Czechoslovakia, after non-communists resign from government

Jun: France joins its German zone to Bizonia to form Trizonia; the West introduces new currency in West Germany; start of Berlin Crisis (Blockade and Airlift)

1949 Jan: Comecon established

Apr: NATO set up

May: Berlin Blockade ended; West Germany (FDR) formally established

Aug: Soviet A-bomb tested

Oct: East German state (GDR) set up

1952 Mar: 'Stalin Notes' on Germany issued

Nov: US explodes H-bomb

1953 Jan: Eisenhower becomes US president

Mar: Stalin dies

Jul: USSR explodes H-bomb

How far was 1946 a turning point?

The growing divide, 1946–47

By the end of 1945, with the Second World War over, tensions between the Allies were already apparent. However, the West was also concerned about developments in the Middle East and the eastern Mediterranean, where the US had what it considered to be vital interests. One area of immediate concern was northern Iran, where the USSR was believed to be spreading its influence. In January 1946, Stalin claimed the USSR had as much right to the Black Sea Straits and Iranian oil as had the West. As early as February of the same year, US secretary of state James Byrnes began to urge the Iranian prime minister to resist any Soviet advances in that important oil-rich region. Truman decided to maintain this firm stand, and Stalin quickly backed down in return for a deal on oil concessions. Although the West believed this showed that, if confronted with determined opposition, Stalin would always give in, the evidence suggests that Stalin was never very serious about expansion in that area.

Similarly half-hearted pressures from Stalin in the spring and summer of 1946 for concessions from Turkey were also resolutely opposed by the West, and the Soviet leader once again backed down. Truman and the West thus concluded that Soviet claims and actions should always be met by determined opposition. In particular, the Turkish 'war scare' and its resolution caused the US under-secretary of state, **Dean Acheson**, to move towards a more confrontational approach to the USSR. In September 1946, Clark Clifford, one of Truman's key advisers, presented a memorandum that also advocated a tough policy. This was opposed by former vice-president and, by then, secretary of commerce Henry Wallace, who favoured a more conciliatory approach. Wallace was later forced to resign from the government.

However, the problems throughout 1946–47 were mostly located in Europe: Germany, peace treaties with Italy and the Axis states of Eastern Europe, the emerging civil war in Greece, atomic weapons, the economic crisis in Western Europe, and increasing Soviet control of Eastern Europe. The decisions made about these issues resulted in more serious divisions between the Allies, in large part because Europe was where Stalin's main security concerns were based.

Kennan's 'Long Telegram'

In 1946, Western governments came to view increasing Soviet control in Eastern Europe as a first step towards the westward spread of communism. Some politicians spoke of possible advances in Greece, Italy and even in France, where communist support was relatively strong. February 1946 saw two significant developments. The first was the failure of the **Baruch Plan**, which ended any hopes of an agreement on the control of nuclear weapons. The second was George Kennan's famous 'Long Telegram', in which he argued that, because of its security fears, internal politics and leadership, and its Marxist–Leninist ideology, the USSR was a dangerous and expansionist state which would never co-operate with the USA. Kennan's telegram hardened attitudes in the US, and played a key role in US foreign policy towards the Soviet Union.

Dean Acheson (1893–1971)
Acheson had been a convinced anti-communist since 1946. He helped develop the Truman Doctrine, the Marshall Plan and NATO, and from 1949 to 1953 he was US secretary of state. He also encouraged support for Nationalist China and US/UN involvement in the Korean War.

Baruch Plan A US plan, presented by political consultant Bernard Baruch to the UN on 15 June 1946, to remove Soviet fears about the USA's nuclear monopoly by eventually placing such weapons under international control. An International Atomic Energy Authority would be set up to control all raw materials and atomic plants. However, the US insisted on its right to continue making nuclear weapons and to retain them for some time. Although adopted by the UN's Atomic Energy Commission on 30 December 1946, the Baruch Plan was vetoed by the USSR in the Security Council.

SOURCE A

We have here a political force committed fanatically to the belief that with the US there can be no permanent *modus vivendi*, that it is desirable and necessary that … the international authority of our state be broken, if Soviet power is to be secure. … Many foreign peoples, in Europe at least, are tired and frightened by experiences of the past, and are less interested in abstract freedom than in security. They are seeking guidance rather than responsibilities. We should be better able than the Russians to give them this. And unless we do, Russians certainly will.

Extract from Kennan's 'Long Telegram', February 1946. Quoted in Gaddis, J. L. and Etzold, T. H. (eds). 1978. Containment: Documents on American Policy and Strategy, 1945–1950. New York, USA. Columbia University Press. pp. 61–63.

Kennan argued in particular that Moscow was 'highly sensitive to the logic of force', and would back down if it encountered 'strong resistance at any point'. Kennan's argument was also based on the belief that, whatever the US did, Soviet policy towards the West could not be altered in the short or medium term. This view rapidly became the basis of US foreign policy, and was the origin of the policy of 'containment' (a term first used by Kennan), which emerged the following year; this was essentially a revival of the Riga Axioms (see pages 50–51).

In March 1946, Winston Churchill made his famous 'Iron Curtain' (see page 18) speech in Fulton, Missouri. Churchill also claimed that the Soviet Union was an expansionist state, arguing for the end of compromise and calling for a stronger Anglo–American alliance. This was an important shift away from the spirit of Yalta and Roosevelt's policy of attempting co-operation with the USSR, and coincided with Kennan's 'Long Telegram'. Stalin compared Churchill to Hitler, and saw the speech as a 'call to war with the Soviet Union'. As a result, the USSR withdrew from the International Monetary Fund (IMF) and stepped up anti-Western propaganda.

> ## Question
>
> What did Kennan's 'Long Telegram' say about Soviet foreign policy?

71

A British cartoon, published in the Daily Mail *on 6 March 1946, following Winston Churchill's 'Iron Curtain' speech*

In essence, Kennan was in favour of a 'fully-fledged and realistic showdown with the Soviet Union' over developments in Eastern Europe. As early as February 1945, he had argued that if the West was not prepared to 'go the whole hog' to block any expansion of Soviet influence in Europe, then the only alternative was to split Germany permanently in two, and to draw a definitive frontier between East and West. He believed the world should be divided into rival spheres of influence and that the US should then conduct a propaganda war against the USSR and communism.

Yet recently released documents indicate not only that Kennan overestimated the importance of ideology as a factor in shaping Soviet foreign policy, but also that in fact the Soviet Union pursued a very flexible approach in the years immediately after 1945. This approach may have had opportunistic and expansionist elements in regard to Eastern Europe, but it was open to compromise and accommodation with the West. As tensions increased, however, those advisers in both camps who favoured a more hardline and confrontational approach began to gain the upper hand.

Using the phrase *Pax Sovietica*, John Foster Dulles argued for military and economic aid to 'endangered' states. At the same time, Dean Acheson warned Truman that any joint Turko–Soviet control of the Black Sea Straits would threaten Greece and the Middle East.

At the same time, Byrnes used international loans and credits to stabilise all economies outside the Soviet sphere, amounting to $5700 million in 1946. He also made it clear that any credits for the USSR would depend on a greater US say in the economic reconstruction of Eastern Europe, and the removal of all trade barriers. This resulted in negotiations being broken off in June 1946.

Economic crisis in Western Europe, 1946–47

Most US officials soon came to support Kennan's views, and some '**doves**', such as Henry Wallace, who believed the USSR was willing to compromise, were forced to resign. However, although a media campaign (helped by Churchill's speech) was launched about the 'new threat' from the Soviet Union, neither the Republican-dominated Congress nor the general public were yet convinced of the need to hand out large loans to allies or to increase the military budget. The Republicans won the congressional elections of November 1946, and actually voted to cut Truman's budget the following year, including military expenditure.

Nevertheless, the economic and political situation in Western Europe from 1946 to 1947 eventually persuaded Congress to support the more active – and costly – foreign policy desired by Truman's administration.

Fact
Joint Turko–Soviet control of the Black Sea Straits had been accepted by Churchill as reasonable in October 1944, while at Potsdam it had been agreed that the USSR had a right to revise the Montreux Convention of 1936.

doves This term is used to describe those who prefer to find peaceful ways to resolve differences. Those who follow more hardline or aggressive policies are sometimes called 'hawks'.

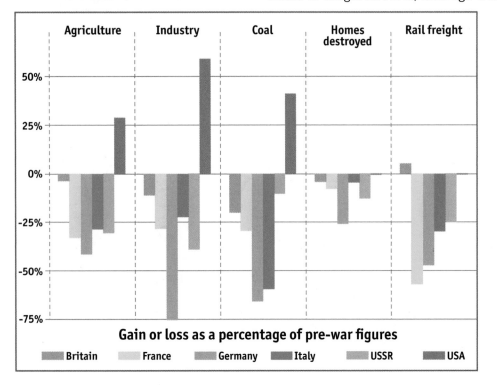

Gain or loss as a percentage of pre-war figures

■ Britain   ■ France   ■ Germany   ■ Italy   ■ USSR   ■ USA

The economic problems facing Europe in 1945. (Adapted from Fisher, P. 1985. The Great Power Conflict After 1945. London, UK. Basil Blackwell. p. 8.)

The economic impact of the Second World War on European countries was incredibly negative compared to the impact on the US. The situation was made worse by poor harvests across Europe in 1946 and a severe winter in 1946–47. At the same time, communist parties in France and Italy were becoming relatively large and popular. This was partly due to the role they had played in resisting fascism during the war. **George C. Marshall**, who replaced Byrnes as secretary of state, estimated that Western Europe would need $17 million of aid in order to recover – but the Republican Congress was still not persuaded.

The turning point came in February 1947, when Britain announced that, because of its economic problems, after March it would no longer be able to give economic or military aid to the Greek royalists in their civil war against the Greek communists. It would also cease aid to Turkey.

By linking loans to the struggle against communism, Dean Acheson was able to gain support for Truman's policy of containment. In particular, Acheson argued that if Greece turned communist, then the Balkans and, ultimately, Africa and Western Europe (especially France and Italy) would be undermined. This 'rotten apple' argument (based on the idea that one communist state would begin to 'spoil' its immediate neighbours) was similar to the Domino Theory that dominated US foreign policy in the following decades. This argument stated that if one country was allowed to 'fall' to communism, then neighbouring states would be the next to go, just like a line of dominoes.

How important were the Truman Doctrine and the Marshall Plan?

Containment and the Truman Doctrine

The change in policy was announced by Truman in his speech to Congress on 12 March 1947. In order to gain the support of the Republican majority, however, he had to exaggerate differences with the Soviet Union and argue that there was a crucial ideological struggle between democracy and communism.

At the same time, Truman's administration exaggerated the military threat posed by the Soviet Union; according to Acheson, the message to the US public had to be 'clearer than the truth'. The USSR, it was implied, was aggressively expansionist and therefore needed to be 'contained', though there was no direct mention of the Soviet Union itself.

In 1947, the US set up new national security organisations – an integrated Defense Department in the Pentagon, the Central Intelligence Agency (CIA) and the National Security Council (NSC). Truman used the same fears in the run-up to the 1948 elections, and domestic politics saw the start of campaigns against communist subversion, which led to the 'witch hunts' in the early 1950s spearheaded by **Joseph McCarthy** (see page 92).

The new policy – which came to be known as the Truman Doctrine – argued that all countries had to choose between the 'freedom of the West or the subjugation of communism'. Truman then announced US readiness to assist any country resisting 'armed minorities' or 'outside pressure'. Congress finally approved aid for Greece ($300 million) and Turkey ($100 million). In addition, US military advisers were sent to Greece. Stalin, who seems to have stuck to the Percentages Agreement not to interfere in Greece, saw this as evidence of the USA's intentions to expand its sphere of influence.

George C. Marshall (1880–1959) Marshall became chief of staff during the Second World War and pushed for an Allied advance through France, believing this was the best way to defeat Germany. As well as being the architect of the Marshall Plan to aid the economic recovery of Western Europe, he also headed the Marshall Mission to China in 1945–46, hoping to maintain the nationalist–communist alliance.

Joseph McCarthy (1909–57) McCarthy became Republican senator for Wisconsin in 1945. In 1950, he began his campaign against suspected communists in the US administration. In 1952, he used the House Un-American Activities Committee, but had no real evidence to back up his claims. He began to lose credibility in 1954, after failing to supply any proof during a televised hearing. He went on to accuse the army and even Eisenhower.

> **Both the USA and the USSR saw the Marshall Plan as an attempt to weaken Soviet control of Eastern Europe, and the Soviet Union saw it an an example of 'dollar imperialism', designed to establish US influence in Europe.**

Historians have put forward various reasons why the policy of containment was adopted so quickly by the US in the late 1940s. For instance, as the US emerged from the Second World War as a truly global power with worldwide interests, developments anywhere in the world might endanger the economic interests and thus the power of the US, and should therefore be resisted. Also, both US industries and the military had benefited from the war economy. Continued growth would be assured if a new threat appeared to take the place of the Axis Powers, as this would maintain the need for high government expenditure. In addition, such military expenditure might help stave off a new Depression in war-torn Europe. This fear was especially prevalent in the 1940s, as communist and socialist parties in Western Europe were quite popular, while nationalist movements in European colonies were threatening vital sources of raw materials and markets.

The Marshall Plan

As well as giving aid to Greece and Turkey, Congress decided to help revive the economies of Western European states by means of US credits and the revival of the German economy. On 17 January 1947, Dulles floated the idea of a European economic union. When the Council of Foreign Ministers, meeting in Moscow in April 1947, failed to reach agreement over the question of Germany (partly because of US opposition to the repeated Soviet request for reparations, and partly because of Soviet intransigence), this idea was linked to economic aid as an anti-communist tool. All this was designed to gain congressional support, especially as an expanded European economy would also be good for US exports. At the same time, it would allow the revival of the German economy within a European framework, thus preventing what France in particular feared – a new German dominance.

SOURCE B

In a similar way, it is a grave error to evaluate or interpret the diplomatic moves of 1945 and 1946 in an economic vacuum. ... The determination to apply the Open Door Policy to eastern Europe ... evolved concurrently with a deep concern over economic affairs in the United States. ... By March 1946, the *New York Times* reported that 'in all groups there is the gnawing fear that after several years of high prosperity, the United States may run into something even graver than the depression of the Thirties.'

Williams, W. A. 1984. The Tragedy of American Diplomacy. New York, USA. Norton. pp. 266–67.

Question

How accurate a picture of the motives for the Marshall Plan do you think Source B gives?

On 23 May 1947, Kennan gave his support to the idea, and the Marshall Plan was announced on 5 June 1947. Technically, this was open to the Soviet Union and states in Eastern Europe, but its political and economic criteria and goals meant Stalin was unlikely to accept it. These criteria included allowing the US to examine the financial records of all applicant countries, and allowing 'free' enterprise. Both the USA and the USSR saw the Marshall Plan as an attempt to weaken Soviet control of Eastern Europe, and the Soviet Union saw it as an

This cartoon appeared in the British magazine Punch *at the time the Marshall Plan was announced*

example of 'dollar imperialism', designed to establish US influence in Europe. In fact, in 1947, Truman stated that 'the Truman Doctrine and the Marshall Plan were always two halves of the same walnut'.

Initially, the US Congress was opposed to the Marshall Plan, and it was not until March 1948 (after the communist coup in Czechoslovakia in February that a figure of $4 billion was agreed. In August, the Western European states calculated that $28 billion were needed, though the US finally reduced this to $17 billion.

At first, the Soviet Union's response to the Marshall Plan was mixed. Although it saw the plan as an extension of the Truman Doctrine, and was not in favour of US economic and political domination of Europe, it also needed US capital and goods. The USSR took part in early discussions in June, but the continued refusal by the US, Britain and France to consider German reparations led to the breakdown of talks. Because this disagreement threatened to delay the Marshall Plan at a time when the economic situation in Britain and France had become serious, it was decided to exclude the Soviet Union from further discussions and to exaggerate the differences between the two sides.

Fact
By the time of the Paris talks in July 1947, the Soviet Union had decided that participation in the proposed scheme would involve too many risks and rejected further negotiations. In fact, by then, Soviet spies in Britain had informed Stalin that the US, Britain and France had held talks earlier in London to preclude Soviet participation.

Question

What connection was there between the Truman Doctrine and the Marshall Plan?

On top of other decisions made in 1946–47, the Truman Doctrine and the Marshall Plan contributed to the collapse of the earlier Soviet policy of co-operation with the USA over western and southern parts of Europe. In this way, along with Soviet actions in Eastern Europe, they both contributed to the split of Europe into two opposing camps.

What were the main points of tension in Europe from 1947 to 1949?

The Cold War deepens, 1947–49

The divisions that emerged during 1946 and the first half of 1947 were exacerbated by developments that took place between the summer of 1947 and 1949. One factor that contributed to these developments was the 'Mr. X' article, written by Kennan and published in July 1947. This further influenced both Truman and the American public.

SOURCE C

It is clear that the main element of any United States policy towards the Soviet Union must be that of a long term, patient but firm and vigilant containment of Russian expansive tendencies. … It must continue to regard the Soviet Union as a rival, not a partner, in the political arena.

Extract from Kennan's 'Mr. X' article. Published in Time *magazine. July 1947.*

As international tensions rose, the CIA intervened in both Italian and French politics to counter local communist influence. It also conducted covert operations in Albania, the Baltic states, Poland and the Ukraine. Such actions only fuelled Stalin's determination to control the states of Eastern Europe even more closely and to eliminate 'imperialist agents' in those satellite states. The Soviet response was twofold: to both increase control of Eastern Europe, and integrate the economies of those states into that of the USSR. While these measures were closely connected to the USSR's need for reparations and economic resources, they only served to increase Cold War tensions.

The Soviet takeover of Eastern Europe

As early as February 1946, the USSR had been attempting to increase influence in 'its' zone or sphere of influence in Eastern Europe, in part due to Stalin's desperation to rebuild the Soviet Union's war-devastated economy. One event that had helped turn the tensions of 1945–46 into a Cold War had been the speech made by James Byrnes in Stuttgart in September 1946. In this speech Byrnes suggested that Germany might be able to 'redraw' its newly established border with Poland, creating an 'enlarged' Germany.

During the summer of 1947, following the implementation of the Truman Doctrine and the Marshall Plan, Soviet influence and control in Eastern Europe was stepped up, resulting in increasingly communist-dominated governments in Poland, Hungary, Romania and Albania.

The USSR soon came to see Europe as being divided into two antagonistic camps, and consequently believed that the strengthened control of Eastern Europe was essential for security.

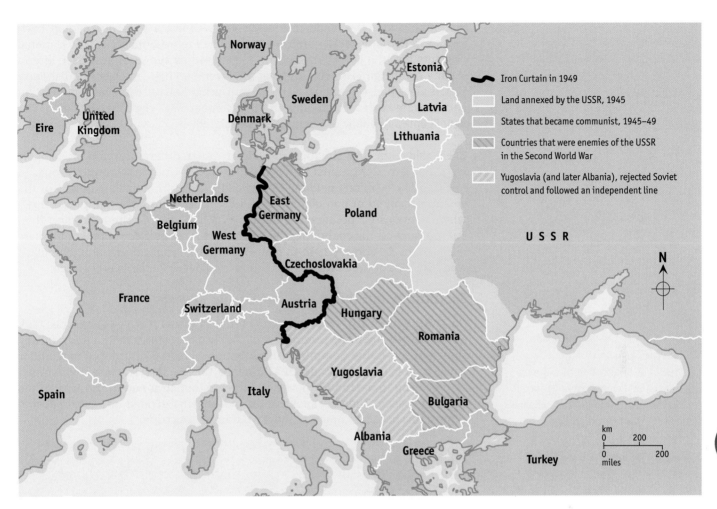

A map of Europe, showing the extent of the Soviet sphere of influence by the end of 1949

The USSR soon came to see Europe as being divided into two antagonistic camps, and consequently believed that strengthened control of Eastern Europe was essential for security. The main steps in this process are detailed below.

Poland: Stanislaw Mikolajczyk, the new deputy prime minister and leader of the important Peasants' Party, was unco-operative and, as a result, the elections due in February 1946 had been postponed until January 1947. Communist manipulation then ensured a communist victory, with Mikolajczyk's party winning only a handful of seats.

Bulgaria: the Communist Party (via the Fatherland Front) had ignored earlier Soviet agreements about allowing representatives of the opposition to have a role in government. After the October 1946 elections, the communists were mainly in control and, during 1947, the activities of the main opposition party were increasingly restricted.

Hungary: the Smallholders' Party (KGP) that had won the October 1945 elections formed a government with Ferenc Nagy as prime minister. Nagy faced a Left bloc made up of the Communist, Social Democrat and National Peasants parties. On 5 March 1946, a coalition government was set up, but by the summer of 1947 Nagy had been forced to resign. New elections, held on 31 August 1947, resulted in a communist victory.

Romania: under the leadership of Dr Petra Groza, a government had been formed in Romania which, after the inclusion of representatives of the National Peasants and the Liberals, had been recognised by the West. However, after a stormy campaign (and vote-rigging) in November 1946, the Communist Party and its allies had won almost all the seats. During 1947, all three main opposition parties were closed down, and on 30 December 1947 the king abdicated. The new People's Republic of Romania was declared.

Czechoslovakia: the situation developed rather differently here, as support for the Czech Communist Party and the Soviet Union was quite strong. In free and fair elections held on 26 May 1946, the communists won 38% of the vote. Harassment of non-communists did not begin until the summer of 1947, when a serious economic crisis developed. The Czech Communist Party then put pressure on the coalition government and most non-communist ministers resigned on 20 February 1948. In new elections, the communists and their allies won over 66% of the seats and the president, Edvard Benes, was replaced.

Cominform and Zhdanov's 'Two Camps' speech

On 22 September 1947, Soviet control of these Eastern European countries took a step further when the communist parties of these states met in Poland. They agreed to set up the Communist Information Bureau (**Cominform**) and, under Soviet politician Andrei Zhdanov's influence, the Marshall Plan was condemned as preparing to extend US power in order to launch a new world war. In his opening speech, Zhdanov spoke of the world being divided into two opposing camps; this became known as the **'Two Camps' Doctrine**.

> **SOURCE D**
>
> A new alignment of political forces has arisen. The more the war recedes into the past, the more distinct become two major trends in post-war international policy, corresponding to the division of the political forces operating on the international arena into two major camps[:] the imperialist and anti-democratic camp, on the one hand, and the anti-imperialist and democratic camp on the other. ... The vague and deliberately guarded formulations of the Marshall Plan amount in essence to a scheme to create blocs of states bound by obligations to the United States, and to grant American credits to European countries as a recompense for their renunciation of economic, and then of political, independence. Moreover, the cornerstone of the Marshall Plan is the restoration of the industrial areas of Western Germany controlled by American monopolies.
>
> *Extract from Zhdanov's 'Two Camps' speech. Quoted in Hunt, M. (ed.). 1996. Crises in US Foreign Policy: An International History Reader. New Haven, USA. Yale University Press. pp. 159–61.*

Cominform was intended to keep the communist parties in Europe under Moscow's control. This was a significant step, and marked the end of the flexible and hesitant foreign policy of the USSR in relation to US actions. The Truman Doctrine, the Marshall Plan and German reconstruction thus proved to be important turning points. The latter policy in particular worried many in those Eastern European states sharing a border with Germany.

Cominform Set up by Stalin in 1945, the Communist Information Bureau was intended to co-ordinate the different communist governments of Eastern Europe and the communist parties in Western Europe. Its headquarters were originally in Belgrade in Yugoslavia, but they shifted to Bucharest in Romania in 1948, when Tito was expelled for not following Stalin's line. Cominform was abolished by Khrushchev in 1956.

'Two Camps' Doctrine This was the Soviet response to the Truman Doctrine, and was announced by Zhdanov at the first conference of Cominform at the end of September 1947. According to Zhdanov, the post-war world was divided into two camps: the Soviet-led, anti-imperialist and democratic camp and the US-led, imperialist and anti-democratic camp. Zhdanov argued that by means of the Truman Doctrine and the Marshall Plan, the US was attempting European domination and preparing for a new war to achieve world domination. He stated that the Soviet bloc was preventing this and trying to preserve world peace.

Yugoslavia

One exception to these developments in Eastern Europe was Yugoslavia, where Tito (see page 30) had already established a communist government, despite Stalin's 'Percentages Agreement' with Churchill (see page 54). Stalin withdrew all Soviet economic and military advisers in March 1948, in an attempt to topple Tito. However, Tito resisted, the Yugoslav Communist Party backed him, and he then arrested Stalin's Yugoslav supporters. In June 1948, Yugoslavia was expelled from Cominform for 'bourgeois nationalism' and, under pressure from the Soviet Union, other Eastern European countries broke off diplomatic and trade links. This was followed by a purge of 'Titoists' in the Eastern European communist parties.

At the same time, communist parties in the West were instructed to campaign against the Marshall Plan, and protest strikes were called in France and Italy during the winter of 1947–48. As Western European politics began to shift to the right in the late 1940s, it was clear that the Cold War was affecting internal as well as international politics.

Sovietisation and the 'peoples' democracies'

With Cominform established, the Soviet Union pushed hard for 'peoples' democracies' to be established in Eastern Europe, with planned economies run along the lines of the Soviet model. As local communist party leaders were increasingly replaced with those selected by Stalin himself, Soviet control over these satellite states was strengthened. However, such actions only served to increase Western support for Truman's policy of containment.

> **Five Ds** Demilitarisation, de-Nazification, democratisation, de-industrialism and decentralisation.

Germany and the problem of reparations

Since its formation in 1871, Germany had enjoyed great geopolitical importance in Europe. After 1945, it was clear that the country would be fundamental to the European (and even global) balance of power – and thus of tremendous importance to Soviet security concerns. As tensions grew into the Cold War, both sides feared Germany becoming part of the opposing camp.

At Potsdam, it had been agreed that, despite a temporary division into four Allied zones of occupation, Germany should be treated as one economic unit administered by the Allied Control Council (ACC). Berlin, deep inside the Soviet zone of Germany, was also to be divided into four zones; it was also agreed that the '**Five Ds**' should be applied to Germany.

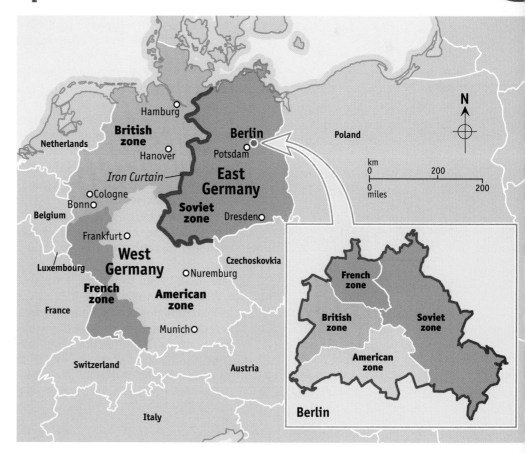

The division of Germany and Berlin after the Second World War

Lucius Clay (1897–1978)
General Clay was commander of US forces in Europe, and military governor of the US zone of Germany, 1947–49. He was best known for his organisation of the Berlin Airlift.

Fact
The USSR's rejection of the plans discussed by the West had been expected and indeed hoped for by Western nations. This outcome (described as a 'successful failure' by German historian Wilfried Loth) enabled the West to continue its plans to establish Bizonia.

Fact
Stalin feared these moves were part of a plan to divide Germany permanently into two halves, and to use the industrial strength of the Ruhr as a base for actions against the USSR.

However, the unresolved question of reparations continued to cause problems between the Soviet Union and the other allies. Although the Soviet Union was the first occupying power to allow democratic parties in its zone, and was a more co-operative member of the Allied Control Commission than France, tensions soon arose over political developments in the Soviet zone. The main issue was economic. The Soviet Union had liked the idea of the 'pastoralisation' of Germany (i.e. that the new post-war Germany should be essentially non-industrial), put forward by US secretary of the treasury Henry Morgenthau. But the US and Britain soon decided that a revival of German industry was essential, partly because it was seen as vital to the recovery of the Western European economies in general, and partly because the US and Britain were unable or unwilling to prop up the German economy indefinitely.

In April 1946, General **Lucius Clay**, the US military governor, had told the US State Department that he believed the Soviet Union was co-operating over the Potsdam agreements and had no plans for aggression. However, Byrnes had decided to test this at the Paris meeting of the Council of Foreign Ministers that began later that month. He proposed that all four Allies should sign a pact to demilitarise Germany for 25 years. Although Molotov, the Soviet foreign minister, did not reject this, the meeting broke up because of the USA's continued refusal to consider the question of reparations.

The creation of Bizonia and Trizonia

On 3 May 1946, because of lack of agreement on an all-German trade policy, Clay was told to stop all reparations deliveries to the Soviet Union. This included 25 million tonnes of coal, which were exported to Western Europe instead. This was seen by the Soviet Union as an attempt to force through the creation of a revived German economy that would be part of the international global capitalist system, and allied to the US. In July, Molotov insisted on $10 billion in reparations from Germany on behalf of the USSR. Once again, Byrnes for the US refused until the German economy had recovered.

On 27 July 1946, Britain and the US agreed to merge their zones to form one economic unit, and in January the following year, the two zones were joined in what became known as Bizonia. In February, Britain threatened to pull out of Bizonia if efforts were not made to revive German heavy industry. At the March–April meeting of the Council of Foreign Ministers in Moscow, the question of reparations was raised again. Although Clay still favoured some concessions on this, Marshall was opposed, while Dulles claimed a revived West German economy would help the economic problems in France. Britain put forward a proposal to revise the Potsdam agreements by getting the USSR to give some of the resources it had already seized to the Western zones, and to accept that there would be no shipments of coal or steel to the USSR until the German economy was thriving. The proposal was rejected by the USSR.

The USSR began to see these steps as an attempt to build up the economy of a Western Germany (with 75% of the German population and the important industrial regions), which might become a military threat in the future as it had been in the past – especially if it were allied to what the Soviet Union perceived as an increasingly hostile USA. During November and December 1947, the Council of Foreign Ministers met in London, and Britain and the US agreed on one last attempt to revive the economy of a unified Germany. However, as they had no intention of agreeing to Soviet demands for reparations, and they knew

A cartoon showing how the Russians feared that Nazi aggression would 'hatch out' again once West Germany was rebuilt

the USSR would not approve the plans without reparations, the talks were expected to fail. They agreed that, in this event, they would develop Bizonia and introduce currency reform as preliminary steps to the establishment of a separate West German state. On 7 June 1948, France agreed to join its zone to Bizonia, to form Trizonia. On 18 June, without consulting the Soviet Union, the West introduced a new currency, the Deutschmark, to replace the Reichsmark. On 23 June, this was extended to West Berlin.

The 1948 Crisis in Berlin – the Berlin Blockade

The Soviet Union, opposed to the idea of a separate West German state, tried to prevent this by putting pressure on West Berlin. On 24 June, the USSR cut off all road, rail and freight traffic to West Berlin. The supply of electricity from East to West Berlin was also cut. This Berlin Crisis – known as the Berlin Blockade – was the first open Cold War conflict between the two sides. However, this crisis did not develop into a 'hot' war. Instead, the Allied response was the massive **Berlin Airlift**, in which tonnes of food, fuel and other basic items were flown from Trizonia into West Berlin to supply its two million citizens. The airlift lasted for almost a year, until May 1949, when the obvious failure of the blockade finally led Stalin to call it off.

Berlin Airlift Aid organised by General Clay. Having a good grasp of the Soviet Union's military weakness – and thus its unwillingness to risk armed conflict – Clay had advocated the use of tanks to break through the road blocks. This advice had been rejected by both Truman and Ernest Bevin, in favour of maintaining links by air.

81

West Berliners cheering an Allied plane bringing in supplies during the Berlin Airlift

Länder This is the name for the separate states that collectively made up the Federal Republic of Germany.

In fact, the Berlin Blockade actually speeded up the very thing it was intended to stop – the establishment of a West German state. The West portrayed the blockade as an attempt by the Soviet Union to drive the Allies out of West Berlin in preparation for taking over the western zones of Germany. The prime ministers of the West German **Länder**, who had at first been reluctant to accept the creation of a separate West German state, now agreed as a way of ensuring US protection against this Soviet 'takeover'. In May 1949, the new Federal Republic of Germany (FDR) was set up.

At first, the USSR was still reluctant to set up a separate East German state. It hoped to avoid a permanent division and instead wanted to see the emergence of a neutral Germany, independent of a US-dominated Western Europe. However, on 7 October, the USSR finally accepted the division of Germany and announced the transformation of its eastern zone into a new state, called the German Democratic Republic (GDR). As with the Allied High Commission in West Germany, the Soviet Control Commission in East Germany retained considerable powers of supervision over the area.

This division of Germany – and Berlin – soon came to represent the division of Europe into two mutually suspicious and hostile camps. Soviet fears that the West wanted a revived Germany closely allied to the US were confirmed in 1955, when West Germany was allowed to join NATO (see page 19).

How did the First Cold War develop in Europe from 1949 to 1953?

US perceptions of the Soviet threat

When Roosevelt had been US president, he had not seen the Soviet Union as a serious threat to his country's security. Mindful of Russian history and fears – and of the fact that, on several occasions, the USSR had come close to defeat during the Second World War – he was prepared to make some concessions. In particular, he believed the Soviet Union desired three things:

- a sphere of influence in Eastern Europe (to include, if possible, those Middle Eastern and Asian states that also had borders with the USSR)
- reparations from former Axis Powers (especially Germany)
- US financial support in reconstructing the USSR.

Roosevelt did not intend to give Stalin everything he wanted, though – he expected that any concessions on these issues would be on American terms.

However, Roosevelt's death and Truman's accession had allowed Byrnes to push for a tougher policy, and concessions would only be forthcoming if the Soviet Union accepted that the US should be the strongest power, based on its nuclear monopoly. When US credits were not forthcoming, Stalin placed reliance on reparations. When these were persistently refused by the US and Britain, the Soviet Union turned to the pursuit of security via tight control over Eastern Europe and the development of its own atomic weapons.

Many Western European countries came to depend on the USA's military strength, as well as looking to it for economic assistance. Britain, for instance, wanted US help to support its interests in Europe and the Middle East; while France needed help to maintain its colonial possessions in Southeast Asia. However, Truman's advisers came to believe that they could win the emerging Cold War by stimulating massive economic growth in the West, which could then 'win' the Eastern European states from the Soviet Union.

By then, some US advisers, including Kennan, had come to believe that the tough stance taken by the West since 1947 had made the USSR ready to negotiate away their sphere of influence. However, others (such as Clay) feared that the overall military weakness of the Soviet Union might lead it to launch a 'defensive' war in the near future, before the imbalance became even greater. The CIA also issued warnings, so, on 17 March 1948, Truman asked Congress to approve military training for all adult males, and selective military service for some. This was unusual in times of peace, and showed the US public how serious the president believed the situation to be.

Fact
Only a few contemporaries – such as General Clay and the historian Isaac Deutscher – publicly questioned the reality of the perceived military threat from the Soviet Union. These two men saw the USSR as militarily, as well as economically, weak.

Ernest Bevin (1881–1951)
Bevin was a British trade unionist and Labour politician. As general secretary of the TGWU, he helped plan the General Strike of 1926. From 1940 to 1945, he was minister of labour and national service. From 1945 to 1951, he held the position of foreign secretary, where he pursued a strong anti-Soviet, pro-US line.

Comecon Set up in 1949, the Council for Mutual Economic Assistance (CMEA), or Comecon, was intended to co-ordinate industrial development and trade in the Soviet Union and its Eastern European satellites, and to prevent trade with the West. Initially, the Soviet Union insisted on preferential terms, especially in relation to the supply of raw materials, which Stalin wanted for the reconstruction of Soviet industry. Later, under Khrushchev, the terms became more equal, and in 1964 a Bank for Socialist Countries was set up.

Military developments and the formation of NATO

Soviet actions in Eastern Europe – especially the communist takeover in Czechoslovakia in February 1948 – led countries in Western Europe to form the Brussels Treaty Organisation (BTO). The Berlin Crisis, which had begun in June 1948, resulted in an increased sense of military insecurity in Western Europe, and led many politicians to conclude that only the US could maintain a 'balance of power' in Europe.

By late 1948, however, Marshall and Kennan had both concluded that the limited response of the Soviet Union over Berlin had shown the Soviet threat to be a political and not a military one. Consequently, they believed it could be contained by mainly non-military means, as Soviet power was at its peak and would soon decline – especially if the economic (as well as military) strength of the West was increased.

After the Berlin Crisis was over, **Ernest Bevin**, the British foreign secretary, worked hard to include the US in a European alliance. The US was more than willing to see the setting up of a global military alliance. On 4 April 1949, the BTO became the North Atlantic Treaty Organisation (NATO), with the US and Canada as new members. The treaty was signed in Washington and the US was clearly the strongest member. In fact, from the beginning, NATO was based on the USA's nuclear monopoly, and the country's nuclear strength remained the main element in NATO strategy throughout the Cold War.

The Soviet reaction

The initial Soviet response to the increasing tensions that followed the Berlin Crisis was more economic than military (though Soviet military expenditure did increase). At first, the Soviet Union came up with the Molotov Plan – a series of bilateral trade agreements between the Eastern European states and the USSR. In January 1949, the Soviet Union announced the formation of **Comecon** – the Council for Mutual Economic Assistance (CMEA), which bound states in Eastern Europe even more closely to the Soviet Union. The creation of NATO raised huge security concerns among the Soviet leadership, as the USSR was at most only a regional power, whereas the USA was already clearly a global superpower. The victory of the Chinese communists, which led to the creation of the People's Republic of China in October 1949, did little to even up the relative standing of the opposing forces in the Cold War.

Soviet fears increased in the 1950s, when similar US-dominated treaties were created in the Pacific and the Middle East. These treaties, which gave the US an even wider spread of foreign bases, only served to underline the global isolation of the Soviet Union.

The nuclear arms race

A significant development in the Cold War, which gave a new dimension to international relations between East and West, occurred in August 1949 when the Soviet Union exploded its first atomic bomb. The US nuclear monopoly was thus ended, and a nuclear arms race began. The US was determined to keep well ahead of Soviet military capabilities, while the USSR was equally determined to match US nuclear capabilities. By 1952, the USA had developed a much more powerful nuclear weapon. The H-bomb ushered in the thermonuclear age, and by 1953 the USSR had matched it.

Stalin's foreign policy, 1949–53

In October 1949, with the creation of the communist People's Republic of China led by Mao Zedong, and then the start of the Korean War in June 1950, Cold War tensions mainly shifted from Europe to Asia (see Unit 2, page 88). However, developments in Asia had an impact on the situation and subsequent developments in Europe itself.

After the Berlin Crisis of 1948–49 and the formation of NATO in April 1949, the Soviet Union followed a dual-track foreign policy in the early 1950s. While its control of Eastern European satellites was consolidated, it also tried to limit the polarisation of Europe into two opposing Cold War camps.

The Stalinisation of Eastern Europe

The effect of the dispute between the Soviet Union and Tito's Yugoslavia in 1948–49, was that Stalin's determination to control the Eastern European bloc was strengthened. In the early 1950s, Titoists were accused of working with the West to restore capitalism in Yugoslavia. There began a witch hunt for Titoists in other Eastern European communist parties, followed by a wave of purges and show trials, which affected even top party and state officials.

All this was part of Stalin's attempt to turn the Eastern European bloc from a Soviet-dominated alliance into a tight monolithic unit controlled from Moscow, with no permitted deviation from Stalin's policies.

Attempts to limit Cold War polarisation

After 1949, Stalin attempted to limit the emerging nuclear arms race by launching what became the first of several 'peace campaigns'. Official statements from Moscow stressed the dangers of a new – nuclear – world war, while communist parties in the West conducted campaigns against the threat posed by nuclear weapons. At the same time, the Soviet Union began to put forward proposals for the neutralisation and demilitarisation of Germany and Central Europe. In part, this was influenced by the huge amounts of money the Soviet Union felt it had to divert to the defence industry in order not to fall too far behind the US. Although the US had also scaled down its forces after 1945 (to 1.5 million troops), it retained a clear nuclear superiority.

According to the Soviet Union, these 'peace campaigns' were a continuation of its pre-1939 attempts to maintain peace in Europe. The encouragement of mass peace movements, which would campaign for disarmament in Western states, thus seemed a logical way to attempt to limit the risk of Western governments launching any military attack on the Soviet Union. This approach, which began to take shape in 1949, reached its peak in the early 1950s, with millions of peace activists campaigning across the world. Similar movements were also established in Eastern Europe, but these were clearly communist-controlled.

Stalin hoped that such wide support would put pressure on Western governments to reduce the international tensions created by the Cold War, and to follow policies more to the liking of the USSR.

Linked to this approach were attempts – after 1949, and the establishment of NATO and the division of Germany – to turn Germany and Austria into a neutral Central European zone. In 1950, following the West's announcement of the

Fact
In Czechoslovakia, the main victim of the witch hunts was Rudolf Slansky. He had been the general secretary of the Czech Communist Party, but in 1952 he and 13 other important communists appeared in a show trial during which all 'confessed' their crimes against socialism. All were found guilty, and Slansky and ten others were executed.

Historical debate

The opinions of historians are still divided on whether the Stalin Notes were a genuine reflection of Soviet policy and what Stalin really wanted to happen to Germany after 1945. Richard Raack (1993) suggests that, as early as June 1945, Stalin had commented to a group of German communists that there would be 'two Germanys' after the war, showing he accepted that Germany would be dismembered. Loth (1998), however, argues that Stalin was still aiming for a unified Germany – though restricted, and with some Soviet influence – as late as 1952.

setting up of a European Defence Community, which would include West Germany, the Soviet Union suggested reuniting Germany, which would then be demilitarised after all occupation troops had been withdrawn. In March 1952, a further series of notes – the 'Stalin Notes' – were presented by the Soviet Union. In the main, they all offered German reunification in return for neutralisation. Though these were repeatedly rejected by the West, Stalin continued to make such offers until his death.

Some historians have suggested that such proposals were merely propaganda ploys – the USSR knew they would be rejected by the West, but believed they would please their supporters in Germany, as well as some NATO countries. Others, such as Caroline Kennedy-Pipe, have stressed this was simply a continuation of post-1945 Soviet security policy, and thus could be seen as both consistent and genuine. According to Geoffrey Roberts, Stalin's preferred option appears to have been a united, left-leaning – but not socialist – Germany. However, the communist victory in China in 1949, and the start of the Korean War in 1950, made the success of such proposals unlikely.

Question

What does this cartoon tell us about Soviet fears?

A cartoon published in the USSR in the 1950s, after West Germany had been allowed to join NATO; the president of the US, Eisenhower, is shown carrying a picture of Hitler

The impact of the Korean War

The start of the Korean War in 1950 increased Cold War tensions and persuaded Truman to act on the policy document NSC-68 (see pages 92–93). This had been drawn up earlier by the State and Defense Departments after Truman had asked the National Security Council to reappraise the USA's Cold War policy. The document called for a trebling of US defence expenditure, so that the Soviet threat could be met anywhere in the world. Truman increased the defence budget from $13.5 billion to $50 billion and, in 1952, plans were drawn up to increase NATO divisions from 14 to 50, and to establish US army, air force and naval forces in Europe. As a result, US military power increased dramatically throughout Western Europe. In addition, it was decided to re-arm West Germany in case the Soviet Union should try to reunite Germany by force, and to expand NATO in Europe by granting membership to Turkey and Greece.

These developments – and the security pacts the US signed with various Pacific states – increased Stalin's fears and forced him to divert huge economic resources from industrial reconstruction and development into defence expenditure. Given the USSR's relative economic weakness, this produced much more negative results for the Soviet economy than military spending did in the United States.

> **Fact**
> NSC-68 was produced by the National Security Council in 1950 (see pages 92–93). It considered four possible US responses, but only recommended one: that the US should drastically increase its armaments in order to maintain a clear superiority over 'the Soviet world'. However, Truman realised that the US voters were not yet ready to approve the massive increase in taxes that would be necessary. Then, in June 1950, according to Dean Acheson, 'Korea came along and saved us'.

Unit summary

You should now have a reasonable understanding of the main problems and developments in Europe in the years 1946–47. In particular, you should have a good knowledge of the details and effects of policies such as the Truman Doctrine and the Marshall Plan, and of Soviet actions in Eastern Europe. In addition, you should be able to evaluate the roles played by key individuals, such as Truman, Churchill and Stalin. You should also understand the main actions and developments that led to the Berlin Blockade and Airlift of 1948–49, the formation of NATO, and the Soviet Union's development of nuclear weapons as well as the impact of such events on the Cold War.

End of unit activities

1 Research and make notes on the historical arguments surrounding the view that the main purpose of the Marshall Plan was to further the economic interests of the USA.

2 Produce a table to summarise the main steps in the Soviet takeover of Eastern Europe in the period 1946–49.

2 Developments in Asia and Indochina

Timeline

1925 Mar: Jiang Jieshi becomes leader of GMD

1937 Jul: Japan invades China

1945 Aug: Korea divided (temporarily) along the 38th parallel; Allied Council set up by the Big Four to administer Japan

Dec: Marshall Mission negotiates GMD–CCP truce

1946 Dec: fighting begins between France and Viet Minh in Indochina

1947 Mar: 'Red Scare' starts in US A

1948 Soviet troops leave North Korea

1949 Jun: US troops leave South Korea

Jul: France grants limited independence to Vietnam, under Bao Dai

Aug–Sep: USSR carries out, then announces, first Soviet A-bomb test

Oct: communist victory in China

1950 Jan: Acheson delivers 'Defensive Perimeter' speech; Ho Chi Minh recognised by USSR and China as legitimate ruler of Vietnam

Feb: Sino–Soviet Treaty signed; McCarthy begins anti-communist campaign in US

Apr: NSC-68

Jun: start of Korean War

Oct: Truman decides on invasion of North Korea; Chinese troops intervene to help North Korea

1951 Jul: peace talks begin

Aug: US forms military alliance with the Philippines; ANZUS Pact signed

Sep: treaty with Japan

1953 Jan: Eisenhower becomes president

Mar: Stalin dies

Jul: armistice signed in Korea

The impact of events and developments in other parts of the world not surprisingly affected the course of the Cold War. After 1949, what had been essentially a European affair became increasingly a global contest. The main developments outside Europe in the First Cold War, from 1946 to 1953, were in Asia: these were the communist victory in China in 1949 and the start of the Korean War the following year. At the same time – but less obviously important at first – were the events beginning to unfold in French **Indochina**.

In the summer of 1949, **Mao Zedong** issued a statement in which he said that, once established, the new China would 'lean to one side' in the new international situation that had emerged after the end of the Second World War. Although Stalin suspected that Mao might not be a reliable friend, he was hopeful that developments in Asia in general would lessen the Soviet Union's isolation.

Consequently, the war that broke out in 1946 in French Indochina, between the French and Ho Chi Minh's Viet Minh guerrilla army, soon became part of the global Cold War. At first the USA was officially opposed to the continuation of European colonialism, and the USSR initially ignored Ho Chi Minh's insurgency. However, in January 1950, first Communist China and then the USSR recognised Ho Chi Minh as the legitimate ruler of Vietnam. The following month, the USA gave its first financial aid to the French attempt to regain control of its former province, and recognised Bao Dai's French-backed government. The French claimed they were fighting communism, while Dean Acheson claimed Ho was a hardline communist rather than a nationalist. Initially, however, the main battle-fronts in the global Cold War were China and Korea.

Key questions

- What attitude did the US take to communism in China before 1949?
- How did the communist victory in China in 1949 affect the Cold War?
- To what extent was the Korean War caused by Cold War factors?
- What were the consequences of the Korean War for the Cold War?

Overview

- At first, the US had not been overly concerned about the civil war in China between the nationalist Guomindang (GMD) and the Chinese Communist Party (CCP).
- However, Japanese aggression – first against Manchuria and then against mainland China – led the US to give increasing support to Jiang Jieshi's nationalist government after 1941.

- In 1945, the US (and the USSR) hoped the two sides in China could form a coalition government; in December 1945, the US Marshall Mission succeeded in bringing about a truce.

- When the truce broke down in early 1946, the US at first continued to support Jiang Jieshi. From 1948, however, as a communist victory seemed imminent, the US began to slow down its aid.

- The US tended to see Communist China as Stalin's tool, and refused to recognise Mao's government. Coming on top of the escalating Cold War in Europe and the loss of the US nuclear monopoly earlier in the year, the 'loss' of China was seen as a defeat for Truman's policy of containment.

- A Sino–Soviet Treaty in 1950 increased US concerns and contributed to the McCarthy 'witch hunts' in the early 1950s. It led Truman to order a review of US foreign policy, resulting in the document known as NSC-68. The US also decided to give aid to the French in their struggle against the communist-led Viet Minh in Indochina.

- In June 1950, Cold War tensions in Asia shifted from China to Korea – which had been temporarily divided in 1945 – when the communist North attacked the South in an attempt to reunify the country.

- The US, which had been backing South Korea, was able to use the Soviet Union's boycott of the UN Security Council to get the UN to agree to sending an army to help the South.

Indochina This was the federation of states in Southeast Asia that were part of the French empire until 1954. The main countries were Vietnam and Cambodia, which were made part of the Union of Indochina in 1887; Laos was added in 1893. After the Second World War, France offered more self-government. Although Cambodia and Laos accepted this, it was rejected by those who wanted total independence for Vietnam. In 1954, France was forced to withdraw completely from Indochina, and the three states became independent at the Geneva meeting of 1954.

Mao Zedong (1893–1976)
Mao was active in the May Fourth Movement, which protested against Japanese demands for Chinese territory after the First World War. He was a founder member of the Chinese Communist Party in 1921, and by 1924 was a member of its Central Committee. In October 1934, he led the Long March of the communist Red Army to the north of China in order to avoid destruction by the Guomindang (see page 90). In 1935 he was elected Chairman of the CCP, a post he retained until his death. Under Mao, China became a one-party state.

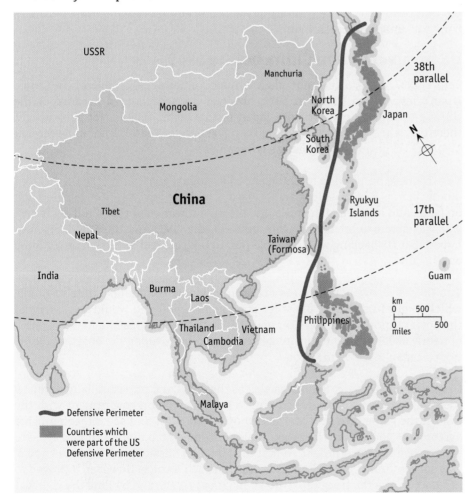

Communist China and its neighbours in 1953; the map also shows the Cold War divisions of Korea and Vietnam, and the US Defensive Perimeter as outlined by Dean Acheson in January 1950 (see pages 94 and 96); Korea and Taiwan were not included

Guomindang A political party set up in China by Sun Yat-sen in 1912. In 1924, Sun announced that the GMD was based on Three Principles – national freedom, democratic government and the people's welfare. The GMD was then reorganised with a Leninist structure. After Sun's death in 1925, Jiang Jieshi assumed leadership and the GMD became more right-wing. Following his defeat by the CCP in 1949, Jiang established a GMD regime in Taiwan, which became known as Nationalist China during the Cold War. Older textbooks refer to the GMD as the Kuomintang.

Jiang Jieshi (1887–1975) Jiang joined Sun Yat-sen's Guomindang Party, and became its leader after Sun's death in 1925. In 1927 he turned on his allies, the CCP. In 1928, Jiang became military dictator of China and concentrated on trying to crush the CCP. His regime was corrupt and unpopular, and after 1946 the civil war between the GMD and the CCP resumed. Defeated in 1949, Jiang retreated to the Chinese island of Formosa (Taiwan). The US claimed his Nationalist China regime there was the legitimate government of the whole of China.

Question

What was the Soviet Union's initial attitude to the Guomindang in China?

- After early victories, the North was pushed back by US/UN forces, commanded by US general Douglas MacArthur. Once the North had been driven from the South, the US/UN forces invaded the North. As they approached the border with China, a massive Chinese army went in to aid the North.
- A clash over strategy, followed by insubordination, led Truman to sack MacArthur, and soon a stalemate in the war was reached. This continued for almost two years, until an armistice was signed in July 1953.
- In the meantime, the US had begun to arrange a series of military alliances in the Pacific, designed to secure what it called the Defensive Perimeter. Crucial to this was the reconstruction of Japan.

What attitude did the US take to communism in China before 1949?

Early Soviet involvement

The Chinese Communist Party was formed in 1921. In its early years, the CCP was advised by the Bolshevik government of Soviet Russia to co-operate with Sun Yat-sen and his nationalist **Guomindang** (GMD) party. However, in 1925, Sun died and was succeeded by **Jiang Jieshi**, who soon moved the party to the right. In 1927, Jiang began what turned out to be a protracted civil war against the CCP. Despite receiving military advisers and equipment from Nazi Germany, Jiang was unable to crush them.

US involvement in China before 1949

Before 1937, the US had not placed much importance on events in China. Japan's invasion of China in 1937, however, caused concern because of the USA's growing competition with Japan in the Pacific region. Not surprisingly, therefore, when Japan attacked the US naval base of Pearl Harbor in December 1941, the US decided to aid Jiang's government.

The Japanese occupation of China ended in August 1945, when the US dropped atomic bombs on Hiroshima and Nagasaki, and the Soviet Union declared war on Japan and invaded Manchuria. By this time it was clear that a full-scale civil war was about to break out again between the GMD and the CCP. Jiang now hoped that US backing would enable him to take control of the whole of China once again.

The US did not want to see the creation of a new communist state in China, which might frustrate its plans for the Pacific region and would certainly end the Soviet Union's isolation. To prevent this, the US organised a massive airlift of nearly 100,000 GMD troops to key cities and ports along the coast, while US troops began to arrive in China.

Despite giving this aid, the US (as well as the USSR) did not want Jiang to renew the civil war; instead, it advised him to form a coalition government with the CCP. At the same time, in order not to upset the West and so risk jeopardising agreements about Eastern Europe, Stalin informed Mao that he should agree to such a coalition government. At first the Marshall Mission, as it became known, was successful in getting both sides to sign such a truce. However, it proved to be short-lived – the truce broke down in January 1946, and by June the civil war was in full swing.

Initially, the US had threatened to halt aid to Jiang if he refused to initiate some social reforms. Though no reforms took place, the US at first continued to send

Jiang massive military aid. Once the Cold War had clearly begun, the Truman Doctrine and the policy of containment led the US to support any regime that was anti-communist. Nonetheless, China was seen as less of a priority than Japan in the USA's overall foreign policy in Asia, even though it was clear that Japanese industrial recovery would be much quicker if it had access to the vast Chinese market and its raw materials.

By the end of 1947, the US – which had so far given Jiang over $200 million in military aid – concluded that the GMD was virtually defeated. Truman was prepared to leave Jiang to his fate as, even at this stage, China was not seen as having any real strategic significance for the US.

Early in 1948, despite the emerging Cold War in Europe, secretary of state George Marshall persuaded Truman to stop any further aid to Jiang. In April, Jiang's capital, Nanjing, fell to the communists and Jiang fled to Taiwan (then known as Formosa). He took with him China's entire gold reserves, 200,000 troops and the imperial art collection from the Forbidden City. On 1 October 1949, Mao proclaimed the birth of the new People's Republic of China.

How did the communist victory in China in 1949 affect the Cold War?

Impact on the US

At first, the USA's decision to withdraw support for Jiang, leaving the way open for a communist takeover, was not considered a serious problem. It was felt that the USA's nuclear monopoly would in itself be enough of a threat to contain communism in China. However, in August 1949, the USSR exploded its first atomic device. One month later, the communists secured their victory in China. These two events caused Truman's government to be accused of being 'soft' on communism and thus responsible for the 'loss of China'. In the summer of 1949, Mao had declared his 'lean to one side' policy in the emerging Cold War.

The question of China – linked to the policy of containment – became more acute in February 1950, when the Soviet Union and China signed the 30-Year Treaty of Friendship, Alliance and Mutual Assistance. As early as December 1949, Mao had gone to Moscow to ask Stalin for economic assistance. Despite his earlier disagreements with Mao over the CCP's decision to continue the civil war in China, Stalin agreed (although he kept Mao waiting to show him who was boss). However, Stalin refused Mao's request for nuclear weapons.

Chairman Mao declares the founding of the People's Republic of China, on 1 October 1949

Question

What did the USA's Marshall Mission to China try to achieve?

Fact

Because of past disagreements with Stalin, Mao had first approached the US for assistance, but Truman had refused to recognise Mao's new government. Mao thus had no choice but to turn to the USSR.

91

The US government's response to this treaty was cautious at first. Despite his dislike of communism, secretary of state Dean Acheson thought that establishing good relations with Mao might be beneficial to US interests. Although the US still refused to recognise the new People's Republic of China, and instead acknowledged Jiang's regime in Taiwan as the legitimate Chinese government, it stopped short at first of guaranteeing US military help should Communist China decide to retake the island. Acheson even argued that recognition of Mao's government might help break up China's new friendship with the Soviet Union. Any progress that may have been made by following this advice was set back by the anti-communist hysteria stirred up by the Republicans during the early 1950s.

McCarthyism and anti-communist hysteria

Events in China coincided with the launch of Republican senator Joseph McCarthy's anti-communist crusade within the USA. In November 1948 – and despite criticism of his China policy – Truman had won the presidential election, but once the Cold War had truly begun in 1947, a 'Red Scare' started to grip increasing numbers of Americans. There were suspicions of 'fifth columnists' (people within a country working to aid an outside enemy) and communist sympathisers. In response to Cold War tensions, the 1946 Congress made increasing use of the House Un-American Activities Committee (**HUAC**).

By 1947, HUAC had turned its attention to Hollywood actors, screenwriters and directors. Media campaigns and statements by churches and other religious groups stirred up the public, and soon the Screen Actors Guild (the film actors' union) began to operate a blacklist against suspected communists. From 1947 to 1952, its president was the actor Ronald Reagan.

In February 1950, after the Sino–Soviet Treaty, the Republican Party decided to step up its campaign against Truman and the Democrats. Also in February 1950, the British announced that Klaus Fuchs (who had worked on the USA's atomic bomb **Manhattan Project**) had been heading a spy ring which had passed nuclear secrets to the Russians. The previous month, Alger Hiss had been found guilty of perjury over the passing of classified US information to the Soviet Union during the late 1930s; a major role in exposing this had been played by the Republican congressman Richard Nixon.

Both these spy scares were used by McCarthy, who began by claiming he had a list of 205 State Department officials who were members of the Communist Party of the USA (CPUSA). He also asserted that the secretary of state had seen this list, but had taken no action. Later he reduced the number of people on the list to 57. This pattern was to be repeated many times – McCarthy would publicly brand people as communists, or communist sympathisers, with no hard evidence and then often change his story. However, his public 'Red-baiting', which became more hysterical after the start of the Korean War in June 1950, helped him win re-election as senator in 1952. In part, Truman was to blame for his own predicament, as in 1947 he had deliberately exaggerated the communist threat in order to get congressional approval for aid to Greece and Turkey and, later, for Marshall Aid.

NSC-68

The events of 1949 in Asia, and growing Republican criticism of his foreign policy, led Truman to call for a complete review of his administration's Cold War policies in January 1950. If nothing else, this would help undermine McCarthy's claims that his administration was 'soft' on communism. The review was

HUAC The US House of Representatives' Un-American Activities Committee, originally set up in 1938. In the early 1950s, it was used by Senator McCarthy in his campaign against communism in the USA. His early activities had pushed Truman into issuing Executive Order 9835 (a 'loyalty' test for civil servants) and, despite Truman's opposition, had persuaded Congress to pass the McCarran-Nixon Internal Security Act (to force all communist organisations to register with the government). Once in charge of the House Committee, McCarthy's 'Red Scare' took off, despite the Senate's Tydings Committee reporting in 1950 that his claims were a 'fraud and a hoax'.

Manhattan Project The Allied military atomic research project set up by Britain and the US soon after the outbreak of the Second World War. Even before the US entered the war in 1941, the research project (codenamed 'Manhattan') was underway in the US. The project was under the authority of US general Leslie Groves, and the lead scientist was J. Robert Oppenheimer. Millions of dollars were spent, and the first atomic device was exploded in the New Mexico desert on 16 July 1945.

carried out by the National Security Council, and the results documented in a report known as NSC-68 in April 1950. This report has been seen by many historians as 'one of the key documents of the Cold War' (Walter LaFeber). Revisionist historians view NSC-68 as an excuse for an always-intended US expansionism, deliberately exaggerating the Soviet Union's own expansionist intentions in order to persuade the US public to agree to a massive increase in defence expenditure – in historian William Chase Taubman's words, 'to put their money where their anti-communist mouths were'.

Essentially, NSC-68 claimed that under Truman US policy was broadly in line with the assessment of the Soviet threat made by Kennan in his 'Long Telegram' of 1946 (see pages 70–71). The review upheld the portrayal of the Soviet Union as a military threat because of its commitment to 'world-wide' revolution and its status as a 'totalitarian dictatorship'.

Acheson argued that the US should prepare for war, as negotiations with the USSR would never result in agreements that would be honoured. NSC-68 also pointed out the continuity of Truman's policies since 1947, attempting to 'contain communism' where it already existed, to erode its influence and power, and to bring about its ultimate downfall. In Asia, the report argued, the key to success was to build Japan into a regional power centre which could, in alliance with the USA, block any moves by the Soviet Union and China (which was seen by the US as Stalin's junior partner, simply acting on his instructions). This, along with strengthening Western Europe, was seen as the means to creating a global balance of power favourable to US interests via a militarised system of alliances and arms races.

Question

Why did Japan become important to US foreign policy after 1949?

One significant change of direction, however, was signalled by the suggestion that US foreign-policy objectives could only be met by a huge increase in US military strength. Previously, the US had mainly relied on its dominant position in the global economy – along with propaganda and a careful selection of specific interests – to wage and win the Cold War.

Now, according to NSC-68, the US needed to expand both its conventional and its nuclear forces. In particular, the report urged an immediate acceleration in the development of the hydrogen bomb in order to restore the USA's nuclear monopoly. US officials argued that the possession of a new type of nuclear weapon would allow the country to deny the USSR any balance of power. This ensured there could be no effective Soviet response to US policies, most importantly plans to expand the US sphere of influence over key areas of the world.

Fact
In part, this shift in policy towards a greater emphasis on the military aspects of containing communism resulted from Paul Nitze replacing George Kennan as head of the State Department's policy planning staff. Nitze was the main author of NSC-68.

Another significant departure suggested in NSC-68 was that containment (which had been based on the belief that the USSR was not a serious long-term threat) should be replaced by confrontation. This confrontation should take the form of an offensive 'roll back' of communism across the world – in Asia as well as Eastern Europe, and eventually in the Soviet Union itself.

Finally, NSC-68 was important in that it envisaged the US having powerful military forces on a permanent basis, even though it was not technically engaged in a war. Previously, during times of peace the US had always reduced its military strength.

Although Truman broadly accepted this analysis and the set of proposals laid out in NSC-68, he calculated that the US electorate was unlikely to accept the massive increase in taxes or the cuts in welfare spending that would be necessary to fund military expansion.

In early April 1950, Truman – concerned about the congressional elections due in November – decided to put everything on hold. Despite this, NSC-68 remained an extremely powerful influence on US policy until the time of détente in the 1970s, and it was revived during the Second Cold War in the late 1970s and early 1980s (see Chapter 6).

To what extent was the Korean War caused by Cold War factors?

The Korean War began in June 1950, when a large North Korean army invaded South Korea in an attempt to reunite the country. (There is some evidence to suggest that South Korea was also preparing an invasion of North Korea.) When the attack happened, it was not obvious at first that it would become an important turning point in the Cold War.

Korea had lost its independence in 1910, when it had been taken over by Japan, and had remained a Japanese colony until August 1945. When Japan surrendered, US and Soviet troops had moved respectively into the south and north of Korea, which had been temporarily divided along the **38th parallel** for the purpose of dealing with Japanese troops. However, as the Cold War began to develop in Europe, these American and Russian zones of occupation had become, in practice, two separate states; this was formalised in 1948.

The Soviet Union – which wanted unification of Korea under the northern leader Kim Il Sung – withdrew its troops in the autumn of 1948. The US – which wanted unification under the southern ruler Syngman Rhee – finally withdrew its troops from Korea in June 1949.

Neither the US nor the USSR seemed too concerned about the immediate future of Korea. Because the USSR shared a border with Korea, Stalin had been concerned about the kind of regime that might take over at the end of the war. However, with Kim Il Sung in charge of the North, Soviet security concerns seemed to have been satisfied.

In January 1950, Acheson made his 'Defensive Perimeter' speech to the Washington Press Club (see pages 89 and 96), in which he named the countries that the US would automatically defend against communist aggression. South Korea was not on the list. Truman supported Acheson, believing that mainland Asia was outside the USA's Pacific Defensive Perimeter. Such comments and measures may have led Stalin to conclude later that the US would not defend South Korea.

Soviet policy – expansionism or security?

Between 1945 and 1950, before the Korean War began, there had been several border clashes between the two rival states of North and South Korea, in which over 100,000 Koreans had died. While US and Soviet troops had remained in their respective zones, they had acted as restraints on the two nationalist Korean leaders. However, their withdrawal in 1948–49 had a destabilising effect and both the local regimes became more aggressive. Kim had warned both Stalin and Mao in advance of his intention to attack South Korea. At first Stalin had put off Kim's requests for support, but in January 1950, after Acheson's speech, the Soviet leader gave cautious approval to Kim's plans. Nevertheless, in April 1950 he made it clear to Kim that, if the US became involved, the USSR would not intervene directly to help him.

38th parallel This is the 38th line of latitude on Earth's surface, which crosses Korea 38° north of the Equator, and divides the country north from south. The division was agreed in 1945 by the USA and the USSR. The communist and industrial North was ruled by Kim Il Sung, while the capitalist and mainly agricultural South was ruled by Syngman Rhee. Both regimes were extremely authoritarian, and both leaders were nationalists who resented the division of their country and wanted to bring about reunification as soon as possible.

Question

Why was Korea divided into North and South after the Second World War?

Fact

Since the collapse of the Soviet Union and the end of the Cold War, access to previously restricted documents has revealed that it was Kim Il Sung who was the main driving force behind the North's decision to invade the South in order to reunite the country.

Stalin's decisions about Korea – like those about Berlin in 1948–49 (see page 81) – were based on serious miscalculations of the likely US response. In particular, he assumed that, as the US had not intervened to prevent Mao's victory in China, it was unlikely to aid South Korea. While he was keenly aware that the Soviet Union could not fight another war, he believed a successful reunification of Korea under Kim's communist government would strengthen Soviet security. It would ensure a friendly state on the USSR's borders, thus reducing his fears of encirclement, and would also give access to Korean hydroelectric power and raw materials which would thus be denied to the USA's most important Pacific ally, Japan. Reunification under the North would therefore reduce Stalin's fears concerning Japan's influence in the region.

Mao was preoccupied with establishing communist rule in China and in dealing with the threat posed by Jiang Jieshi's regime in Taiwan, which Mao wanted to invade. The Chinese leader therefore refused to make any guarantees of military assistance.

It thus seems that it was Kim, not Stalin or Mao, who pushed for the attack in June 1950. He was encouraged by Rhee's unpopularity and evidence of growing support for the communist party in the South. He believed most Koreans would see him as a national hero if he reunited the country. Japan had been a harsh ruler of Korea and Kim resented US post-war attempts to rebuild Japan as a pro-Western regional power. Mindful of US backing for Jiang Jieshi in China's civil war, he feared the same assistance might be given to South Korea.

Several historians have argued that the 1950 invasion was in many ways a continuation of a much longer civil war between North and South Korea. US historian Bruce Cumings, for example, has suggested that the North Korean invasion was the result of Kim's strong nationalist and revolutionary ideals, and had very little to do with Soviet wishes. Eventually, Kim was able to persuade Stalin that an invasion would result in a quick victory. Consequently, Stalin saw no need to end the Soviet delegation's boycott of the UN Security Council, which was a protest against the USA's refusal to allow Communist China a seat. Acheson's Defensive Perimeter speech also encouraged Kim to push ahead with his invasion plans.

US strategy

The importance of Japan

Although US Cold War policy was mainly focused on 'containing' Soviet influence in Europe, there was also a strong drive to contain what was seen as the threat of Soviet expansion across the world. While this led to support for Jiang's anti-communist regime in China, the main focus of US policy in Asia was Japan.

By 1947 and the start of the Cold War, US strategy towards Japan had altered. Essentially, control of the country was seen as crucial for the balance of power in the whole Asian region, especially in view of its vast industrial potential. Thus it was seen as essential to tie Japan into a close alliance with the US, and to rapidly rebuild its economic strength. Japan's industry and agriculture had been badly damaged in the closing stages of the war, while the Communist Party of Japan was growing in popularity. The US reaction was to rebuild the economy and remove earlier restrictions on industrial production. In 1949, Congress voted to give $500 million in aid for the purchase of food, and for raw materials for Japanese industry.

> **Although US Cold War policy was mainly focused on 'containing' Soviet influence in Europe, there was also a strong drive to contain what was seen as the threat of Soviet expansion across the world.**

> **Fact**
> After August 1945, the Big Four set up a joint Allied Council to administer Japan, but the real power lay with the USA – the only ally with an army in Japan. Consequently, Soviet requests for the temporary division of Japan into four zones of occupation, as in Germany, were immediately refused.

Defensive Perimeter Strategy
A US military plan developed in relation to Asia. War plans were drawn up to defend a crescent of offshore Pacific islands against any possible communist threat from the Soviet Union or China. These islands were Japan, the Ryukyu islands, Guam and the Philippines. They formed an inverted U-shape, and all had US airbases and garrisons.

Douglas MacArthur (1880–1964) MacArthur fought in the First World War and became the youngest commander in the US army in France. In 1930, he was promoted to chief of staff and, during the Second World War, took charge of the military campaign against Japan in the Pacific. He accepted Japan's formal surrender in 1945, and was in charge of the administration there until 1951. In 1950, at the age of 70, he was appointed commander of the UN forces in Korea, but was dismissed the following year for opposing Truman's strategy and for acts of insubordination, including publicly criticising Truman's decision to negotiate with China.

The Defensive Perimeter

While China, South Korea and even for a time Vietnam were not seen as vitally important to US security, it was decided that communism should be contained on the periphery of Asia. A new policy, known as the **Defensive Perimeter Strategy**, was drawn up to defend a belt of offshore Pacific islands in Asia against further Soviet expansion.

As the Cold War developed, it was also decided that anti-communist forces in China, South Korea and Vietnam should be given substantial financial assistance. At this time, US policy was firmly against deploying US troops in any conflict on the Asian mainland.

However, by 1950, the USA's communism-containment strategy in Asia had not enjoyed much success. Although Japan was showing signs of a strong economic revival and was closely allied to the US, China had been 'lost'. At the same time, communist forces were clearly growing in popularity and strength in Indochina (see Chapter 5 for developments in this area).

In part, this lack of success was because most of the USA's resources were devoted to Europe, which was seen as being of greater strategic importance than Asia. However, communist movements in Asia were much more popular than those in Europe, partly because they were linked to strong desires for national independence from colonial powers such as France. This, even more than the relative lack of US aid, was the major reason why communism in Asia proved so much more difficult to 'contain'.

The US response

Truman's immediate reaction to the North Korean invasion on 25 June 1950 was to rush military supplies to South Korea. Two days later, taking advantage of the USSR's boycott (see page 95), the US pushed a resolution through the UN Security Council calling for military action to be taken by UN members against North Korea.

In theory this was a UN military venture – 15 other UN members, including Britain, sent troops – but it was essentially a US enterprise. The vast majority of troops were non-Korean (260,000 out of just under 300,000 were American), and both the UN forces and those of South Korea were placed under the command of US General **Douglas MacArthur**, who was directly accountable to Truman, not to the UN.

The reasons for these US actions were varied. One major factor was the belief that Kim was not acting independently, but merely as Stalin's puppet, as part of the Soviet Union's attempt at world domination. Truman acted on what later became known as the Domino Theory (see pages 121–22) – if South Korea fell to the communists then the rest of Asia would follow, putting the Near East and even Europe under threat. A firm response was also seen as evidence of the USA's determination to resist communism anywhere in the world. In addition, it provided an opportunity to get public acceptance for the NSC-68 proposals that had been drawn up just two months before. Finally, Truman claimed that Korea was an important test for the new United Nations.

SOURCE A

In my generation, this was not the first time that the strong had attacked the weak. I recalled some earlier instances: Manchuria, Ethiopia, Austria. I remembered how each time the democracies failed to act, it had encouraged the aggressors to keep going ahead. Communism was acting in Korea just as Hitler, Mussolini and the Japanese had acted. ... If this were allowed to go unchallenged it would mean a third World War, just as similar instances had brought on a Second World War.

Truman, Harry S. 1956. Years of Trial and Hope, 1946–1953. London, UK. Hodder & Stoughton. p. 351.

Questions

Why might the date and nature of Source A make its expressed views unreliable? Does this mean that the source is of no use to historians trying to uncover the reasons for US actions in 1950?

The course of the Korean War, 1950–53

Initially the war went extremely well for North Korea. By August, the North Koreans had captured Seoul, the South Korean capital, and by September they had conquered the whole country, with the exception of an area around the south-eastern port of Pusan.

In this desperate situation, MacArthur launched a seaborne counter-invasion at Inchon, well behind North Korean lines. Soon he was pushing northwards to the 38th parallel. At the same time, UN forces were able to fight their way out of Pusan and begin pushing the North Koreans back.

The US had originally stated its aim as merely to expel the North Koreans from the South across the 38th parallel, but in October 1950 Truman – keen to demonstrate his anti-communist stance in light of impending elections – instructed MacArthur to invade North Korea.

In part, this was because an easy victory seemed possible, as US intelligence reports suggested that neither the Soviet Union nor China would intervene on behalf of the North Koreans. However, the USA's coalition partners were concerned by this step, which was against the UN mandate and showed that the USA had clearly moved beyond a policy of containment to one of 'roll-back', as outlined in NSC-68 (see pages 92–93).

MacArthur quickly captured Pyongyang, the North Korean capital, and continued to push north. By November 1950, MacArthur was rushing on to the Yalu River, which marked the border between North Korea and China. Up until then, Mao had wanted to keep out of the Korean War. But, as US troops approached the Chinese border, he came under increasing pressure from Stalin, and especially from sections of the CCP leadership, to take action to defend Chinese independence and national security. With no official diplomatic contact with the US, Mao genuinely feared the US might invade China through North Korea.

roll-back A policy that actively attempted to undermine and bring down the governments of communist states – as opposed to containment, which accepted communism in states where it already existed, but tried to prevent its spread.

97

By 1953, the main features of the Cold War were firmly established: a globalised military and ideological confrontation between the main powers and their allies in various systems of allegiance.

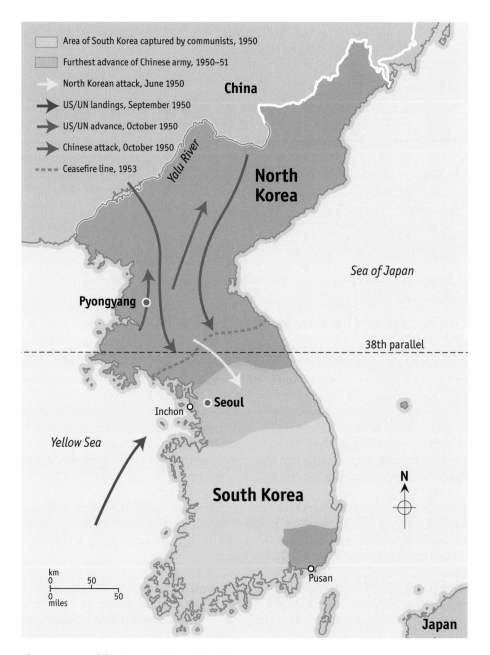

Area of South Korea captured by communists, 1950

Furthest advance of Chinese army, 1950–51

North Korean attack, June 1950

US/UN landings, September 1950

US/UN advance, October 1950

Chinese attack, October 1950

Ceasefire line, 1953

China

Yalu River

North Korea

Sea of Japan

Pyongyang

38th parallel

Inchon   Seoul

Yellow Sea

South Korea

N

km
0   50
0   50
miles

Pusan

Japan

The progress of the Korean War, 1950–53

The decision to send troops to aid Kim was coloured by the hope that a US invasion of China could be prevented by fighting in Korea. The tension was heightened by fears that Jiang, with US military help, might choose this moment to launch an invasion of mainland China from Taiwan. Eventually Mao convinced Stalin to agree to provide Soviet-manned planes with North Korean markings to give air cover – but only behind friendly lines. All sides were keen to avoid direct confrontations that might lead to another world war.

A small force of Chinese 'volunteers' crossed into North Korea on 25 October to help stop MacArthur's advance, but they then retreated. When MacArthur renewed his advance, over 250,000 Chinese troops crossed the Yalu River. After a successful counter-offensive, Chinese and North Korean forces recaptured Pyongyang and, in January 1951, pushed south and retook Seoul.

For a time, Truman and his administration considered MacArthur's call for the use of nuclear weapons against China. In the end, after strong opposition from British prime minister Clement Attlee and worries that such action might end in a nuclear war with the Soviet Union, this option was rejected.

Truman and Acheson decided to go back to the original US policy of simply expelling North Korea from the South. The US was now committed to fighting a limited war, which it believed the Soviet Union would not oppose. This decision was not supported by MacArthur. When he publicly criticised Truman's policies, he was dismissed as military commander in April 1951, and was replaced by General Matthew Ridgway. The Republicans supported MacArthur, and there was much public criticism of Truman's actions.

In fact, as soon as the war had started, Stalin had withdrawn all Soviet military advisers from North Korea and had recalled Soviet ships on their way to North Korea with military supplies. At the end of 1950, despite US advances up to the Chinese border, Stalin broke his promises to Mao on providing air cover and military equipment for the advancing Chinese troops.

A photograph of some of the many civilians who suffered during the Korean War

Fact
These fears were based on the incorrect assumptions that Stalin had ordered the Chinese in, and would honour the Sino–Soviet Treaty of 1950 if China was attacked.

Fact
Even later on, when Stalin did decide to give some help to China and North Korea, he made sure that the help was limited, and that no Soviet personnel were directly involved in the fighting, though advisers remained and others helped supervise airbases.

Truman stuck to the new policy that Korea was not the place to risk an all-out war against communism. From March 1951, however, the two sides reached a military stalemate. Although talks for a truce began as early as July 1951, they dragged on until 1953.

By 1952, with many of the NSC-68 recommendations already implemented – including development of the H-bomb – some in the US military believed the USSR could now be defeated. Stalin, though, was not prepared to be bullied. He calculated that the US could not win a conventional war against China and North Korea, and had information that the US would not use nuclear weapons.

The logjam was broken in 1953. In January, Eisenhower became president and warned China, via the Indian ambassador, that the US would consider using the A-bomb if no progress was made at the talks taking place at Panmunjon. This was part of what was called the 'New Look' US foreign policy and was closely associated with Eisenhower and his secretary of state, John Foster Dulles. In public, Dulles spoke openly about 'brinkmanship', based on a willingness to use nuclear weapons (see page 108). In practice, though, this proved to be more rhetoric than reality. In fact, there was not much change from Truman's earlier policy of containment. Then, in March, Stalin died. This allowed an armistice to be signed in July 1953, despite resistance from South Korea. The main feature of the armistice was an agreement that a line, roughly along the 38th parallel, would be the border between North and South Korea. Thus, after three years of war and almost ten million either dead or injured, very little had changed.

(see page 108)

What were the consequences of the Korean War for the Cold War?

The US and NSC-68

The Korean War gave NSC-68 supporters the opportunity they needed to gain acceptance of its policy and its military implications. Before then, supporters of NSC-68 realised that the US Congress and the general public wanted reduced taxation. Essentially, Truman, the US military and the right in general used the Korean War as an opportunity to launch a new, much more aggressive Cold War policy. In many ways the Korean War marked the start of the Cold War arms race – both conventional and nuclear – and the more limited 'hot' wars, albeit via 'client' states in the Developing World. After 1953, the Cold War clearly became a global phenomenon.

For the US to take on the role of global 'policeman' against communism, it had to maintain near-parity in conventional forces with the Soviet Union and clear superiority in nuclear weapons. Thus, huge increases in the military budget and a massive increase in military production were essential. After the war began in 1950, Truman got Congress to approve a significant increase in military spending – $10 billion on the armed forces, $260 million for the H-bomb project and $4 billion in military aid for US allies across the world. In 1950, US defence expenditure had been $13.1 billion; by 1953, it had reached $50.4 billion.

Asia

Apart from having an impact on US policy in Europe, the Korean War also affected developments in Asia. In September 1951, the US (along with 48 other nations) signed the San Francisco Peace Treaty with Japan, restoring sovereignty

---

Question

What was China's involvement in the Korean War?

Fact

Although US defence expenditure declined after the Korean War, it never dropped below an annual figure of $40 billion for the rest of the decade. By 1953, US military production was 700% higher than it had been in 1950.

to Japan and promising the end of US occupation by 1952. In return, Japan signed a Mutual Security Agreement with the US, guaranteeing that US military bases could remain. By the Yoshida Letter, Japan agreed to a trade boycott against Communist China.

The Yoshida Letter also promised that Japan would trade with Jiang's Taiwan which, from the very start of the Korean War, became more important to the USA. Massive US military and economic aid was given to Jiang, as it was believed that Taiwan was important in blocking any expansion of Communist China in Asia. To confirm this, the US signed a mutual defence treaty with Taiwan in 1954. The US intervention in Korea, and its continued support for Taiwan as representative of the whole of China in the UN, led to a 20-year period of Sino–American hostility. The Korean War also had a significant impact on subsequent US policy in Indochina, as we will examine in the next chapter.

Question

What was the Yoshida Letter, published in 1952?

Cold War treaties

Just as the Korean War had an impact on NATO, the fighting in the Pacific Rim also resulted in US security commitments to Australia and New Zealand, in addition to those given to Japan. These were formalised in the signing of two new Cold War treaties. In August 1951, the US agreed a military alliance with the Philippines. However, the US build-up of Japan had worried both Australia and New Zealand, which saw Japan as an economic competitor and, in view of recent history, as a potential military threat.

To allay these fears, the US proposed the ANZUS Pact, which offered US support against any military aggression, while Australia and New Zealand promised to help the US stand against communist activities in the Pacific region. The pact was signed in September 1951. Stalin's hopes of a North Korean victory, to weaken the Western encirclement that he feared, were dashed. In fact, the USA's commitments to Japan actually resulted in a range of new anti-Soviet allies for the US in Asia.

All these new developments had been considered by the US before 1950, but the start of the Korean War speeded up their implementation. It is significant that, by the end of the Korean War, all the key proposals of NSC-68 had been put into operation. By 1953, the US was committed to a global military strategy of opposing communist 'aggression' and defending the 'free' world whenever necessary, up to and including putting US troops into combat. This was to remain the cornerstone of US Cold War policy for the next two decades.

Conclusion

By 1953, the main features of the Cold War were firmly established: a globalised military and ideological confrontation between the main powers and their allies in various systems of allegiance (though, as yet, the USSR had nothing like NATO, as Cominform and Comecon were not military organisations). Other results were: nuclear and conventional arms races, a succession of vicious 'limited' regional wars between proxy or 'client' states, especially in Vietnam; spying and covert operations of sabotage and murder; and vigorous propaganda campaigns and security service pressures on civilians to conform – whether to 'Marxism–Leninism' in the Soviet bloc, or to 'Uncle Sam' and 'free enterprise' in the West. The Cold War had intensified.

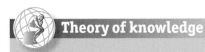

Historical information and interpretations

Consider the events leading up to the Korean War. In pairs, discuss how and why perspectives in the Soviet Union, in the USA and in China would have differed at the time of the crisis. How does hindsight and the end of the Cold War affect our understanding of the causes of the Korean War?

Unit summary

Study of this unit should have provided you with an understanding of US interests in mainland China, and of the impact of the victory of the Chinese Communist Party in 1949 on US foreign policy and internal politics. You should have an understanding of the significance of the US document NSC-68, and how it affected subsequent US diplomacy. Finally, you should have a good appreciation of the reasons for the Korean War, the main events during this war, and the different ways in which it affected relations between the two main Cold War blocs.

End of unit activities

1 Find out more about, and make notes on, US interest and involvement in China in the period 1900–49. Write a couple of brief paragraphs to argue whether or not US policies in China were those of an imperialist power.

2 Research and summarise the different historical views surrounding the significance of NSC-68 for future Cold War developments.

3 Produce a chart to show the main events and outcomes of the Korean War.

Discussion point

According to US historian Geir Lundestad, the USA was drawn into the creation of NATO by the states of Western Europe – so creating a US 'empire by invitation' rather than one by design. How far do you agree with this view? To help reach a conclusion, try searching on the internet for material relating to the formation of NATO, as well as researching other books.

End of chapter activities

Paper 1 exam practice

Question

What message is presented in Source A below about the likely impact of the US nuclear monopoly on Soviet foreign policy in Europe?
[2 marks]

Skill

Comprehension of the message of a source

SOURCE A

No atomic bombardment could destroy the Red Army; it could destroy only the industrial means of supplying it. The Russian defence to atomic attack is, therefore, self-evident; it is to overrun continental Europe with infantry, and defy us to drop atomic bombs on Poland, Czechoslovakia, Austria. ... The more we threaten to demolish Russian cities, the more obvious it is that the Russian defence would be to ensconce themselves in European cities which we could not demolish without massacring hundreds of thousands of our own friends.

Extract from an article written by Walter Lippmann, an American journalist, published in the Nashville Tennessean, *15 March 1946. Quoted in Rayner, E. G. 1992.* The Cold War. *London, UK. Hodder Murray. p. 12.*

Examiner's tips

Comprehension questions are the most straightforward questions you will face in Paper 1. They simply require you to understand the message presented by a source **and** to extract one or two relevant points that relate to the particular question and show/explain your understanding.

As only 2 marks are available for this question, make sure you don't waste valuable exam time that should be spent on the higher-scoring questions by writing a long answer here. All that's needed are a couple of short sentences, giving the necessary information to show you have understood the main message of the source. Basically, try to give an overall view of the source, along with a couple of pieces of information to illustrate your points.

Common mistakes

When asked to show your comprehension/understanding of a particular source, make sure you don't just paraphrase the source (or copy out a few sentences from it). Give a couple of sentences that briefly point out the view/message of the source.

Simplified markscheme

For **each point/item of relevant/correct understanding/information** identified, award **1 mark** – up to a **maximum of 2 marks**.

Student answer

> *Source A is trying to say that by threatening to destroy Soviet cities with its nuclear weapons, the USA in fact is merely likely to provoke the USSR to 'overrun continental Europe' with its infantry.*

Examiner's comments

The candidate has selected **one** relevant and explicit piece of information from the source that helps illustrate a basic point. This is certainly enough to gain 1 mark. However, it's not much more than a paraphrase; what's really needed to gain the other mark available is an overall concluding sentence that briefly pulls together the main message.

Activity

Look again at the source, and the student answer above. Now try to write a brief sentence to give an **overall** view of the message the author is trying to get across.

Summary activities

1   Complete a spider diagram to show the main developments in the Cold War from 1946 to 1953. Use the information from this chapter and any other resources available to you.

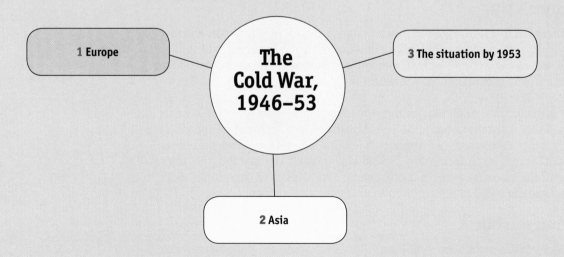

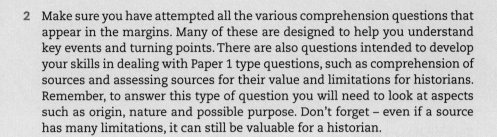

2 Make sure you have attempted all the various comprehension questions that appear in the margins. Many of these are designed to help you understand key events and turning points. There are also questions intended to develop your skills in dealing with Paper 1 type questions, such as comprehension of sources and assessing sources for their value and limitations for historians. Remember, to answer this type of question you will need to look at aspects such as origin, nature and possible purpose. Don't forget – even if a source has many limitations, it can still be valuable for a historian.

Practice paper 2 questions

1 Assess the impact of the Truman Doctrine and the Marshall Plan on the development of the Cold War between 1946 and 1953.

2 Analyse the role of Germany in the development of the Cold War between 1946 and 1953.

3 To what extent was the Berlin Crisis of 1948–49 a serious danger to international peace?

4 Examine the impact on the Cold War of the victory of the Chinese communists in 1949.

5 In what ways, and with what results, was Korea a key focus of the Cold War in the period up to 1953?

6 Compare and contrast the policies of the USA and the USSR towards Asia between 1945 and 1953.

Further reading

Try reading the relevant chapters/sections of the following books:

Crockatt, Richard. 1995. *The Fifty Years War*. London, UK. Routledge.

Walker, Martin. 1994. *The Cold War*. London, UK. Fourth Estate.

Roberts, Geoffrey. 2006. *Stalin's Wars: From Cold War to Cold War*. New Haven and London. Yale University Press.

Williamson, David. 2006. *Europe and the Cold War, 1945–91*. London, UK. Hodder Education.

Mastny, Vojtech. 1996. *The Cold War and Soviet Insecurity – the Stalin Years*. Oxford, UK. Oxford University Press.

Foot, Rosemary. 1995. *The Practice of Power: US Relations with China Since 1949*. Oxford, UK. Clarendon Press.

Introduction

While the years after 1949 saw Cold War tensions spread from Europe to Asia, the period 1953–68 saw it become a truly global conflict that particularly affected certain countries in both Asia and the Americas, as well as those in Europe. In addition to producing a highly visible image of Cold War divisions – the Berlin Wall in 1961 – this period also included the Cuban Missile Crisis of 1962, which almost resulted in a nuclear Third World War.

During these years, the USA became increasingly involved in one of the cruellest of the Cold War's regional 'hot wars' – Vietnam. This war not only had disastrous results for the people of Vietnam and the rest of Indochina, it also had a huge impact on the US itself, and on the way the Cold War was to develop after 1968. It also provided the world with some of the Cold War's most horrific images.

This chapter is divided into three units, which deal with the main aspects of the development and impact of the Cold War in Europe, Asia and the Americas during the period 1953–68. These years saw important crises in all three regions, showing just how global the Cold War had become.

In particular, the chapter will examine the continuing problem of Germany, and how this problem was 'resolved' in the early 1960s. It also looks at some of the serious problems the USSR faced in its satellite states in Eastern Europe, notably in Hungary in 1956 and in Czechoslovakia in 1968.

It will also examine the reasons for and the impact of growing US involvement in the war in Vietnam, and how this escalated after 1965. Finally, it will explore the problems surrounding the small island of Cuba in the Caribbean which, in the eyes of many contemporaries, seemed for a time on the edge of bringing about the end of the world by nuclear warfare.

As the various incidents and crises are examined, issues surrounding nuclear weapons and the much-discussed 'missile gap' will be explored, especially how the various technological developments affected the course of the Cold War.

Questions

What impact did photographs such as this have on people in the US and the rest of the world? Does this photograph give a fair reflection of US actions in Vietnam during this period? Does it help to explain why the US was eventually forced to withdraw from Vietnam?

106

Vietnamese children (including a badly burned ten-year-old girl) flee from their village after a US napalm attack; this photograph became one of the most enduring images of the Vietnam War

1 Developments in Europe

Key questions

- To what extent did relations between the two camps begin to alter in the period 1953–55?
- How did Khrushchev's 'Peaceful Coexistence' differ from previous Soviet foreign policy?
- What impact did the fall of Khrushchev have on the Cold War?
- How significant were events in Czechoslovakia in 1968 for East–West relations?

Overview

- From 1949, with the communist victory in China and then the start of the Korean War the following year, Cold War tensions had shifted mainly to Asia. In Europe, the Cold War had been heightened by the US exploding its first H-bomb in 1952.
- A thaw in Cold War tensions had begun to emerge after Stalin's death in March 1953, despite the USSR exploding its first H-bomb shortly afterwards. The new Soviet leadership soon announced a willingness to negotiate over Cold War problems, as did both Eisenhower and Churchill.
- Relations fluctuated, especially after West Germany joined NATO. Although the USSR responded with the Warsaw Pact, a treaty establishing Austria's neutrality was agreed. In July 1955, a summit meeting took place in Geneva.
- The Suez and Hungarian crises renewed tensions in 1956. New disagreements over Berlin in 1958 seemed to be resolved by the 1959 Camp David meeting.
- The relaxation of tensions was undermined by the U-2 spy-plane incident, which broke up the May 1960 Paris Summit. In November, Kennedy was elected president of the USA.
- Renewed tensions over Berlin led to the building of the Berlin Wall in 1961. Despite this (and the Cuban Missile Crisis of 1962), a Nuclear Test Ban Treaty was signed in August 1963, and the thaw continued.
- In 1968 came the Warsaw Pact invasion of Czechoslovakia and the announcement of the Brezhnev Doctrine. Despite criticisms from the West about the invasion, relations between the superpowers continued to improve.

Timeline

1953 Mar: Stalin dies

1954 Feb: further Soviet offers on German reunification rejected by the West at summit of Foreign Ministers

1955 Feb: Khrushchev emerges as main Soviet leader

May: West Germany joins NATO; Warsaw Pact formed; Treaty on Austrian neutrality signed

Jul: Geneva Summit

1956 Feb: 20th Congress of CPSU

Apr: Cominform dissolved

Jun: unrest in Poland results in reforms

Oct: Hungarian Revolt

Nov: Soviet troops invade Hungary

1957 Oct: USSR launches *Sputnik*

1958 Nov: Khrushchev's Ultimatum and start of second crisis over Berlin

1959 Sep: Camp David meeting

1960 May: Paris Summit; U-2 spy-plane incident

1961 Mar: Soviet manned spaceflight

Jun: Vienna Summit

Aug: Berlin Wall built

1964 Oct: Khrushchev replaced by Brezhnev and Kosygin

1968 Apr: Dubcek begins 'Prague Spring' in Czechoslovakia

Jul: Warsaw Letter written

Aug: Bratislava Declaration; Warsaw Pact forces invade Czechoslovakia

Nov: Brezhnev Doctrine

Fact
According to several historians, including Fred Halliday, 1953 marked the end of the First Cold War. The period 1953/4–1968/9 was one of fluctuating relations between the two superpowers – what Halliday terms 'oscillatory antagonism' – in which attempts to lessen confrontation and reach agreement were periodically frustrated by the emergence of new tensions and crises.

To what extent did relations between the two camps begin to alter in the period 1953–55?

Stalin's death and changes in the USSR

In Chapter 4 we examined how the last two years of Stalin's rule had seen various Cold War confrontations and related problems. As well as Korea, there had been tensions with Yugoslavia and a purge in the Eastern European states under Soviet control. However, when Stalin died in March 1953 – just two months after Eisenhower had become the new US president – the top communists in the Soviet Union acted quickly for change. Internally, they decided to establish a collective leadership to avoid the domination of one individual. The new chairman of the Council of Ministers (prime minister) was Georgy Malenkov, with **Nikita Khrushchev** as first secretary of the Communist Party. Also part of the new collective leadership were Vyacheslav Molotov (foreign minister), Nikolai Bulganin (minister of defence) and Lavrenty Beria (minister of internal affairs). Beria, however, was arrested and shot in July 1953, accused of plotting to set himself up as dictator.

The 'thaw', 1953–55

This new Soviet leadership attempted to 'thaw' Cold War tensions – it was one of the reasons why an armistice was signed in July 1953, to end the fighting in Korea. Another factor was the possible strain that continued fighting in Korea might place on the Soviet economy. This was also a concern for the new US administration which, like its Soviet counterpart, appeared more interested in negotiations rather than conflict as a way of dealing with international problems than Truman's government had been.

In general, the new Soviet leadership followed Malenkov's idea of a 'New Course' with the West. This thaw continued despite an increased nuclear arms race: the US had exploded its first H-bomb in November 1952, and the USSR followed suit in July 1953.

As noted above, one important Soviet motive for attempting to lessen tensions was concern over the impact on the economy of the increased defence spending resulting from the continuing arms race. Approximately 30% of the Soviet economy was spent on armaments, in order not to fall too far behind the US. Consequently, with a much smaller and weaker economy than the US, the new Soviet leaders were keen to reduce military expenditure in order to divert money to modernising industry and technology, and to consumer consumption to improve living standards.

Eisenhower and the 'New Look'

This thaw developed despite the fact that the Republicans, led by **Dwight D. Eisenhower**, had won the 1952 elections in the US. Their 'New Look' defence policy was, at least on the surface, a significant departure from that followed by Truman in the years 1945–53. It was symbolised by the appointment of John Foster Dulles as secretary of state. Dulles continued to take a hardline stance in the Cold War, talking of the need for massive retaliation and 'brinkmanship'. By 'brinkmanship', Dulles meant that the US should adopt a much more confrontational and aggressive stance towards the USSR and China, up to and including the use of nuclear weapons. This was based on the belief that the USA's nuclear superiority would force concessions.

You have to take chances for peace, just as you must take chances in war. Some say that we were brought to the verge of war. Of course we were brought to the verge of war. The ability to get to the verge without getting into the war is the necessary art. If you cannot master it, you inevitably get into wars. If you try to run away from it, if you are scared to go to the brink, you are lost.

Extract from an interview Dulles gave to Life *magazine in 1952, to explain the policy of brinkmanship.*

Dulles had attacked containment as an 'immoral' policy that had abandoned all those living in the Soviet bloc, and had called for the 'rolling back' of communism and the 'liberation' of Eastern Europe. This emphasis on nuclear weapons was linked to the Republicans' desire, as the party of big business, to reduce taxation while employing a more aggressive Cold War foreign policy. Building up a stockpile of nuclear weapons was cheaper than maintaining large conventional forces. This policy was characterised by the phrase 'a bigger bang for the buck'. Dulles also wanted to use CIA-run covert operations more widely.

In fact, Eisenhower and Dulles continued in essence with Truman's containment policy – only the emphasis and style differed in the main. Eisenhower also wanted to surround the USSR with a series of military alliances headed by the US. Nevertheless, the president's apparently conciliatory 'Chance for Peace' speech in April 1953 (like his later 'Open Skies' proposal of 1955) – made in response to the hints coming from the new Soviet leaders – was actually constructed in ways designed to ensure rejection by the USSR. The main significance of these speeches was that such proposals had been made at all.

The period 1952–62 included several crises, in Europe and in other regions of the world, that seemed to take the two superpowers to the 'brink' of war. At a lower level both sides continued the propaganda war against their rival.

The continuing Cold War problem of Germany

The new Soviet leadership was determined to continue Stalin's attempts to achieve an easing of East–West tensions, especially in relation to Germany, via negotiated agreements and compromises.

So, in February 1954, at the Council of Foreign Ministers, the Soviet Union again offered unification of Germany in return for neutralisation. Once more this was rejected by the West, as some feared a united Germany might go over to the Soviet bloc. In fact, one Soviet motive for offering reunification was to increase West German opposition to rearmament and NATO. The Soviet Union then suggested that it should join NATO. The idea was to create an organisation of collective security for the whole of Europe, and was in part inspired by Soviet fears that West Germany was about to be re-armed and allowed to join NATO. Once again, the West turned down this proposal.

Dwight D. Eisenhower (1890–1969) The Republican Eisenhower started as a soldier and commanded both the invasion of North Africa (1942) and the Allied invasion of Europe (1944). He was then appointed US army chief of staff and, in 1949, commander of NATO. He won the presidency in 1952. His views about the Soviet Union were similar to Truman's. He helped end the Korean War, but authorised the U-2 flights over the USSR and also began the plans for an invasion of Cuba, which was later put into effect by John F. Kennedy.

109

Question

How did Eisenhower's 'New Look' policy, including the idea of massive retaliation, differ from Truman's policy of containment?

Fact

According to historians Vladislav Zubok and Constantine Pleshakov, the USSR may have been 'ready to sell the Socialist GDR for détente with the West', on the basis of a neutralised, demilitarised and reunited Germany.

How far did Khrushchev's 'Peaceful Coexistence' differ from previous Soviet foreign policy?

The emergence of Khrushchev, 1955

A power struggle followed Stalin's death. After much manoeuvring, in February 1955 Khrushchev was able to bring about Malenkov's dismissal as Soviet premier. Like the rest of the Soviet leadership, Khrushchev had been profoundly affected by the **Great Patriotic War** of 1941–45. Fully aware of the human and economic devastation his country had suffered, and genuinely fearful of the risks posed by the escalating nuclear arms race, Khrushchev is particularly associated with his version of the traditional Soviet policy of 'Peaceful Coexistence'.

Khrushchev's pursuit of this policy during the period 1955–64 was at times inconsistent. He was more of a risk-taker than either Stalin or the collective leadership that had replaced him in the years 1953–55, both of which had followed a cautious foreign policy. Nonetheless, Khrushchev tried to achieve real détente between East and West, to avoid the risk of a devastating nuclear world war. With regard to Europe, Khrushchev believed the situation was sufficiently stable for the Soviet Union to make concessions in peripheral areas. He offered to pull Soviet troops out of Austria as long as the country's neutrality was guaranteed, and to return the Porkkala naval base to Finland. The most important of these agreements was the one concerning Austria which, like Germany, had been divided into four occupation zones at the end of the war.

Under Khrushchev, the USSR – which preferred the idea of Austrian neutrality to partition – held talks to resolve this issue. In the end, the US decided to accept the idea of Austrian neutrality, which was favoured by the leaders of the Western zones, and a reduction of direct US influence over Austria.

However, under Khrushchev 'Peaceful Coexistence' also involved a clearly competitive element (again, not new in itself) based on the belief that the socialist system would soon prove to be economically superior to the capitalist system. Ultimately, he argued, there could be a peaceful global transition to socialism.

The formation of the Warsaw Pact, 1955

In May 1955, just as the USSR had feared, West Germany became a member of NATO. Shortly thereafter, the Soviet Union announced the formation of its own military alliance. The Warsaw Pact – so called because the treaty was signed in Warsaw – was a mutual military assistance alliance that included the Soviet Union and all the Eastern European allies. In particular, it included East Germany, as the lack of agreement on the German question had finally persuaded the Soviet Union of the need to prop up the communist government in East Germany.

However, the USSR did not give up on the possibility of achieving a European agreement on collective security. In fact, the Warsaw Pact even had a clause (Article 11) which stated that, if a general European treaty on collective security was signed, then the Warsaw Pact would be dissolved. Thus, Soviet attempts to reduce polarisation and possible confrontation between the two Cold War blocs in Europe seem to have been as genuine as those of the West.

Great Patriotic War This was the Russian name for the campaign on the Eastern Front during the Second World War, from 1941 to 1945.

Fact
By 1952, some US leaders had come to see Austria as 'Europe's Korea', and the secret rearming of the Western zones (begun as early as 1948) was stepped up.

Question
What were the main features of Khrushchev's policy of 'Peaceful Coexistence'?

Fact
The formation of the Warsaw Pact marked the Soviet Union's final acceptance that the division of Germany was now permanent.

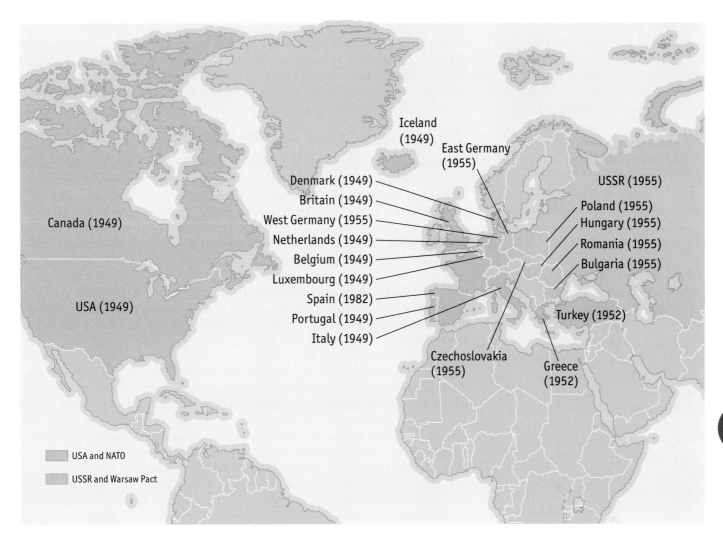

The superpower alliances and the dates they joined NATO or the Warsaw Pact

The Geneva Summit, July 1955

In July 1955, the first of a series of summit meetings between the leaders of the Big Four took place in Geneva. This – the first meeting of the leaders since the Potsdam Conference in July 1945 – was not significant for any particular agreements, but rather for the spirit of friendship in which the meeting was conducted. Nuclear weapons and Germany were the main items on the agenda. Eisenhower and Dulles recognised the need to develop a less confrontational image on the world stage, while fear of war and domestic pressures also helped push them in the direction of talks. Despite the lack of concrete progress in some areas, at least discussion was taking place – an improvement on the situation under Truman and Stalin.

This 'spirit of Geneva' saw some general agreement on the need for less confrontation and more co-operation. It also agreed on a moratorium on nuclear testing. However, Soviet proposals on disarmament, European security (such as mutual disbandment of NATO and the Warsaw Pact, and the withdrawal of all foreign troops from Europe), and control of nuclear weapons were again rejected by the US and its allies.

U-2 spy plane This was a US reconnaissance (spy) aircraft that flew at an altitude beyond the range of Soviet fighters and ground-to-air missiles. At first the USSR could do nothing about these US flights above their territory. However, improved air-to-air missiles finally allowed the Soviet Union to shoot one down and capture its pilot, Gary Powers. This incident ended the May 1960 Paris Summit after only one day (see pages 114–15), and prevented agreements on Berlin and a test-ban treaty.

de-Stalinisation This refers to the process in which Khrushchev (and later Gorbachev) attempted to reverse Stalin's imposition of strict central controls from Moscow on the Soviet Union and the leaderships of Eastern European communist parties and states. These attempts to restore independent action and control, and to reduce censorship, can be seen as attempts to return to the original 'Leninist' norms or practices of democratic centralism. Normally applied to the years 1969–79, in fact there were several such attempts between 1945 and 1991 to improve East–West relations.

They also rejected the USSR's renewed offers to resolve the German question by free elections for a reunited Germany. At the same time, Eisenhower's 'Open Skies' proposal that each side allow the other to undertake aerial reconnaissance of military sites was – as expected – rejected by Khrushchev. The US went ahead with its **U-2 spy plane** flights over Soviet territory anyway. Nonetheless, progress was made: in September, the Soviet Union established diplomatic relations and trade links with West Germany.

Khrushchev's 'secret' speech, 1956

On assuming control in 1953, the Soviet collective leadership had immediately begun attempts to repair relations with Yugoslavia and to improve those with its Eastern European satellites. In February 1956, Khrushchev announced his foreign policy at the 20th Party Congress of the CPSU. This had important implications for Soviet foreign policy towards both Europe and the Developing World, as Khrushchev argued that, in the new nuclear age, peaceful coexistence was both possible and necessary.

However, Khrushchev also made another important (secret) speech at this Congress. Although intended to have only a domestic impact – to achieve '**de-Stalinisation**' or liberalisation – it rapidly caused serious problems in Eastern Europe.

In this secret speech, Khrushchev attacked Stalin's policies and accepted that there could be 'national roads to socialism' that did not necessarily have to follow the Soviet model. In fact, as early as 1955, Khrushchev had made attempts to secure Yugoslavia as a definite ally of the Soviet Union. Khrushchev soon announced the dissolution of Cominform, from which Stalin had expelled Yugoslavia, and he encouraged its membership of the Warsaw Pact. Tito refused to go this far, and only agreed to restore diplomatic relations.

The secret speech was soon unofficially circulated in the Eastern European satellites, where it gave hope to reform communists and non-communists who sought a reduction in Soviet control of their countries. Two countries particularly affected were Poland and Hungary.

Revolt and reform in Poland, 1956

Protests by Polish factory workers over increased production quotas turned into a serious riot in Poznan in June 1956. The Polish communists (the Polish United Workers Party, PUWP) responded by moving towards a programme of reform and liberalisation, headed by Wladyslaw Gomulka. Gomulka had been the leader of the Polish communists but had been imprisoned during the Eastern European purges of the late 1940s, and had only been released and rehabilitated after Stalin's death.

In the context of the Cold War, the Soviet leadership feared the consequences of a Poland independent of Soviet control, so a meeting was arranged with Gomulka in Warsaw in late October 1956. Gomulka persuaded Khrushchev that he had no intention of leaving the Warsaw Pact, or of dismantling the communist framework. On 21 October, Khrushchev finally decided to trust Gomulka, and calculated that no military intervention was needed to ensure Soviet security. These events led the new Soviet leaders to urge the promotion of previously purged reform-minded communist leaders in other Eastern European states, to prevent unrest spreading from Poland. These leaders included Imre Nagy in Hungary.

The Hungarian Revolt, 1956

The situation in Hungary was more serious. During 1956, following Khrushchev's secret speech and the developments in Poland, protests became increasingly widespread. On 23 October, a large illegal demonstration in Budapest, called in support of the Polish reform communists, was soon out of control. Before long an armed revolt had broken out, which led to the government calling in Soviet troops for assistance. However, the fighting then spread to other major cities.

Initially, the Soviets attempted a peaceful solution like that reached in Poland. Consequently, the reform communist Imre Nagy was allowed to form a new government. However, Nagy's decision to allow opposition parties, and especially indications that he would withdraw Hungary from the Warsaw Pact, persuaded the majority of the Soviet leadership to opt for military intervention. This was the decision taken on 31 October. It was partly the result of fear that if Hungary were allowed to leave, other states might follow suit, thus breaking up the European buffer zone on which Soviet security depended. Fears were increased by the USA which, attempting to exploit the opportunities offered by de-Stalinisation, issued statements and propaganda. These seemed to suggest that the US supported the idea of a neutral Hungary along the lines of Yugoslavia or Austria.

On 1 November 1956, Nagy announced Hungary's withdrawal from the Warsaw Pact. On 4 November, the Soviet Union launched its military intervention. After some intense fighting, a new pro-Soviet government was installed, headed by Janos Kadar. In the purge that followed, many were expelled from party and state posts, while Nagy was taken to the Soviet Union and, in 1958, executed.

Once the crisis was over, Soviet armed forces were withdrawn from several Warsaw Pact states. In addition, the Soviet Union began to give credits and subsidies to help prop up the weaker economies of Eastern Europe.

Sputnik and its impact, October 1957

On 4 October 1957, much to the surprise of the West, the Soviet Union launched the world's first satellite, *Sputnik*, into space. Eisenhower had begun his second term of office in January 1957, and he had wanted the USSR to be the first to take this step. In this way, he believed the USA would be seen as justified in developing its own ICBM system (see page 32), which was in fact already well advanced.

In reality, as its U-2 spy flights confirmed, the US continued to have an overwhelming nuclear superiority throughout the decade – even by 1960, the USSR had only four ICBMs and 145 long-range bombers. However, the launch of *Sputnik* gave Eisenhower the opportunity to support the establishment of NASA (the National Aeronautics and Space Administration) in 1958, to further promote US development of missiles and space exploration.

However, despite (or possibly because of) the Soviet Union's relative weakness, Khrushchev decided to pursue a more active foreign policy. In particular, he tried to get both West Germany and Britain to leave NATO. Although he had been encouraged by the Geneva Conference and by the USA's reluctance to use nuclear weapons during the various crises of the mid 1950s, his turn to a more risky foreign policy was also an attempt to deflect internal criticisms of some of his economic policies.

Fact
That Khrushchev's main concerns were security-based is suggested by the fact that, once the situation had stabilised, new Hungarian leader Janos Kadar actually implemented several of the reforms promised earlier by Nagy. In fact, as the historian R. C. Nation has suggested, Khrushchev was also prepared to accept a limited reduction in Soviet control. On 30 October, while the Hungarian Crisis was still at its height, the USSR had issued a declaration promising a more equal relationship between the Soviet Union and the Eastern European states.

Activity
Using the information in the earlier chapters of this book, and any other materials you have used, write a couple of paragraphs to explain what criticisms – if any – you would make of the West's policy in relation to the Hungarian Uprising of 1956.

113

Sputnik The world's first orbiting satellite, launched by the USSR in October 1957. The word means 'traveller'. The Soviet Union went on to achieve a series of other space firsts, including the first man to orbit Earth in space.

Fact

At this stage, NATO already had nuclear-capable artillery and fighter bombers, and the US was rapidly building up its arsenal of tactical (short-range) nuclear weapons and ballistic missiles. However, as argued by James L. Richardson, these Soviet actions were in part driven by the GDR leader, Walter Ulbricht. Ulbricht threatened to take unilateral and possibly provocative action if Khrushchev did not try to do something about the existence of West Berlin – which was, after all, deep within GDR territory.

The Second Berlin Crisis, 1958–61

A second crisis over Berlin developed late in 1958 when, on 27 November, Khrushchev issued his first Berlin Ultimatum. This was an attempt to push the West into concluding a formal peace with Germany and agreeing that West Berlin should become an international and demilitarised area. Khrushchev warned that if such agreements were not forthcoming, the Soviet Union would sign a separate peace with the GDR that would include handing over control of the access routes into West Berlin.

These moves were intended partly to force the West to reopen negotiations on the future of Germany, and in particular to prevent NATO's attempts to make West Germany a nuclear power. This was something the Soviet Union greatly feared, and in 1958, NATO did in fact consider taking such a step. The prospect obviously alarmed the Soviet and the East German leaders.

Initially, Khrushchev was keen to impress the Chinese communists and to improve his standing within the Soviet leadership. He had therefore insisted on agreement being reached within six months (by 27 May 1959), but the negotiations continued at Geneva during the summer of 1959.

Camp David, September 1959

In an attempt to break the deadlock, Eisenhower invited Khrushchev to Camp David in the US for talks. These went well and Khrushchev withdrew his ultimatum, even though he was not given any indication that the West intended to make concessions. It was also agreed that further discussions would take place at the Paris Summit planned for May 1960.

The Paris Summit and the U-2 incident, May 1960

By the time the leaders met in Paris, the situation had already altered. The US had discovered, via its spy planes, that the USSR was already well behind the US in terms of ICBMs, while West Germany was no longer prepared to make any concessions on West Berlin. Then, on 1 May 1960, came the announcement that a Soviet missile had successfully brought down a US U-2 spy plane over the USSR. Eisenhower, embarrassed that his previous denials of spy planes had been revealed (he had claimed they were merely weather planes), and concerned at the effectiveness of Soviet missile technology, refused to apologise for the incident. Khrushchev cancelled Eisenhower's proposed visit to the Soviet Union. The incident doomed the Paris Summit to failure.

A Soviet cartoon about the U-2 incident, showing Eisenhower painting a dove (the symbol of peace) on a spy plane

The Soviets proposed a confederation between the two German states, with both leaving their respective military alliances (NATO and the Warsaw Pact). They also suggested the internationalisation and demilitarisation of Berlin. These proposals were countered by the Western powers by suggestions for a united Germany and all-German elections, along with some German disarmament. One reason the West was keen to resist the moves outlined by the Soviet Union was that Berlin was an important propaganda, espionage and intelligence base behind the Iron Curtain.

In reality, there was little hope of an immediate reunification of Germany, but Khrushchev wanted the West to recognise the East German state, as the USSR had done with West Germany. The West, however, refused to do so until free elections were held in the GDR. The stalemate continued for the next two years.

As these discussions dragged on, an increasing number of East Germans migrated to the West. By 1959, these numbered around 200,000 a year – many of them young technicians and other skilled workers. This had a serious effect on the weak East German economy, and was thus encouraged by the West. Not surprisingly, the GDR leader, Walter Ulbricht, began to press for action.

Ideally, Ulbricht wanted West Berlin to be added to East Berlin, removing the Western presence in the GDR. Khrushchev, however, preferred the continued division of Berlin if it allowed him to gain concessions from the West over West German rearmament – in particular, to prevent West Germany possessing nuclear weapons. Encouraged by another Soviet technological first – manned space flight – and the failure of the US-backed Bay of Pigs incident in Cuba (see page 138), Khrushchev thought he might secure a better deal with the new US president, **John F. Kennedy**.

The Vienna Summit, June 1961

The first meeting between Kennedy and Khrushchev was not a success, as Kennedy still refused to make concessions on Berlin or Germany. Although moving away from Eisenhower's idea of massive retaliation, Kennedy was still determined to 'contain communism'. He increased US military spending and ordered more nuclear fallout shelters for the civil defence programme in the USA.

At the end of June, Khrushchev gave provisional permission for Ulbricht to begin preparations for physically dividing Berlin. He then announced that he was reimposing a six-month deadline for an initial peace to be signed with Germany and for West Berlin to become an international demilitarised zone.

The Berlin Wall, August 1961

As tensions increased, the number of East German refugees increased dramatically, to over 20,000 a month, and was soon almost double the rate for the 1950s. So, on 3–5 August, urged by a desperate East German leadership, Khrushchev agreed to the Warsaw Pact calling on the GDR to take action to secure the border with West Berlin. At first, a barbed-wire fence was erected. The West did not react, so on 13 August, the GDR authorities rapidly completed the building of the Berlin Wall. The wall stopped the mass emigration from the East and this, along with Soviet aid, eased the GDR's economic problems.

John F. Kennedy (1917–63)
Kennedy was born into a wealthy and politically powerful family. He fought in the US Navy during the Second World War, and became a Democrat congressman in 1947. In 1960, he became the youngest – and the first Catholic – president of the USA. He was a strong anti-communist, but was also in favour of social and welfare reform in the US. He was assassinated in November 1963.

115

Fact
Kennedy later said that the Berlin Wall was 'not a very nice solution but … a hell of a lot better than a war'.

Question

What were the reasons for the building of the Berlin Wall in 1961?

Parents hold their children up to show them to relatives on the other side of the Berlin Wall

The Berlin Wall remained a very visible image of the Cold War division between East and West until it was pulled down in November 1989. However, it also removed Germany as a key issue in the Cold War, and the focus of the conflict moved away from Europe.

What impact did the fall of Khrushchev have on the Cold War?

Khrushchev's fall, October 1964

Many Soviet leaders had been unhappy with the way Khrushchev had conducted his foreign policy, including his handling of the Cuban Missile Crisis (see pages 138–41), but much so more with elements of domestic policy. In October 1964, his opponents were able to secure a majority in the Central Committee for his removal. At first, power was shared between **Leonid Brezhnev**, the new first secretary of the CPSU, and Alexei Kosygin, the new premier.

Leonid Brezhnev (1906–82)

Brezhnev became a secretary to the CPSU Central Committee in 1952, and joined the leadership in 1957. He helped bring about Khrushchev's fall in 1964, and soon took over, although Alexei Kosygin had equal power at first. By the late 1960s, however, Brezhnev was clearly dominant.

A Soviet cartoon of 1963 about the building of the Berlin Wall; the notice reads 'The border of the GDR is closed to all enemies'

As tensions increased, the number of East German refugees increased dramatically, to over 20,000 a month, and was soon almost double the rate for the 1950s.

Under Brezhnev and Kosygin, the de-Stalinisation and limited liberalisation associated with Khrushchev came to an end, and economic policy grew much more conservative. However, at the same time, the USSR began to move from being just a regional power towards the status of an increasingly global superpower. This was achieved without the great crises of Cold War relations that had characterised Khrushchev's conduct of foreign policy. This was because Brezhnev and Kosygin began to pursue a policy of détente. For the Soviet Union, détente was essentially a continuation of the traditional Soviet policy of attempting to achieve peaceful coexistence with the capitalist West. Brezhnev and Kosygin hoped détente with the West would stabilise and gain acceptance of their Eastern European bloc and help prevent any US–China alliance directed at the Soviet Union.

Détente and the USA

At the same time, the idea of détente appealed to the US. It seemed a way of obtaining Soviet help in securing an 'acceptable' settlement to the Vietnam War (see page 121), and in curbing any expansionist aims the USSR might have. Brezhnev and Kosygin revived the Soviet policy of attempting to achieve a pan-European collective security system, which it had been pursuing on and off since the 1950s. However, it is important to remember that détente was nothing more than a desire by both sides, for similar and different reasons, to ease tensions.

Fact
By the mid 1960s, the Soviet and Eastern European economies were attempting to make significant technological improvements, and so desired more trade with the West.

117

How significant were events in Czechoslovakia in 1968 for East–West relations?

Despite these optimistic signs, détente got off to a poor start in 1968 because of the crisis that arose over Czechoslovakia. In January 1968, the hardline Stalinist leader of Czechoslovakia, Antonin Novotny, was replaced by the reform communist Alexander Dubcek. As the new first secretary of the Czech Communist Party, Dubcek launched a series of political and economic reforms – the Action Programme – in April 1968.

Czechoslovakia and the 'Prague Spring', 1968

This 'Prague Spring', as it came to be called, alarmed hardliners such as Brezhnev, who feared it might set an example for domestic reforms elsewhere in the Eastern bloc. The Soviet Union, worried about possible US reaction, was given to understand by the US president Lyndon B. Johnson that the Czech crisis was seen as an intra-communist dispute.

Consequently, the Brezhnev leadership began to feel free to put pressure on Dubcek to slow down the reforms, while also encouraging the hardliners in the Czech party to oppose him. However, the crisis continued and on 14–15 July 1968, the leaders of five Eastern European communist parties (in the Soviet Union, the GDR, Hungary, Poland and Bulgaria) met in Warsaw to discuss the situation. On 15 July they sent an open letter – the 'Warsaw Letter' – to the Czech Communist Party. The letter stated that the internal developments in Czechoslovakia were of vital concern to the security of all the states signing the letter. In particular, the Warsaw Letter claimed Dubcek's policies were allowing counter-revolutionary forces to threaten the existence of socialism in Czechoslovakia. Dubcek's reply was to reassert his commitment to socialism and the Warsaw Pact, while defending his Action Programme which, he said, would continue.

On 3 August, all the states that had signed the Warsaw Letter met with Czech representatives in Bratislava. Here, all parties issued the Bratislava Declaration, which confirmed their commitment to defending socialism in Eastern Europe. It appeared that Dubcek had been forced to limit his 'Prague Spring'. However, there was pressure from the more hardline rulers in Eastern Europe (Gomulka of Poland and especially Ulbricht in the GDR) to put a complete end to Dubcek's reforms. At the same time, hardliners in the Czech party continued to urge the Soviet Union to intervene.

The Warsaw Pact invasion

On 20–21 August, the five signatories of the Warsaw Letter sent a combined military force into Czechoslovakia. Instead of armed resistance (as in Hungary in 1956), the Soviet-led force met passive resistance and peaceful protest. Dubcek and some other leaders were arrested and taken to Moscow. After difficult discussions, a joint statement was issued on 27 August, in which Dubcek promised 'normalisation' of the situation. In other words, he agreed to end the 'Prague Spring' and to return to pre-1968 methods of rule.

The Brezhnev Doctrine

In November 1968, Brezhnev issued what became known as the 'Brezhnev Doctrine' at a congress of the Polish Communist Party. In this, he asserted that the sovereignty or independence of each of the Eastern European states was

> **Prague Spring** This refers to the attempt in the late 1960s by reform communists in Czechoslovakia to liberalise and develop a democratic communist state – what Dubcek called 'socialism with a human face'.

limited by their duty to the Soviet Union, their own 'socialist' system and the security of the rest of the Warsaw Pact. As well as attempting to limit dissent within the communist movement (many communists, especially in the West, had supported Dubcek and had condemned the Warsaw Pact invasion), it was intended to underline to the West that this was an internal matter within the Eastern bloc, not an example of Soviet expansionism. Therefore, it was hoped, the US would not make the Czech crisis an excuse to call off the new policy of détente.

SOURCE B

First, a nuclear war was utterly unacceptable, as the Cuban crisis had clearly demonstrated. Second, there was the enormous burden of military expenditures. ... Third, the process of improving relations between the Soviet Union and Western Europe, especially with the Federal Republic of Germany ... would become extremely complicated if the United States were to try to impede it. Fourth, there was a sharp aggravation in Soviet–Chinese relations.

Extract from Dobrynin, A. 1995. In Confidence: Moscow's Ambassador to America's Six Cold War Presidents. Quoted in Sewell, M. 2002. The Cold War. Cambridge, UK. Cambridge University Press. pp. 97–98.

Question

What value and limitations does Source B have for historians wishing to understand the reasons for détente?

119

Unit summary

You should now have a good understanding of the main developments in the USSR following the death of Stalin in 1953. You should also have a sound understanding of the roles of key individuals such as Khrushchev, Eisenhower and Kennedy. You should be able to answer questions that focus on developments in Eastern Europe – such as the formation of the Warsaw Pact, Khrushchev's secret speech in 1956, and events in Poland and Hungary – and how these affected the course of the Cold War in the period up to 1968. In addition, you should have a sound understanding of the key policies and factors that led to the building of the Berlin Wall in 1961, and to the Warsaw Pact's actions against Czechoslovakia in 1968. Finally, you should have some appreciation of how Cold War relations fluctuated during this period

End of unit activities

1 Find out more about, and make notes on, Khrushchev's policy of 'Peaceful Coexistence' and Eisenhower's 'New Look' policy.

2 Produce a chart to summarise the main circumstances and outcomes of the major summit meetings in the period 1955–61.

2 Developments in Asia

Timeline

1946 Fighting begins between France and the Viet Minh

1949 France grants limited independence to Vietnam, under Bao Dai

1950 Ho Chi Minh recognised by USSR and China as legitimate ruler of Vietnam

1954 May: US decides to increase aid to France in war against the Viet Minh; French defeated at Dien Bien Phu

Jul: Geneva Accords – Vietnam temporarily divided along 17th parallel

Sep: US sets up SEATO; Taiwan Straits crisis

1956 South Vietnam, backed by US, refuses to hold unification elections

1958 Viet Cong set up in South Vietnam and begins guerrilla war against government

1958 Second Taiwan crisis

1959 Jun: Soviet technicians withdrawn from China

Sep: Sino–Indian border dispute

1960 NLF set up and receives aid from North Vietnam

1961 Jan: Kennedy becomes president

1963 Nov: Diem murdered after military coup (with CIA assistance); Kennedy assassinated and replaced by Johnson

1964 Aug: Gulf of Tonkin incident; Tonkin Gulf Resolution

1965 Mar: start of Operation Thunder; first US troops sent to South Vietnam

Jul: 180,000 US troops sent to South Vietnam

1968 Jan: Tet Offensive

May: My Lai Massacre; peace negotiations start in Paris

Oct: Johnson announces temporary halt to US bombing of North Vietnam

As well as significant Cold War developments in Europe during this period, there were also major changes in Asia (this time involving Indochina) and especially Vietnam. These events had far-reaching consequences for the course of the Cold War in the period 1954–68, and had a particular impact on the US economy and its politics, as well as its ability to take aggressive action in other parts of the world. According to most – but not all – historians, Vietnam was the most striking failure of the US policy of containment.

Map of Indochina showing the division of Vietnam

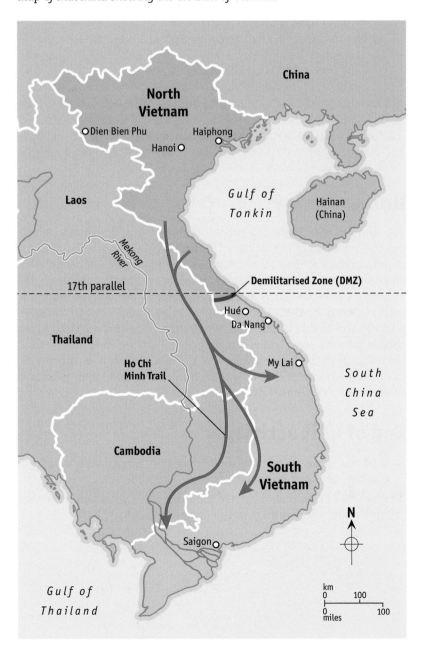

Key questions

- Why did the US get involved in Vietnam after 1954?
- What impact did Indochina have on the Cold War?
- Why did US involvement in Vietnam increase after 1964?

Overview

- In 1945, the US was against the French returning to Indochina as a colonial power. However, a war broke out between the communist-led Viet Minh and the French in 1946; after developments elsewhere in Asia in 1949–50, the US decided to give aid to the French in order to 'contain' communism.
- In 1954, the Vienna Conference seemed to promise agreements on Korea and Indochina, but then the French suffered a heavy defeat at Dien Bien Phu.
- The Geneva Accords later that year led to the temporary division of Vietnam into North and South along the 17th parallel, with unification elections to be held in 1956. The US immediately set up a military mission, and gave economic and military aid to the South.
- Convinced that the communist leader of North Vietnam, Ho Chi Minh, would win the elections, the US-backed South refused to hold them.
- In 1958, the Viet Cong began a guerrilla war against the government of South Vietnam and, in 1960, the National Liberation Front was set up to include all those against the South.
- The US increased its military aid to the South and, with Kennedy's approval, the CIA helped the South Vietnamese army to overthrow Ngo Dinh Diem in November 1963. However, although Kennedy increased the number of US military advisers in South Vietnam, he refused to send regular combat troops there.
- Following Kennedy's assassination, vice-president Lyndon B. Johnson took over. Unlike Kennedy, Johnson was prepared to commit US troops to the war in Vietnam, which had become a major Cold War issue.
- The Gulf of Tonkin incident in 1964 led to the US Congress passing the Tonkin Gulf Resolution; this resulted in the bombing of North Vietnam and the sending of regular US troops to the South.
- Under Johnson, US involvement – and the war – soon escalated. By late 1967, over 540,000 US troops were in South Vietnam. However, US tactics were unsuccessful, and even counter-productive; massive anti-war protests began to take place in the US and elsewhere.
- In January 1968, the Viet Cong and the Viet Minh launched the Tet Offensive; though they were defeated with heavy losses, this showed that the US was far from winning the war.

Why did the US get involved in Vietnam after 1954?

Containment and the Domino Theory

Since 1947, US policy towards the Soviet Union and communism had been based on the Truman Doctrine and the policy of containment (see page 73). After 1949, US policy was based on the Domino Theory – the idea that when one country turned communist, bordering countries would soon follow, one after another (see page 122).

Fact
The Domino Theory was particularly associated with Eisenhower who, talking about the situation in Southeast Asia during a speech in April 1954, compared these countries to 'a row of dominoes'. To prevent other states 'falling' to communism, he argued that the US needed to support anti-communist governments in the region – especially in Vietnam. The theory was applied in Southeast Asia by both Kennedy and Johnson.

The Domino Theory

Truman had only been prepared to make a military stand on what was called the Defensive Perimeter – that is, the Pacific islands ringing the Asian mainland (see page 96). As far as the mainland was concerned, US policy was to give economic aid to anti-communist forces. Indochina, and particularly Vietnam, was seen as being vital in blocking communist access to the rice-growing areas of the region. The outbreak of the Korean War in June 1950 had been a turning point in US policy towards Vietnam. Once North Korea had begun its invasion of the South, Truman and his administration quickly implemented the NSC-68 proposals. One of its main ideas was that the economies of the US and the West could not afford to 'lose' significantly more population, territory and resources to the other side. This was accepted by John Foster Dulles. Within a short time, Truman decided to increase aid to the French to help in their struggle against the communist-led Viet Minh forces in Vietnam. Soon the US was providing $1 billion a year.

The French and Indochina

Before the Second World War, Indochina (Vietnam, Cambodia and Laos) had been part of the French empire. During the war, the region had been taken over by Japan but, after 1945, the French were keen to return and regain their Southeast Asian colonies.

Their main problem was strong opposition from the **Viet Minh**, a communist–nationalist movement wanting independence. Led by the communist **Ho Chi Minh**, the Viet Minh had liberated much of the country from Japanese occupation before 1945, and at the end of the war they announced the formation of the Democratic Republic of Vietnam.

Viet Minh The Vietnam League for Independence (Viet Minh) was set up by Ho Chi Minh in 1941, while he was in exile in China. After the Japanese invasion, the Viet Minh formed its own army and, from 1943, conducted a military campaign against the Japanese army. By 1945, they had liberated much of the country, but France refused to grant independence. In 1954, the guerrilla warfare conducted by the Viet Minh culminated in the battle of Dien Bien Phu. The French were defeated and withdrew from Indochina.

Initially, the US had wanted such countries to be independent and allied to the US, and had applied pressure on France to withdraw. Ho had felt encouraged to ask the US for aid, but had been turned down – US policy hardened once Truman assumed the presidency. However, in 1946 fighting broke out between the French and the Viet Minh. This turned out to be a long guerrilla war, first against the French and then against the US.

As the Cold War developed and national communist movements seemed to be growing in popularity, the US decided to help the French stay in Indochina. In 1949, the French offered a form of limited independence for Vietnam. Under this scheme, Bao Dai was appointed head of a new government. However, this reform was rejected by the Viet Minh. In 1950, Ho was recognised by Stalin and Mao as the legitimate leader of Vietnam. The US then recognised Bao Dai as ruler of Vietnam. After 1950, the US concluded that Ho, like Kim in North Korea, was acting on instructions from Moscow. Beginning in March 1950, the US began to send military aid to the French in the hope of defeating the Viet Minh.

Eisenhower's 'New Look' and Vietnam

In November 1952, Eisenhower won the US presidential election and he took office in January 1953. Along with Dulles, he was associated with the 'New Look' foreign policy, which was supposed to be significantly different from Truman's pursuit of containment. Like Truman, Eisenhower saw Ho as an instrument of international communism, and believed in the Domino Theory. In particular, Vietnam was seen as key to preventing Laos, Cambodia, Thailand, Burma, Malaya, Indonesia, and even Singapore and Japan, from 'going communist'. Following the loss of China in 1949, Eisenhower and Dulles believed the loss of Indochina would have drastic results for the rest of Southeast Asia, which was vital to US interests.

SOURCE A

b. Communist control of all of South-east Asia would render the US position in the Pacific offshore islands precarious and would seriously jeopardise fundamental US security interests in the Far East.
c. South-east Asia, especially Malaya and Indonesia, is the principal world source of natural rubber and tin, and a producer of petroleum and other strategically important commodities. …
d. The loss of South-east Asia, especially of Malaya and Indonesia, could result in such economic and political pressures as to make it extremely difficult to prevent Japan's eventual accommodation to communism.

Extracts from NSC-124/2, June 1952. The Pentagon Papers. 1971. Quoted in Rayner, E. G. 1992. The Cold War. London, UK. Hodder Murray. p. 54.

By the end of 1953, with the Korean War over, Eisenhower's 'New Look' strategy had emerged, with its much greater emphasis on maintaining a clear nuclear superiority in order to force concessions from the USSR and China. By then, it was clear that the French were finding it increasingly difficult to maintain their position in Vietnam, in the face of determined resistance by the Viet Minh.

Ho Chi Minh (1890–1969)
Ho's real name was Nguyen That Thanh. By 1945, his Viet Minh controlled most of Vietnam, and he was declared president of an independent Vietnam. But as the Cold War developed, the US backed the return of the French. Ho established a one-party communist state in the North, but died in 1969 before the reunification of his country. He was a popular nationalist leader (despite the political repression of opposition views), and was nicknamed 'Uncle Ho'.

123

Question
How does this document link to the 'Domino Theory'?

Fact
The US also saw military aid to the French as important for European security, as a defeat for France might strengthen the French Communist Party. At the same time, such US support was seen as buying French approval for the rebuilding of West Germany's economic and military strength, something the US believed was crucial to containing communism in Europe.

Fact

There is some evidence to suggest that Eisenhower was also much more prepared than Truman to sanction 'covert operations' to contain communism, as such methods were quick, cheap and beyond the scrutiny of Congress. However, the evidence is inconclusive.

Vo Nguyen Giap (b. 1911)

Giap was a Vietnamese communist and a brilliant general. He was familiar with the guerrilla warfare tactics used by the Chinese communists, but also developed his own strategies over many years of war. He had commanded the Viet Minh troops that had entered Saigon after the defeat of Japan, and had been responsible for the defeat of the French at Dien Bien Phu in 1954. He commanded North Vietnam's armies during the Vietnam War, and organised the Tet Offensive in 1968. After reunification in 1975, he became deputy prime minister.

Question

What was agreed about Vietnam in the Geneva Accords of 1954?

SOURCE B

You have the specific value of a locality in its production of materials that the world needs. You have the possibility that many human beings pass under a dictatorship that is inimical to the free world. You have the broader considerations that might follow what you would call the 'falling domino' principle. … You have a row of dominoes set up, you knock over the first one, and what will happen to the last one is the certainty that it will go over very quickly.

Comments made by Eisenhower in April 1954, in support of his decision to give continued aid to the French. The Pentagon Papers. 1971. Quoted in Rogers, K. and Thomas, J. 2008. The Cold War. London, UK. Heinemann. p. 61.

Initially, Eisenhower continued giving massive aid to French forces in Vietnam and sending US 'advisers'. By 1954, the US was funding almost 80% of the French military budget in Indochina, and had given over $4 billion in aid. At this stage, however, the US had no desire to get involved in another Korean situation by sending in troops, with its likely price of heavy US casualties (this had proved increasingly unpopular with the American public). Eisenhower had also calculated that direct US involvement might provoke the Chinese into intervening.

In March 1954, a crucial stage was reached when the French were clearly facing a heavy defeat in the battle of Dien Bien Phu. Eisenhower ruled out the use of US troops when Congress made it clear they wanted 'no more Koreas', and Britain refused to join in. Another suggestion was made by the Pentagon: three tactical nuclear weapons should be dropped to destroy the Viet Minh troops, led by General **Vo Nguyen Giap**, surrounding the French forces at Dien Bien Phu. This idea was also rejected. Dien Bien Phu fell to the Viet Minh on 7 May 1954, effectively ending French colonial rule of Indochina. In practice, therefore, Eisenhower's 'New Look' policy seemed little different from Truman's containment policy.

The division of Vietnam

After the defeat at Dien Bien Phu, the French decided to withdraw from Vietnam. However, both the US and the communist states of the USSR and China were prepared to negotiate an end to the conflict. In particular, the Soviet leadership put pressure on Ho to accept the temporary division of Vietnam into North and South, along the 17th parallel, even though the Viet Minh controlled about two-thirds of the country. This was finally agreed at the Geneva Conference, in what were known as the Geneva Accords, in July 1954. Ho accepted the Accords, to stop the fighting and because it was agreed that national elections would be held within two years.

However, the US refused to sign the Accords, although it did promise not to break them by the use of force. Both Ho and the US believed the communist-led Viet Minh would win any unification elections.

The growth of US involvement

At the same time, the US began attempts to train a South Vietnamese army and set up a military mission to offer advice. It started to prop up South Vietnam as a block to communism advancing from the North (similar to South Korea) in what was effectively the start of US involvement in the longest war in its history.

This war took place in a small, underdeveloped state over 16,000 km (10,000 miles) from the USA, yet despite being the world's dominant superpower, the US was forced to admit defeat and make a humiliating withdrawal in the years 1973–75. By July 1955, most of the French troops had been withdrawn; the US then quickly removed the French-backed Bao Dai and instead picked **Ngo Dinh Diem** to be the head of a new South Vietnam government. Diem was a Catholic and had been educated in the US. One of his first acts – on Eisenhower's instructions – was to announce that the national unification elections would not be held. Both Diem and the US feared the communists would win such elections (several estimates predicted Ho would win about 80% of the vote).

The USA's main aim now was to create a viable state in South Vietnam which could prevent the advance of communism. The US also moved to create a new anti-communist treaty, SEATO (see page 129). This was in defiance of the Geneva Accords, which stated that Laos and Cambodia should be neutral. SEATO set up both these countries, along with South Vietnam, as 'protected areas'. Diem's rule soon became corrupt and increasingly repressive, and he began to lose the support of much of the population in the South.

The Viet Cong

The communists in the South began to organise resistance and guerrilla warfare. These communists became known as the Viet Cong (Vietnamese communists) or VC – a term of abuse used by Diem and the USA. Diem's troops found it almost impossible to combat these communist guerrillas – coming from the South, they were familiar with the local terrain.

In 1959, North Vietnam announced its intention to reunite Vietnam, and in 1960 Ho encouraged the Viet Cong to form the National Liberation Front (NLF) in alliance with other anti-Diem forces. This acted as the political arm of the Viet Cong. China then gave its backing to the growing insurgency movement. The USSR had advised against the resumption of fighting in 1959, and agreed to the neutralisation of Laos. It did not really concern itself with Vietnam until after the US massively increased its involvement in 1965.

Despite the growing unpopularity of Diem's regime, the US continued to give him massive economic and military aid, in order to prevent a communist victory in South Vietnam.

Kennedy's 'Flexible Response'

The 1960 presidential elections were won by John F. Kennedy. Although Kennedy was a Democrat he basically shared Eisenhower's world view, and since the late 1940s, he had been a staunch Cold War warrior. He had attacked Truman over the 'loss' of China, had supported McCarthy's campaign, and had even accused Eisenhower of allowing the USSR to open up a 'missile gap' with the US. In fact, on taking office, Kennedy discovered that his country still had a clear lead, which he was determined to maintain. In 1956, he had made a speech arguing that Vietnam was 'the cornerstone of the free world in Southeast Asia'.

Ngo Dinh Diem (1901–63)
A nationalist and a US protégé, Diem was opposed to both the French and the communists. In 1954, he was appointed as prime minister of South Vietnam. At first, he was supported by the US but his regime became increasingly brutal and corrupt. Soon the mainly Buddhist population was being alienated, while support for the Viet Cong increased. The US began to look for a more acceptable and competent ruler, and gave assistance to a coup by some South Vietnamese generals in 1963. Diem and his brother were murdered by the plotters.

Question

Who were the Viet Cong?

Fact
In all, the US gave over $1 billion in aid to Diem in the years 1955–61. Though this propped up Diem's increasingly unpopular regime, it did nothing to solve the problems faced by the South Vietnamese peasants, such as the high rents they had to pay to landlords.

Questions

What reasons are given in this speech concerning the importance of Vietnam to the US? How does this speech show that Kennedy supported the Domino Theory?

Dean Rusk (1909–94) Rusk was a Democrat politician and was involved in the US decision to enter the Korean War in 1950. From 1961 to 1969 he was secretary of state, in which position he both advocated and defended US involvement in Vietnam.

Robert McNamara (1916–2009) From 1961 to 1968 McNamara was US secretary of defense. He began to have serious doubts about US policies and actions in Vietnam (though these were not publicly articulated until years later), and eventually resigned. He was later president of the World Bank.

SOURCE C

Vietnam represents the cornerstone of the Free World in South-east Asia, the keystone to the arch, the finger in the dike. Burma, Thailand, India, Japan, the Philippines, and, obviously, Laos and Cambodia are among those whose security would be threatened if the red tide of communism overflowed into Vietnam. … Moreover the independence of Free Vietnam is crucial to the free world in fields other than the military. Her economy is essential to the economy of all South-east Asia; and her political liberty is an inspiration to all those seeking to obtain or maintain their liberty in all parts of Asia – and indeed the world.

Extract from a speech by Kennedy to the American Friends of Vietnam in June 1956. Quoted in Rayner, E. G. 1992. The Cold War. London, UK. Hodder Murray. p. 54.

By the time Kennedy assumed office in January 1961, Cold War tensions were reaching a dangerous level, and the US had come to regard Vietnam – and Southeast Asia in general – as indispensable for US security. Though prepared to concede the loss of North Vietnam, Eisenhower had not wanted to be the president who lost Indochina, and Kennedy was equally reluctant. Fearing that the Democrats would lose the next presidential election if South Vietnam turned communist, he immediately appointed fervent anti-communists to key posts, including some Republicans. Also important were appointees such as **Dean Rusk** and **Robert McNamara**.

These politicians believed that China was behind North Vietnam and that behind China was the Soviet Union. They rapidly drew up and adopted a new containment strategy, known as the 'Flexible Response'. This was based on increasing US conventional military forces to enable the country to fight limited wars in Asia and, if necessary, in Europe. It was presented as a critique of Eisenhower's public reliance on nuclear weapons and massive retaliation, even though the New Look had not worked this way in practice. It was also seen as a way of bringing some control and stability to warfare in the nuclear age.

Kennedy's first crisis in Indochina, however, was in Laos. Here he showed his determination to take action, as he believed that a communist victory in Laos would threaten the survival of South Vietnam as an anti-communist state. Kennedy protested at Soviet aid to the Pathet Lao. This group, formed in 1950, was originally a nationalist–communist coalition that fought for independence from France. The communists in the Pathet Lao, who were supported by communists in Vietnam, soon came to dominate the group.

Kennedy sent the Seventh Fleet to the Gulf of Thailand, and put all US forces in the Far East on alert. At the same time, he persuaded several SEATO members to pledge military support for any US-led action. Khrushchev agreed to put pressure on the Pathet Lao to conclude a ceasefire with the US-backed royal government of Laos. In 1962, the USSR and US signed an agreement in Geneva accepting and guaranteeing the neutrality of Laos.

In fact, fighting was resumed almost immediately – the US resorted to covert operations, while the Soviet Union renewed military aid to the Pathet Lao. However, Kennedy was determined to hang on to South Vietnam, as he and his advisers saw the country as having tremendous geopolitical importance which, if 'lost', would tilt the balance of power globally in favour of the communist 'bloc'.

Kennedy increased economic aid and sent extra military advisers to South Vietnam; he allowed these advisers to engage in combat (such as flying South Vietnamese troops into battle) and authorised counter-insurgency operations such as the 'strategic hamlets' programme, designed to grind down the NLF by a policy of attrition. He even authorised '**search and destroy**' missions. By 1963, over 100 US soldiers had been killed in Vietnam.

American soldiers during a search and destroy mission in South Vietnam

By this time, however, it was clear that such strategies were not working, mainly because Diem's repressive policies and anti-Buddhist actions, and his refusal to carry out the social and political reforms suggested by US advisers, continued to alienate the majority of the South Vietnamese population, some 90% of whom were Buddhists. Diem and his brother, Ngo Dinh Nhu, the head of the secret police, tended only to appoint Catholics, who were a minority. In the summer of 1963, Buddhists organised massive demonstrations, which were fired on by the police. In protest, a Buddhist monk set himself on fire in Saigon, and this practice of self-immolation soon spread.

search and destroy This was one of the military strategies used by the US in Vietnam. After Vietnamese civilians had been 'persuaded' to move into 'strategic hamlets' in areas controlled by the South Vietnamese army and the US (to remove them from contact with the Viet Cong), US troops were sent into these cleared areas to 'search and destroy' the Viet Cong. It was assumed that any Vietnamese who remained in such areas must be members or supporters of the Viet Cong, so troops were encouraged to achieve a high body count. This strategy led to the My Lai Massacre in 1968 (see page 173).

napalm Developed during the Second World War and widely used by the US in the Vietnam War, this inflammable petroleum jelly is put into bombs. When they explode, the flaming petrol spreads widely and sticks to anything it touches. Many Vietnamese civilians, as well as Viet Cong soldiers, were horribly burnt or killed.

Agent Orange A chemical defoliant spray designed to remove the leaves from the trees in the jungle, to deprive the Viet Cong of cover and to expose their position to American bombers. However, it also damaged crops and timber (an important export crop). It also had serious effects on unborn babies, resulting in deformities.

Lyndon B. Johnson (1908–73) As a Democrat member of the House of Representatives (1937–48) and then the Senate (1948–60), Johnson became known as a liberal. However, this reputation, and his 'Great Society' programme, were overshadowed by his escalation of the USA's involvement in the Vietnam War, which he began after assuming the presidency in 1963. Under him, the war became increasingly costly and unpopular and, in March 1968, he announced that he would not stand for re-election.

Kennedy gave permission for the use of **napalm** and defoliants, such as **Agent Orange**. Later, the Taylor-Rostow Report suggested sending 8000 US troops, ostensibly as a 'flood relief' team. However, twice in 1961 Kennedy rejected advice to send in regular US combat troops, even though his vice-president, **Lyndon B. Johnson**, was in favour. Just before his assassination, Kennedy did authorise the CIA to assist in a coup by South Vietnamese generals against the increasingly corrupt and inefficient Diem. On 1 November 1963, Diem was overthrown and he and his brother were murdered.

Thus Kennedy consciously followed his own policy of 'Flexible Response' (as did Johnson later); there is little evidence that Kennedy and the US just drifted into the war, or that they were tricked into it by the military.

What impact did Indochina have on the Cold War?

The search for new alliances

As noted above, tensions over Indochina led the US to create a NATO-type alliance for Asia to contain the spread of communism in what was now seen as a key area. On 8 September 1954, Dulles set up the South East Asia Treaty Organisation (**SEATO**). In addition to the US, its members were France, Britain, Australia, New Zealand (these last two countries were already allied to the US via the ANZUS Pact of 1951), Thailand, the Philippines and Pakistan. SEATO members were united in viewing South Vietnam, Laos and Cambodia as being of great strategic importance. Interestingly, three states – Indonesia, India (two of the most important states in the region) and Burma – rejected membership, as they believed the US was exaggerating the communist threat in the area.

The official basis of SEATO was that member countries would intervene in states where communists were poised to take power by force. Dulles assured the US Congress that intervention would only be considered if communist forces were clearly dominant. He also stated that the first military action would be taken by the air force, not by ground troops, and promised that no interventions would take place without the approval of the Senate. However, another clause in the treaty stated that intervention might also take place in a country in which a communist party seemed likely to win elections.

The Soviet response to SEATO, and to growing US influence in Asia, was to give its support to the non-aligned grouping of African and Asian states that had been set up at the **Bandung Conference** in Indonesia. During November and December 1955, Khrushchev and the Soviet prime minister, Bulganin, visited India, Burma and Afghanistan. Moreover, President Sukarno of Indonesia visited Moscow and was promised economic and military aid, even though he also received aid from the US. Sukarno was supported by the Indonesian Communist Party so, in 1958, Eisenhower instructed the CIA to incite Sumatra, the largest of Indonesia's islands, to break away from Indonesia politically. This failed.

China's reaction – crises over the Taiwan Straits

Mao was alarmed by the formation of SEATO, and calculated that the US would now try to separate Taiwan permanently from mainland China. This resulted in Communist China shelling some of the offshore islands – the Jinmen (Quemoy) and Mazu (Matsu) groups – in September 1954. This shelling was an attempt to persuade the US not to commit too closely to Jiang Jieshi's regime, which had troops on these islands, and which had recently announced an imminent attack on China in what was to be a new 'holy war' against communism.

In 1955, China began shelling the Tachen islands, also occupied by Jiang's troops. During this Taiwan Straits crisis in the years 1954–55, the US military once again recommended the use of nuclear weapons, and once again (after some hesitation) Eisenhower refused, believing it would prove difficult to limit such action. Dulles suspected Jiang might be trying to provoke a war with China so that he could retake the mainland, but the US refused to back down. Because the situation in Asia generally was seen as threatening, the US believed it had to be seen to stand by Taiwan. The result was a firm mutual defence pact between the US and Taiwan.

The US then attempted to get China to give a commitment never to use force to regain Taiwan. Mao at first refused, pointing out that the island belonged to China and that the dispute was merely a leftover from the Chinese civil war. However, when China seized the Tachen islands, Eisenhower threatened to use nuclear weapons if China attacked Taiwan. Congress passed the Taiwan Resolution, which authorised the president to take whatever military action he deemed necessary. Zhou Enlai, the Chinese premier, responded that China would only use peaceful means to regain Taiwan.

In 1958, a second crisis broke out when China resumed its shelling of the Jinmen and Mazu islands. Dulles declared it to be the first stage in a Chinese invasion of Taiwan. The Seventh Fleet was sent to the Taiwan Straits, US forces were placed on alert, and the US once again began to threaten the use of nuclear weapons. However, both China and the US were prepared to negotiate, and another ceasefire was arranged. At the same time, Dulles once again made it clear to Jiang that, although the US would support the independence of Taiwan, it would not help him in any invasion of mainland China.

The USSR and China

This tension over SEATO and the situation in Asia also led to worsening relations between the USSR and China. Once the US had broken off talks with China in 1957, Mao had asked Khrushchev for Soviet support for a Chinese offensive to regain the islands of Jinmen and Mazu. However, Khrushchev had refused to provide any offensive military aid and said that the Soviet Union would only intervene if China was directly invaded by the US. At the same time, the US threat of a nuclear response if the attacks persisted had forced Mao to back down. This resulted in increased bitterness between the two communist powers (especially as the Soviet Union still refused to give China access to atomic-bomb technology) and to a growing split that soon affected the communist movement around the world.

In fact, as early as the first Taiwan Straits crisis in 1954, Dulles had realised that, as well as sending a clear signal to all concerned that the US was prepared to take military action in Southeast Asia, a firm US stance on these islands might help bring about a collapse of the Sino–Soviet alliance. He calculated that a strong US line would dissuade the USSR from actively supporting China, and that this would drive a wedge between them. However, he and Eisenhower were forced to stick to the 'Two Chinas' policy – supporting Jiang's nationalist regime against Mao's communist one – by the continued activity

SEATO The South East Asia Treaty Organisation, set up by the US in 1954, in Manila (its headquarters were in Bangkok) to contain the spread of communism in Asia. As well as the US and various Asian states, it also included Britain and France. In 1965, both Pakistan and France withdrew, not wishing to become involved in the Vietnam War. In 1955, a similar Cold War organisation was set up by the US – the Baghdad Pact – which included Turkey, Iraq, Iran and Pakistan, as well as Britain and the US.

Bandung Conference A meeting held in Bandung (the capital of the Indonesian island of West Java). It was attended by 29 non-aligned Asian and African states. They were opposed to colonialism and racism, and wanted to gain recognition of the 'Third World', as well as staying out of the Cold War.

Fact
Also important in this split was the process of limited de-Stalinisation being undertaken in the USSR after Khrushchev's secret speech of 1956. Mao and the CCP believed the old Stalinist methods of rule should be maintained.

of the US 'China Lobby'. This group persisted in pressuring the US government to help Jiang invade mainland China. Had it not been so vociferous, it is possible that direct Washington–Beijing negotiations might have taken place long before they eventually did in 1971.

On 20 June 1959, the growing Sino–Soviet split resulted in the USSR suddenly withdrawing all its experts from China, at a critical time for the Chinese economy. Soon another tension developed in Asia, this time resulting from what proved to be the first Sino–Indian border dispute, which began on 9 September 1959. Mao was infuriated by the Soviet Union's decision to stay neutral. This quickly resulted in the communist movement splitting into either pro-Moscow or pro-Beijing parties.

Why did US involvement in Vietnam increase after 1964?

Johnson and escalation

By the time of Kennedy's assassination in November 1963, the Viet Cong had control of more than half of rural South Vietnam. Meanwhile, in the cities, they were able to launch a terrorist campaign against government officials and police commanders. When Johnson took over, he was determined to step up – *escalate* – US involvement in the war in South Vietnam. However, to do this he needed a 'justification' that would convince both the US Congress and the electorate.

US credibility was seen as being at stake in what was claimed to be Chinese-backed external aggression against South Vietnam. Chinese backing for North Vietnam, in part based on Mao's fears of 'Western imperialist' encirclement, put increasing pressure on the USSR to get involved.

The Gulf of Tonkin and Operation Rolling Thunder

On 2 August 1964, a US destroyer close to the North Vietnamese coast in the Gulf of Tonkin (and so in North Vietnam's territorial waters) was attacked by North Vietnamese ships. Although no serious damage was done, two days later two other US destroyers were allegedly fired on, although no physical proof of these later attacks was found. Johnson used this supposed Gulf of Tonkin incident as an excuse to order the bombing of the North's naval bases, even though no state of war had been declared. The US Congress was persuaded to pass the Tonkin Resolution, giving the president power to 'take all necessary steps, including the use of armed force', to defend the South. In effect, this was a blank cheque for Johnson to conduct the war as he saw fit, without having to consult Congress further. By March 1965, US bombers were flying regular bombing missions against the North, in a campaign known as Operation Rolling Thunder.

US tactics

For several years, Johnson had favoured sending a large US army into the South to destroy the Viet Cong. In March, he deployed some US ground forces to South Vietnam, initially to protect the US airbase at Da Nang. Then, in July 1965, Johnson ordered in 180,000 US troops. By 1968, the number of US troops in Vietnam had reached 540,000.

The US bombing of both North and South Vietnam was repeatedly stepped up. It is estimated that more bombs were dropped on North Vietnam in three

Fact
During the presidential election in November 1964, Johnson – seen as the 'peace' candidate – nonetheless declared he would not see Southeast Asia 'go the way China went', thus indicating his belief in containment and the Domino Theory, and a desire not to be seen as soft on communism.

Fact
Under Johnson, about 10% of young American men were being drafted (conscripted) to fight in Vietnam; their average age was 19, and many did not want to be there. Though the arrival of such large numbers of American soldiers helped prevent the total collapse of Diem's South Vietnamese military regime, the increasingly heavy fighting did not succeed in destroying the Viet Cong.

years than the total amount of bombs dropped on Germany, Italy and Japan during the whole of the Second World War. As far as détente was concerned, this massive US escalation after 1965 at first placed real obstacles in the way of further significant negotiations over other Cold War issues.

A female Viet Cong fighter uses an anti-tank gun during the Vietnam War; the Viet Cong had both men and women fighters

The Viet Cong were increasingly aided by equipment and troops from North Vietnam, which itself began to receive military equipment from the Soviet Union in 1964. The Viet Cong were able to survive by digging a vast network of underground tunnels. Furthermore, the vast experience of the Viet Cong in guerrilla warfare meant they frequently outmanoeuvred the US troops.

Unable to match the expertise of the Viet Cong in setting ambushes and booby-traps, US military commanders decided to rely on their massive firepower advantage. In addition to traditional bombing, the US continued to make heavy use of napalm, defoliants (such as Agent Orange) and anti-personnel bombs. However, these frequently killed civilians and caused mounting opposition to US involvement and tactics, both in Vietnam and abroad – including in the United States itself.

The events of the Korean War had had an impact, though: the US decided not to send troops across the 17th parallel. While China warned of nuclear war, and encouraged the North to resist US peace initiatives during 1965–68, Mao was equally determined to avoid serious risks.

It is estimated that more bombs were dropped on North Vietnam in three years than the total amount of bombs dropped on Germany, Italy and Japan during the whole of the Second World War.

131

Fact

Johnson's advisers, including Dean Acheson, began to think that the US could not prevent the communists from winning in the South. In particular, the Tet Offensive showed that the US was far from achieving an overall victory, and that the communists' resistance was as determined as ever. Many US politicians became disillusioned with the war, and the anti-war movement in the US grew considerably.

Great Society This was Johnson's attempt to tackle the poverty and inequality that existed for millions of people (white and black) in the USA. In order to build a 'Great Society', in 1964, he initiated the most ambitious legislative programme since Roosevelt's New Deal. This included a 'War on Poverty', a Medical Care for the Aged Act, a Social Security Act, educational and urban renewal initiatives, and measures to give real civil rights to African-Americans. However, much of this was undermined by the escalating costs of the Vietnam War.

The Tet Offensive, January 1968

The lack of success being achieved by the policy of attrition and US tactics generally was dramatically demonstrated in January 1968. During the Tet religious New Year festival, Viet Cong and North Vietnamese troops launched a massive attack against many towns and US military bases across South Vietnam. They even attacked the US embassy in Saigon, the South Vietnamese capital. For the next three months there was intense and bitter fighting, as the US attempted to recapture the towns taken in January. By the end of March 1968, over 50,000 communist troops had been killed and virtually all their gains had been lost. The Tet Offensive proved to be a defeat for the communists, but in the long term it marked the beginning of the USA's reappraisal of its involvement.

One more immediate result was that in March 1968 Johnson announced his decision not to stand for re-election. His claims of 'progress' were shown to be false, and many important establishment figures who had previously backed the war came out against further escalation. The war, with its mounting civilian casualties, had turned Johnson into the USA's most unpopular president. A common chant by anti-war protestors was: 'Hey, hey, LBJ. How many kids did you kill today?'

Increasingly, public opinion in the US began to turn against the war, in part as a result of widespread television coverage. Despite massive expenditure – which had helped undermine Johnson's '**Great Society**' project – it was clear that the US was slowly losing the war. By then, the conflict was costing $28 billion a year, and over 300 US soldiers were being killed each week. Johnson announced that the bombing would be scaled down and called for peace talks with Hanoi. The North Vietnamese government agreed, and negotiations began in Paris in May 1968. No real progress was made, despite Soviet pressure on the North, but in October 1968 Johnson called a temporary halt to the bombing of North Vietnam.

Unit summary

You should now have a solid understanding of how, before 1960, the US became increasingly involved in developments in French Indochina – and especially of what was happening in Vietnam. You should have a good knowledge of the factors leading to French withdrawal from Indochina, and of the main points of the Geneva Conference in 1954. You should also be able to show how the Domino Theory relates to the steps taken by US presidents such as Kennedy and Johnson, which ended in escalating US intervention. Finally, you should have an understanding of the main tensions between China and the US over Taiwan and the offshore islands during this period, and the outcomes of these tensions.

End of unit activities

1   Produce a timeline to show the main steps in growing US involvement in Vietnam in the period 1954–68.

2   Find out more about the tensions and disputes between China and the US over Taiwan and the offshore islands during this period. Then make notes on this – and on how these affected relations between the USSR and Communist China.

3 Developments in the Americas

The Cold War during this period also moved much closer to home for the US, after a revolution took place in Cuba in 1959. While the actions taken by the US can be seen as a response to Cold War developments, some historians have viewed them as yet another example of the US government intervening anywhere in the Americas against radical regimes it considered a threat to its immediate interests or 'stability' in the region. This foreign policy had existed long before the start of the Cold War, and even before the Russian Revolution of 1917. It stretched right back to the Monroe Doctrine of 1823.

Key questions

- Why did the US consider Cuba so important?
- Why did the Cuban Missile Crisis happen?
- What impact did the Cuban Revolution have on the Cold War?

Overview

- Historically, the US had always claimed its right to see the Americas as its 'backyard', and had fought a war against Spain in 1898 which, in practice, established its control of the region.
- This attitude was strengthened by the development of the First Cold War, and had resulted in the Rio Pact and the formation of the OAS in the period 1947–48.
- Concern about the reform policies of Arbenz, the president of Guatemala, resulted in the CIA helping to topple him in a coup in 1954.
- Since 1898, the US had dominated Cuba; this control seemed threatened by a revolution in 1959, led by Fidel Castro. Pressure from the US led Castro to turn to the USSR for help, and soon Cuba became part of the Cold War.
- After a failed attempt to overthrow Castro in 1961, Cuba appealed to Khrushchev for protection. Khrushchev responded by sending intermediate-range ballistic missiles. When these were spotted by US spy planes, the Cuban Missile Crisis unfolded.
- Despite the real risk of nuclear war during this crisis, Kennedy and Khrushchev were able to agree a compromise. Afterwards, Soviet–US relations were improved by the establishment of a hotline between Moscow and Washington, and the signing of a partial Nuclear Test-Ban Treaty.
- After the crisis, however, the US maintained its hostility towards Cuba, while Cuba tried to encourage other revolutions in the Americas.

Timeline

1947 Sep: Rio Pact signed

1948 Mar: OAS formed

1951 Mar: Arbenz elected president of Guatemala

1953 Arbenz nationalises some US-owned land (including some owned by the United Fruit Company) to begin land reform

1954 Jun: CIA helps Armas to overthrow Arbenz

1956 Dec: Castro's force lands in Cuba, to begin guerrilla war against Batista

1959 Jan: Castro's revolutionary government takes control of Cuba

1961 Jan: US breaks off diplomatic relations with Cuba

Apr: Bay of Pigs invasion

1962 Oct: Cuban Missile Crisis

Nov: Kennedy authorises resumption of covert operations in Cuba

1963 Jun: hotline established

Aug: Nuclear Test-Ban Treaty agreed

1965 Che Guevara goes to Bolivia to help revolution there

1967 Oct: Che Guevara captured and shot

134

Question

Why did the US set up the Organisation of American States in 1948?

Fulgencio Batista (1901–74)
Batista was a sergeant in the Cuban army, before leading a successful coup in 1933. At first he ruled through a series of 'puppet' presidents until, in 1940, he took full control after being 'elected' president himself. He retired in 1944 and moved to Florida, but organised a military coup in 1952 and ruled as a dictator until he was overthrown by Castro in 1959.

Why did the US consider Cuba so important?

The US, Latin America and the Caribbean before 1945

Historically, the US had always seen Latin America and the Caribbean as its 'backyard', and the **Monroe Doctrine** of 1823 had made it abundantly clear that the US intended to be the overwhelmingly dominant power in the region. In 1904, US president Theodore Roosevelt – who said that, in dealing with Latin America, the US should 'speak softly and carry a big stick' – had announced what became known as the 'Roosevelt Corollary' to the Monroe Doctrine. This basically justified any US intervention in Latin and Central America: to protect private property, to maintain order or to protect American lives. There were, in fact, several armed interventions in the years before 1933, when the US adopted its 'Good Neighbor' policy under Franklin Roosevelt.

Impact of the Cold War

As soon as the First Cold War began, the US took steps to ensure that no communist or pro-communist state could ever be established in the Americas. In 1947, the US signed the Rio Pact with almost all the nations of Central and South America. This was the first post-war security treaty agreed by the US. It stated that an attack on any country on the American continent would be treated as an attack on all. In March 1948, the US set up the Organisation of American States (OAS) as the political movement of the Rio Pact signatories. Its charter included an unequivocal statement that 'international communism' was incompatible with 'American freedom'.

US intervention in Guatemala

The first apparent challenge to the USA's policy in the region was presented by developments in the Central American state of Guatemala, a poor agrarian country, where most of the land was in the hands of a wealthy minority. As a result, over half the population owned only 3% of the land.

In 1950, the elected reforming president had handed over to the defence minister, Colonel Jacobo Arbenz Guzman. Arbenz then headed a centre-left coalition that won elections later in the year, and he was installed as president in 1951.

Arbenz wanted to carry out land reform and, in June 1952, pushed through an act allowing the government to nationalise uncultivated areas of land in the large plantations. Compensation would be paid for any land so taken. However, in 1953, some unused land owned by the US United Fruit Company (UFCO) was taken. This company owned huge areas of land in Guatemala, 85% of which was unused. In order to avoid paying tax, the company had consistently undervalued the land it owned.

Eisenhower, who became president in 1953, had (like Truman before him) been worried by Arbenz's election in 1951 and his subsequent land-reform programme. The US president seized on the fact that Arbenz was supported by the communists as an opportunity to take action. In particular, Eisenhower claimed that the land-reform programme was the first step in a communist takeover, even though there were only four communists in the Guatemalan parliament.

In August 1953, Dulles tried to get the members of the OAS to agree that action should be taken under the terms of the Rio Pact, claiming outside influence in

Guatemala and that, if Guatemala fell, the rest of Central America was in danger (an example of the Domino Theory). However, an OAS meeting in early 1954 failed to support the USA's call for action. As a result, Eisenhower opted for covert action and authorised the CIA to develop a plan to overthrow Arbenz's government. This plan centred on a coup to be led by Castillo Armas, a fervent anti-communist. Armas was given funds for a small group of mercenaries, and provided with a base in neighbouring Honduras from which he could launch his coup.

Meanwhile, the US government kept up its demands for massive compensation for the loss of US property. Aware of the growing threat, Arbenz decided to buy small arms from the Eastern bloc. However, in June 1954, Armas launched his 'invasion'; the CIA had provided him with two planes, flown by US pilots, which bombed civilian targets. This led Arbenz to believe that there was a large invasion force, and in the ensuing panic the armed forces deserted him and he fled to Mexico. After the coup, Armas ordered the execution of hundreds of political opponents. Once installed as military dictator, Armas proved to be a corrupt but reliable ally for the US – but only for a short time. He was soon overthrown.

According to revisionist historians, the issue was complicated by the fact that many in Eisenhower's administration were closely involved with or connected to the UFCO. For example, the secretary of state, John Foster Dulles, and his brother, Allen Dulles (director of the CIA), had both come from a law firm with close links to UFCO. However, other historians have pointed out that the coup was actually opposed by UFCO, and that Eisenhower's Justice Department eventually prosecuted UFCO under the anti-trust laws.

The importance of Cuba

A more obvious challenge to US hegemony in the region occurred following events in Cuba which, since the Spanish–American War of 1898, had been dominated by the US (as had Puerto Rico and the Philippines). Cuba, nominally independent since December 1898, is a Caribbean island, about 145 km (90 miles) south of Florida. Initially, Cuba had been under US military occupation, but in 1901 the US allowed Cuba to draft a constitution. To achieve this, the Cubans were forced to include the Platt Amendment, which stated that the US had the right to 'oversee' the Cuban economy, veto any international agreements and intervene in Cuba's domestic politics. Thus Cuba was, in practice though not in law, a US protectorate. By 1934, when Roosevelt ended the Platt Amendment, the Cuban economy was highly dependent on sugar production and effectively controlled by US business interests.

Since 1934, Cuba had been ruled by the right-wing military dictator General **Fulgencio Batista**, supported by the US. Under his rule from 1934 to 1959, the US acquired increasing control of the Cuban economy as well as of political developments on the island. Soon, most of Cuba's land, industries and even public utilities were owned by US companies, while the capital Havana became a playground for rich American businessmen and the Mafia (Havana was nicknamed the 'whorehouse of America'). In addition, the US still retained an important naval base at Guantanamo.

Castro – radical or communist?

Many were opposed to Batista's regime and to Cuba being little more than a US satellite. One group was led by a young student radical called **Fidel Castro** who, though left of centre, was not associated with the larger and

Fidel Castro (b. 1926) Castro was the son of a wealthy sugar-plantation owner. He studied law at the University of Havana from 1945 to 1948. He practised law from 1950 to 1952, and stood for Congress in 1952. After the disastrous attack on the army's Moncada Barracks in 1953, he was imprisoned. Released in 1955, he went into exile in Mexico where, along with several supporters (including Raul, one of his brothers), he founded the 26th of July Movement. Despite claims to the contrary, he did not turn to communism until 1961.

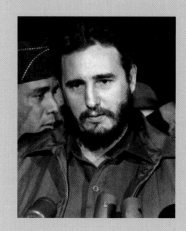

136

better-organised communist student group. On 26 July 1953, his group had carried out an attack on the army's Moncada Barracks. This was a total failure, and Fidel and his brother, Raul, surrendered in an attempt to halt Batista's slaughter of suspects.

Castro was sentenced to 15 years in prison but was released in an amnesty, with several others, in 1954. He then went into exile in Mexico, where he met up with a young Argentine doctor and revolutionary called **Ernesto 'Che' Guevara**. In Mexico, Castro's 26th of July Movement, named after the failed attack on the barracks, issued two official manifestos. Though they wanted a radical social revolution, Castro made great efforts to establish their lack of involvement with communism.

In December 1956, a small force of revolutionaries led by Castro landed in Cuba. At this stage, the revolutionaries were still essentially middle-class liberal reformers and, in February 1958, religious leaders in Cuba were sufficiently reassured to issue a call for a government of national unity. In March, however, the US (embarrassed by public criticism of its support for Batista's repressive regime) placed an embargo on arms shipments to both sides. A bitter guerrilla war ensued, during which Eisenhower's government came increasingly to believe that continued support for Batista was endangering US interests in Cuba. However, Batista suddenly decided to flee to the Dominican Republic, and on 1 January 1959 Castro's forces were able to enter Havana.

US concerns

Castro's revolution

Initially, the new government was headed by Manuel Urrutia (president) and José Miro Cardona (prime minister), but real power rested with Fidel Castro, commander-in-chief of the armed forces. By February, Cardona had resigned in protest at his lack of power and Castro took over his post.

At first Castro looked to the US for aid. However, the USA was seriously worried by Castro's agrarian reform law of May 1959. Not only did this limit all estates to 1000 acres – with compensation in bonds, based on 1958 tax valuations – but it also stated that foreigners would no longer be allowed to own agricultural land in Cuba. Of particular concern was the fact that Castro appointed the communist Nunez Jimenez as head of the National Institute of Agrarian Reform (INRA). The US began to see Castro, with his plans for land, health and welfare reforms, as another Arbenz.

Eventually Castro strengthened his position and, in September 1959, he announced at the UN that neutrality was the only realistic position for Developing World states in the Cold War. With Cuban exiles already flying bombing missions from Florida and firing sugar-cane fields, Castro began to accuse the US of plotting the return of Batista. In fact, from late 1959, the CIA was making use of Cuban exiles and hatching plans to disrupt the Cuban economy and destabilise Castro's government.

During 1960, tensions increased when Castro ordered the US-owned oil refineries in Cuba to process Soviet crude oil, which was cheaper than the oil normally purchased from Venezuela. When they refused to do so (breaking Cuban law), Castro nationalised the US oil companies. In response, in July 1960, Eisenhower suspended the Cuban sugar quota in the US; this was cut off permanently in December. Castro replied by nationalising almost all US-owned companies in Cuba, so the US placed an embargo on virtually all trade to Cuba. By then, Cuba had signed a trade agreement with the USSR (February 1960), which gave Cuba $100 million credit for the purchase of equipment, while the Soviet Union promised to purchase two million tonnes of sugar a year for the next four years. In the same month, Castro further upset the US by concluding a trade agreement with Communist China.

As 1960 progressed, Castro began a general programme of nationalisation of the Cuban economy and – although not a member himself – came to rely increasingly on the Cuban Communist Party to provide administrators for his reform programmes. In March 1960, the CIA persuaded Eisenhower to approve the training of an invasion force of right-wing Cuban exiles to overthrow Castro; serious training began in July.

A Soviet cartoon from 1960; the sign (held by the US secretary of state) reads: 'I forbid you to make friends with the Soviet Union'

Then, in September 1960, the US were angered – and the USSR disappointed – when Cuba became the first Latin American state to establish diplomatic relations with Mao's China. In January the following year, Eisenhower broke off diplomatic relations with Cuba, while Castro moved closer and closer to the Soviet bloc. A small island in the USA's 'backyard' was now an important factor in the Cold War, offering a direct challenge to the USA's containment policy. By mid 1961, Castro had established diplomatic and trade relations with every communist state, including North Korea and North Vietnam.

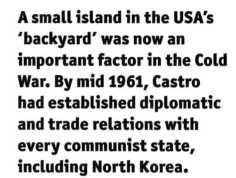

A small island in the USA's 'backyard' was now an important factor in the Cold War. By mid 1961, Castro had established diplomatic and trade relations with every communist state, including North Korea.

137

Fact
In response to growing fears about the possibility of imminent counter-revolution and a US invasion, many political freedoms were removed by Castro's government.

The Bay of Pigs, 1961

Eisenhower's economic blockade of Cuba and his invasion plans were inherited by Kennedy, who had won the presidential election in November 1960. Kennedy shared Eisenhower's hostility towards Castro's government, and had even accused Eisenhower of having 'lost' Cuba by being too passive. He authorised the CIA to continue with the project. On 15 April 1961, Cuban exiles (with CIA pilots) carried out preliminary air-raids to knock out the Cuban air force. Castro's immediate response, on 16 April, was to announce that Cuba intended to follow a 'socialist' road in order to complete its revolution. At the same time, negotiations continued with the Soviet Union for a large aid package, including weapons.

Since 1959, Castro's attempts to purchase small arms, in order to build up a Cuban army strong enough to resist any attempt by Batista to return, had been blocked by the US. From February 1960, the USSR had begun providing such weapons, along with military advisers. These weapons and advisers proved useful in dealing with the land invasion that followed the air-raids, on 17 April 1961. The landings, of about 1400 Cuban exiles, took place in the Bahia de Cochinos (Bay of Pigs) in a remote part of the island. Though Kennedy had ordered that no Americans should take part – and had withdrawn air support – the US provided the transport and weapons needed. In fact, the first invader to touch Cuban soil was an American.

This attempted invasion was quickly defeated and the whole venture became a deeply humiliating fiasco for Kennedy, the new Cold War warrior president of the USA. It meant a loss of prestige for his administration, both within the US and across the rest of the world, and made it difficult for his country to pose as an 'anti-colonial' power in the Developing World. Many Latin American countries saw the invasion as an example of traditional 'Yankee imperialism'. Later, Kennedy admitted that US support for Batista had probably resulted in increased support for communism in Cuba.

In all, 1179 of the Cuban exiles were captured. In order to get them back, the US had to give $53 million to Cuba in the form of baby food, medicines and medical equipment. Not only had the CIA seriously underestimated the strength of the Cuban armed forces, it had also failed to realise the extent of popular support for the Castro regime.

Why did the Cuban Missile Crisis happen?

US plans had clearly suffered a serious setback with the Bay of Pigs incident, but Kennedy remained determined to bring about Castro's overthrow, so he authorised CIA operations to continue. These included bizarre schemes to assassinate Castro, as well as using 'private' planes to bomb or napalm sugar and tobacco fields. CIA agents also sabotaged oil refineries and sank Cuban merchant ships. As early as 30 November 1961, Kennedy authorised another attempt to overthrow Castro. Cuban security police also captured documents which said that, if Castro had not been overthrown by October 1962, then the US would have to take more drastic action. In addition, the US had Cuba expelled from the OAS, while 40,000 US troops staged a 'mock' invasion of Puerto Rico – clearly intended as a warning to Castro.

Fearing another possible US-backed invasion, Castro appealed to Khrushchev for protection. Relations between Kennedy and Khrushchev had not recovered from the Vienna Summit of June 1961 (see page 115), where Khrushchev had formed a low opinion of a 'callous' Kennedy. From May 1962, Soviet weapons deliveries to Cuba increased dramatically.

The 'missile gap' and Soviet concerns

Castro's request came at a time when the Soviet Union was growing increasingly concerned and insecure about the nuclear missiles that the US had placed in Turkey – on the Black Sea coast, close to the USSR – and in Italy. Khrushchev was also worried in general about the 'missile gap' between the USSR and the USA.

In February 1962, the USA publicly announced that any missile gap was in its favour. This contributed to the growing criticism Khrushchev faced at home over cuts in Soviet armed forces, some economic failures and his reforms in general. The development of thermonuclear weapons added a new dimension to fears of nuclear war. Hence Khrushchev felt under pressure to achieve a foreign-policy success that would increase Soviet security and bolster his own position within the Soviet Communist Party. In addition, according to historians such as Gaddis, and Zubok and Pleshakov, Khrushchev genuinely feared there might be another US-sponsored invasion of Cuba.

> **Fact**
> By 1962, the USSR still had only a small number of ICBMs, while the US had 294 and, more importantly, already had 144 Polaris SLBMs. In fact, the US was fully aware – thanks to its spy planes – of its lead over the USSR in regard to both missiles and warheads.

SOURCE A

The fate of Cuba and the maintenance of Soviet prestige in that part of the world preoccupied me. ... We had to establish a tangible and effective deterrent to American interference in the Caribbean. ... The logical answer was missiles. We knew that American missiles were aimed against us in Turkey and Italy, to say nothing of West Germany.

Extract from the memoirs of Nikita Khrushchev, Khrushchev Remembers. *Crankshaw, E. (ed.). 1970. Quoted in Rayner, E. G. 1992.* The Cold War. *London, UK. Hodder Murray. pp. 50–51.*

During a visit to Bulgaria in May 1962, Khrushchev began to consider how placing Soviet missiles on Cuba might serve a dual purpose. Castro would gain the protection he had requested against further US aggression, while the Soviet Union would be able to counter the threat posed by the US missiles in Turkey and Italy with a similar threat against the US. During 1961–62, Khrushchev grew increasingly concerned by the vulnerability of the USSR to US attack, in addition to the tensions over Berlin and criticisms from China. There were even rumours that the USA was considering a surprise nuclear first strike.

By September 1962, the Soviet Union had begun to install and equip missile sites in Cuba, as well as increasing the number of tanks, bombers and fighters supplied to Castro's armed forces. There were soon over 5000 Soviet technicians and engineers working on the missile sites, which were under Soviet rather than Cuban control. Khrushchev hoped that these moves would remain secret until the missiles were fully operational.

> **Fact**
> In fact, many of these technicians and engineers were military personnel. The total Soviet presence in Cuba eventually reached 42,000.

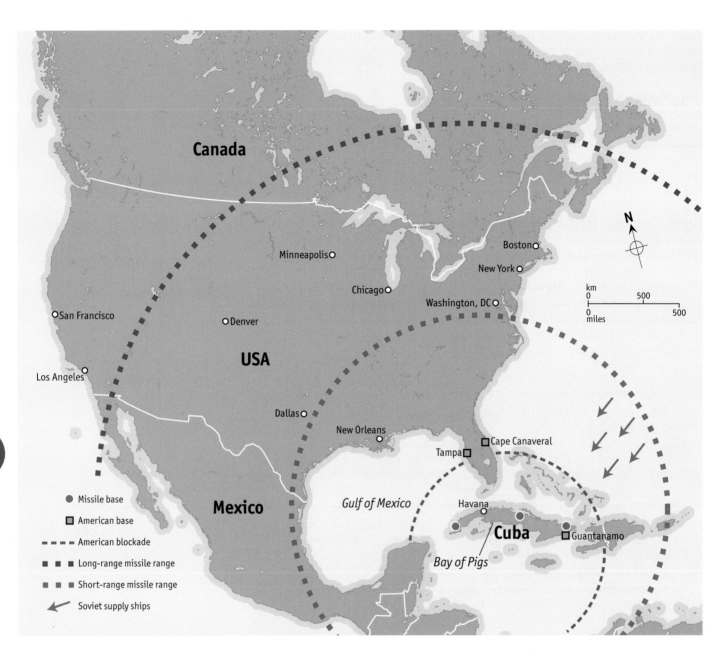

The Cuban Missile Crisis, October 1962

Kennedy – statesman or dangerous bungler?

On 11 September, Kennedy warned Khrushchev that the US would prevent the installation of Soviet nuclear missiles on Cuba by 'whatever means might be necessary'. Khrushchev replied that the Soviet Union had no intention of providing such missiles for Cuba. In part, Khrushchev felt able to take such a risky step because the crisis over Berlin had blown over after the building of the Berlin Wall in 1961, leaving him free to focus on other problems. More importantly, the failure over Berlin led him to seek a success elsewhere. However, these Soviet short- and intermediate-range missiles, while not altering the overall global nuclear superiority of the US, were seen by Kennedy as altering the strategic balance of forces in a region long considered a US sphere of influence. In particular, they would reduce the warning time for missiles fired at the US, which the US public would see as a serious failure on the part of Kennedy's government.

On 14 October, a US U-2 spy plane returned from a reconnaissance mission over Cuba with photos of an intermediate-range ballistic missile site under construction. These missiles, with a range of 1600 km (1000 miles), would turn most of the USA's major cities into potential targets. Two days later, on 16 October, these photographs were handed to Kennedy. They seemed to show that Soviet missiles had arrived, but not yet been made ready for use. This initiated a serious crisis, which has become known as 'The Thirteen Days' – the closest the USA and USSR came to war.

For six days, a few members of the US government (the Executive Committee of the NSC – ExComm) discussed the various response options without consulting any allies, including its closest ally Britain. As a first step, Robert McNamara ordered preparations for an invasion of Cuba to be ready by 20 October. Only on 21 October, after Kennedy had decided on what action to take, was Britain informed about the missiles.

In fact, Kennedy had decided on two responses: the US would first mount a naval blockade of Cuba; then, US troops would invade the island. The blockade, or 'quarantine', was announced publicly on 22 October. The days from then until 29 October – when Khrushchev made a broadcast stating that Soviet missiles would be withdrawn from Cuba – were arguably the most tense days of the entire Cold War, especially as, on 23 October, Khrushchev issued a reply that Soviet ships would not respect the blockade. However, the following day, 18 Soviet ships (possibly containing warheads for the missiles) stopped or turned back just before reaching the limit set by the US.

A US destroyer shadows a Soviet supply ship during the period of 'quarantine' in the Cuban Missile Crisis

Fact
In fact, Kennedy took most of the important decisions outside ExComm, relying mostly on his brother Robert, Dean Rusk (secretary of state), Robert McNamara (secretary of defense) and McGeorge Bundy (national security adviser).

Fact

The US stated that, from 24 October, it would stop and search all ships bound for Cuba. Opinion continues to be divided on whether or not the USA's actions were technically an act of war.

Fact

Mention of the UN presented difficulties for the US, as it had never publicly admitted to having missiles in Turkey. In addition, Kennedy did not wish to be seen backing down or making concessions to the USSR.

Fact

The US missiles were removed from Turkey in April 1963, but the American public was not told about this until 1969. In fact, the Soviet Union gained very little from the deal, as the US had already decided to remove its missiles, since land-based sites had been rendered obsolete by the introduction of SLBMs, which were much more difficult to detect and hence to destroy.

The risk of nuclear war increased when the US announced that, if the missiles were not removed at once, Cuba would be invaded. On 25 October, the US began to put into effect plans for an air-strike against the missile sites, to take place on 29 or 30 October. Castro – and even some Soviet generals – urged Khrushchev to launch some missiles in order to prevent the threatened US invasion of Cuba. Khrushchev rejected these calls and instead, on 26 October, sent a personal letter to Kennedy.

The compromises

The letter offered the withdrawal of Soviet missiles from Cuba and promised no more would be sent, on condition that the US lifted its blockade of Cuba and promised not to invade the island. On 27 October, before receiving a response from the US, Khrushchev sent a second letter, with different demands. This time he offered to remove Soviet missiles from Cuba if the US would reciprocate by removing its own Jupiter missiles from Turkey. Khrushchev further suggested that this be done via the UN.

SOURCE B

You are worried over Cuba. You say that it worries you because it lies 90 miles across the sea from the shores of the United States. However, Turkey lies next to us. You have stationed devastating rocket weapons in Turkey, literally right next to us. This is why I make this proposal: We agree to remove the weapons from Cuba. We agree to this and to state this commitment in the United Nations. Your representatives will make a statement that the United States, on its part, will evacuate its similar weapons from Turkey.

Extract from Khrushchev's letter to Kennedy, 28 October 1962. Quoted in McAleavy, T. 1996. Modern World History. Cambridge, UK. Cambridge University Press. p. 131.

The US military chiefs pressed Kennedy to launch an air attack on Cuba – especially when, on 27 October, a US spy-plane was shot down over Cuba, resulting in the death of the pilot. However, Kennedy was hesitant. After some intense discussions, it was agreed by ExComm that Khrushchev's second letter should be ignored. Instead, Kennedy replied to the first letter and offered to give a commitment not to invade Cuba, provided that the Soviet missiles were withdrawn first. Later that same day, Robert Kennedy, the president's brother, was sent to have discussions with Anatoly Dobrynin, the Soviet ambassador in the US. Robert Kennedy had been instructed to give an unofficial ultimatum – and offer – to the ambassador: if the Soviet Union had not promised by 28 October to remove its missiles, the US would attack and destroy them. However, the offer was that once the missiles were withdrawn, the US would remove theirs from Turkey at some point in the near future.

He stressed that this would not be part of any public deal. Dobrynin reported back to Khrushchev, who accepted this compromise on 28 October, so ending the crisis.

Results of the crisis

The end of what proved, for 13 days, to be the most serious crisis of the entire Cold War was portrayed in the West as a victory for Kennedy and a defeat for Khrushchev, as the deal over Cuba and US missiles in Turkey was kept secret. Although Khrushchev had secured unofficial promises about US attacks on Cuba, many leading Soviet communists were unhappy at the USSR's public climb-down. The Cuban Missile Crisis undoubtedly played a part in Khrushchev's removal from power in 1964. At the same time, his agreements confirmed to the Chinese communists that the Soviet leader was unwilling to stand up to the US. China therefore continued to develop its own independent foreign policy, widening the split in the world communist movement. However, although Kennedy had recognised the legitimacy of Soviet security concerns, Khrushchev still faced inequalities between his own country's nuclear force and that of the USA.

In Western Europe there was some anger at how little the US had consulted its allies during this emergency, despite the risk that any conflict between the US and the USSR would probably have involved other NATO members. France, in particular, was resentful. This was one of the reasons why French leader Charles de Gaulle decided to withdraw France from NATO, and tried to encourage the rest of Western Europe to adopt an independent foreign policy.

The hotline and the Test-Ban Treaty

Both sides had been shocked by how close they had come to nuclear war and were determined to avoid such serious tensions in the future. The Cuban Missile Crisis was therefore a turning point in the Cold War, and contributed to the development of détente.

It was agreed almost immediately to install a special telephone 'hotline' between the Kremlin and the White House, so that the leaders could communicate quickly and directly with each other during any future crisis. This hotline was in operation by June 1963. Although the Cold War continued, the level of tension between the US and the USSR never again reached that of October 1962. Such 'brinkmanship' was seen as too dangerous in the nuclear age.

This crisis also helped bring about a partial thaw in East–West relations. In what came to be seen as the first step towards halting the nuclear arms race, the Soviet Union and the US signed a Nuclear Test-Ban Treaty in August 1963. This did not limit or reduce the building and deployment of nuclear weapons, but it did attempt to control the testing of such devices.

Although the Cuban Missile Crisis helped change Cold War confrontation, it did not end it. For instance, the 1963 Test-Ban Treaty (and the later Non-Proliferation Treaty of 1969) did not end the arms race. However, from 1962, Cold War conflict remained confined to the Developing World, and the world as a whole seemed a more secure place after the Cuban Missile Crisis than it had before.

Both sides had been shocked by how close they had come to nuclear war and were determined to avoid such serious tensions in the future. The Cuban Missile Crisis was a turning point in the Cold War.

143

Fact
In addition to – and separate from – the Test-Ban Treaty, the US agreed to sell the Soviet Union surplus grain worth $250 million. A Treaty for the Non-Proliferation of Nuclear Weapons was drawn up, but was not actually signed until the era of détente in 1969.

What impact did the Cuban Revolution have on the Cold War?

Cuba and Latin America

Despite the 1962 agreements, the US remained extremely hostile to Cuba. In addition, the promises the US gave Khrushchev not to attack Cuba fell by the wayside as they were dependent on UN inspection of the missile sites – something Castro refused to allow, as he saw it as an infringement of Cuban sovereignty. As early as June 1963, Kennedy ordered the resumption of covert operations in Cuba. The CIA thus continued to carry out acts of sabotage and small military raids, while plans to assassinate Castro continued to be drawn up.

Because of continuing US hostility to Cuba after the Missile Crisis of 1962, Castro hoped the example of the Cuban Revolution would inspire similar revolutions in Central and Latin America and the Caribbean, as such a development would end Cuba's isolation in the region. This is precisely what the USA – and many Latin American rulers – feared. In fact, the first attempt by Castro (who, along with other leading Cuban revolutionaries, had a strong commitment to the idea of international revolution) to spread revolution in the region came as early as 1959, with an unsuccessful intervention in the Dominican Republic. However, despite several groups appearing which claimed inspiration from the Cuban Revolution, and the supply of weapons and training by Cuba, nothing significant occurred. Even a personal attempt by Che Guevara – who had spearheaded the drive to spread revolution in the region – to stimulate a revolution in Bolivia in 1965 failed. He was eventually captured by US-trained Bolivian Ranger counter-insurgency forces, interrogated and then summarily executed in 1967.

> **Fact**
> One of Guevara's aims – and Castro's hopes – had been to create 'many Vietnams', in order to weaken the USA's ability to intervene in the Developing World and crush incipient revolutions.

144

> **Historical debate**
>
> There has been considerable debate amongst historians about Kennedy's handling of the Cuban Missile Crisis. The orthodox view maintains that Kennedy conducted himself extremely ably from the very beginning of the crisis, and all the way through it until its resolution.
>
> However, revisionist historians claim that Kennedy and his advisers almost turned a negotiable Cold War problem into a nuclear Third World War.
>
> Some post-revisionist historians have revisited the crisis, and many now conclude that, overall, Kennedy handled the negotiations in a statesman-like way, and stood up to the 'hawks' who were pushing for some sort of military response.

Until 1968, Cuba had tended towards a foreign policy somewhat at variance with that favoured by the USSR, despite its economic and military dependence on the communist superpower. In particular, the Soviet Union did not approve of Castro's attempts to 'export' revolution. One reason for these differences was that, following the Cuban Missile Crisis of 1962, Castro came to believe that the USSR had used Cuba in its global contest with the USA.

However, after Guevara's failure and death in Bolivia, Castro began to follow a line more in keeping with Moscow's preferences. The first sign of this came in 1968, when Castro publicly supported the Warsaw Pact's invasion of Czechoslovakia. This shift later intensified after Cuba experienced serious economic problems in 1969 and 1970, and so became increasingly dependent on Soviet aid. However, Castro remained committed to the idea of internationalism, although he became a much more reliable ally of the Soviet Union in the Developing World.

Unit summary

You should have built up an understanding of the significance of the Monroe Doctrine for US policy in Latin America and the Caribbean. In particular, you should be aware of various US interventions in the area – and of the particular importance of Cuba to US economic and strategic interests.

You should also have a sound understanding of the main factors and events that led to worsening relations between the US and Cuba after Castro came to power in 1959. In particular, you should be able to grasp the reasons for the Cuban Missile Crisis, the roles played by Kennedy and Khrushchev, and how the crisis was resolved. Finally, you should be able to demonstrate an understanding of the results of the crisis and its impact on Cold War relations between the two superpowers.

End of unit activities

1   Carry out further research on the Monroe Doctrine. Then produce a chart to show US interventions in Central and Latin America and the Caribbean in the period 1900–59.

2   Find out more about Castro's political beliefs, and the impact of US actions on them before 1962. Then write a brief summary of your findings.

3   Produce a timeline to show the main events of the Cuban Missile Crisis.

4   See what further information you can find about Kennedy's handling of the Cuban Missile Crisis.

> **Question**
>
> What impact did the Cuban Missile Crisis of 1962 have on the Cold War?

End of chapter activities

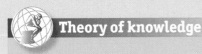
Theory of knowledge

Facts and perceptions

Has the advent of photographic, film and TV images and 'evidence' made it easier for historians to establish the 'truth' of recent historical events? To what extent – and for what reasons – does historical truth change over time? Discuss this in relation to one of the following events covered in this chapter: the building of the Berlin Wall, the Tet Offensive, or the Cuban Missile Crisis.

Historical debate

What are the similarities and differences between the methods used by historians and scientists to establish the 'truth'? Is scientific knowledge always more 'objective' than historical knowledge?

Paper 1 exam practice

Question

Compare and contrast the reasons for the invasion of Czechoslovakia as expressed in Sources A and B opposite.
[6 marks]

Skill

Cross-referencing

Examiner's tips

Cross-referencing questions require you to compare **AND** contrast the information/content/nature of **two** sources, relating to a particular issue. Before you write your answer, draw a rough chart or diagram to show the **similarities** and the **differences** between the two sources. That way, you should ensure you address **BOTH** aspects/elements of the question.

Common mistakes

When asked to compare and contrast two sources, make sure you don't just comment on **one** of them! A few candidates make this mistake every year – and lose 4 of the 6 marks available.

Simplified markscheme

Band		Marks
1	**Both** sources **linked**, with **detailed references** to the two sources, identifying **both** similarities **and** differences.	6
2	**Both** sources **linked**, with **detailed references** to the two sources, identifying **either** similarities **or** differences.	4–5
3	Comments on both sources, **but** treating each one **separately**.	3
4	Discusses/comments on just **one** source.	0–2

SOURCE A

The Soviet retreat from Cuba, the growing atmosphere of détente and the Sino–Soviet split all combined to weaken Soviet control over Eastern Europe and provide some opportunities for the satellite states to pursue their own policies. ... The Soviet government's efforts to consolidate its control over Eastern Europe ... suffered a serious setback when in January 1968 Alexander Dubcek became the First Secretary of the Czech Communist Party. ... He attempted to create a socialist system that would be based on the consent of the people. In April 1968 he revealed his program for democratic change and modernization of the economy, which marked the start of what was called the Prague Spring. In June he abolished censorship, which led to a flood of anti-Soviet propaganda being published in Czechoslovakia. These developments began to worry Brezhnev and the other leaders of the Warsaw Pact.

Williamson, D. 2001. Europe and the Cold War, 1945–91. London, UK. Hodder Murray. p. 140.

SOURCE B

The measures taken by the Soviet Union, jointly with other socialist countries, in defending the socialist gains of the Czechoslovak people are of great significance for strengthening the socialist states. ... The CPSU (Communist Party of the Soviet Union) has always asserted that every socialist country must determine its own development on the path of socialism, in accordance with national circumstances. But when there is a threat to the cause of socialism in that country – a threat to the security of the socialist states as a whole – this becomes the concern of all socialist countries. ...

Clearly, such action as military aid to suppress a threat to the socialist order is an extraordinary, forced measure which can be provoked only by the direct activity of the enemies of socialism. ... Czechoslovakia's detachment from the socialist states, would have brought it into conflict with its own vital interests and would have been dangerous (or threatening) to the other socialist states.

Extract from a speech by Leonid Brezhnev, given on 12 November 1968.

Student answer

Sources A and B give quite different reasons for the invasion of Czecho-slovakia. Source B, from Brezhnev, explains the invasion was to defend the 'socialist gains of the Czechoslovak people' and to 'strengthen the socialist states'. Essentially, then, Brezhnev felt there was a threat to the cause of socialism in Czechoslovakia, and to the security of the socialist states as a whole. This was as a result of the 'direct activity of the enemies of socialism'.

However, Source A refers to different reasons for the invasion – 'the Soviet retreat from Cuba, the growing atmosphere of détente and the Sino–Soviet split' as having weakened Soviet control of Eastern Europe. None of these factors is mentioned in Source B. Also, another differ-ence is that Source A doesn't say anywhere that there was a threat to socialism as stated in Source B. Instead, Source A talks about Dubcek's 'program for democratic change and modernization' of the Czechoslovak economy – neither of which are mentioned in Source B.

Examiner's comments

There are several clear/precise references to **both** the sources, and several **differences/contrasts** are identified. Also, the sources are clearly linked in the second paragraph, rather than being dealt with separately. The candidate has thus done enough to get into Band 2, and so be awarded 4 or 5 marks. However, as no similarities/comparisons are made, this answer fails to get into Band 1.

Activity

Look again at the two sources, the simplified markscheme, and the student answer above. Now try to write a paragraph or two to push the answer up into Band 1, and so obtain the full 6 marks.

Summary activities

1 Produce three sets of revision cards – one for each of the **three regions**: Europe, Asia and the Americas – to cover (via bullet points) the main events and developments in the Cold War from 1954 to 1968. Then produce a final card to summarise the main points of the state of superpower relations by 1968. To do this, use the information from this chapter, and any other resources available to you. Make sure you include **all** the main events and turning points.

2 Make sure you have attempted all the various comprehension questions that appear in the margins. Many of these are designed to help you understand key events and turning points. There are also questions designed to develop your skills in dealing with Paper 1-type questions, such as comprehension of sources, and assessing sources for their value and limitations for historians. Remember, to answer this type of question you will need to look at aspects such as origin, nature and possible purpose. Don't forget – even if a source has many limitations, it can still be valuable for a historian.

148

Practice Paper 2 questions

1 Compare and contrast the significance of the Berlin crises and also of Czechoslovakia's 'Prague Spring' in the development of the Cold War in Europe during the period 1953–68.

2 In what ways and to what extent did Khrushchev's policy of 'Peaceful Coexistence' alter the nature of the Cold War in Europe during the period 1953–64?

3 Analyse the part played by **either** Kennedy **or** Khrushchev in the development of the Cold War in Europe between 1960–64.

4 'The USA decided to become involved in the war in Vietnam because it wished to preserve the freedom of the people of South Vietnam.' To what extent do you agree with this statement about the reasons for US involvement in the Vietnam War during the period 1954–68?

5 In what ways did developments in Vietnam affect the Cold War between 1954 and 1968?

6 Analyse the part played by Cuba in the development of the Cold War in the period 1959–68.

7 Examine the impact of the Cuban Missile Crisis of 1962 on the development of the Cold War.

Further reading

Try reading the relevant chapters/sections of the following books:

Gaddis, John Lewis. 2007. *The Cold War: A New History*. London, UK. Penguin.

Williamson, David. 2006. *Europe and the Cold War, 1945–91*. London, UK. Hodder Education.

Zubok, Vladislav. and Pleshakov, Constantine. 1996. *Inside the Kremlin's Cold War: From Stalin to Khrushchev*, 1996. Cambridge, USA. Harvard University Press.

Beschloss, Michael R. 1991. *The Crisis Years: Kennedy and Khrushchev, 1960–1963*, London, UK. HarperCollins.

Freedman, Lawrence. 2001. *Kennedy's Wars: Berlin, Cuba, Laos and Vietnam*. Oxford, UK. Oxford University Press.

Lowe, Peter (ed.). 1998. *The Vietnam War*. London, UK. Palgrave Macmillan.

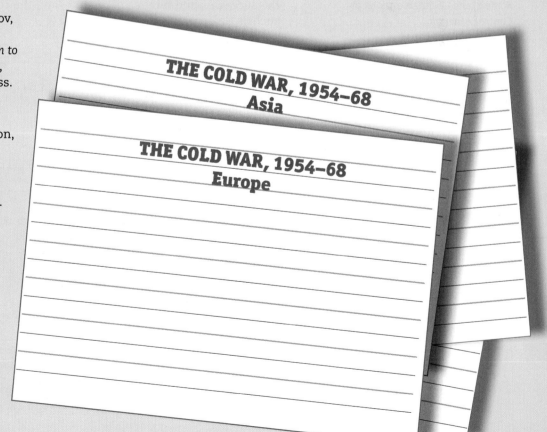

THE COLD WAR, 1954–68
Asia

THE COLD WAR, 1954–68
Europe

From détente to the Second Cold War (1969–85)

Introduction

The period 1969–85 saw some significant developments in the Cold War, ranging from a period of détente to the start of what most historians see as a Second Cold War. Once again, events were not confined to Europe, but also affected Asia, the Americas and Africa.

This chapter will cover, among other issues, the impact of the rapprochement between the US and Communist China – making Cold War politics 'triangular' or even 'multi-polar'. As well as looking at the reasons for the end of the Vietnam War, the effect of the changing international relations on Europe – both East and West – will be explored, as will further developments in the Americas and in parts of Africa.

Central to this period, though, was the emergence of détente, its global and regional impacts, the various attempts at limiting the nuclear arms race, and the reasons for its end and eventual replacement by the Second Cold War.

By the end of this chapter, you should be able to compare and contrast the events and impacts of the Cold War that took place in the different regions of the world, and to understand the increasingly complex international relations that arose in the period 1969–85. You should also be able to give your views on the successes and failures of détente, and the roles played by key individuals such as Nixon, Kissinger and Brezhnev.

Some of the US interventions in Central America

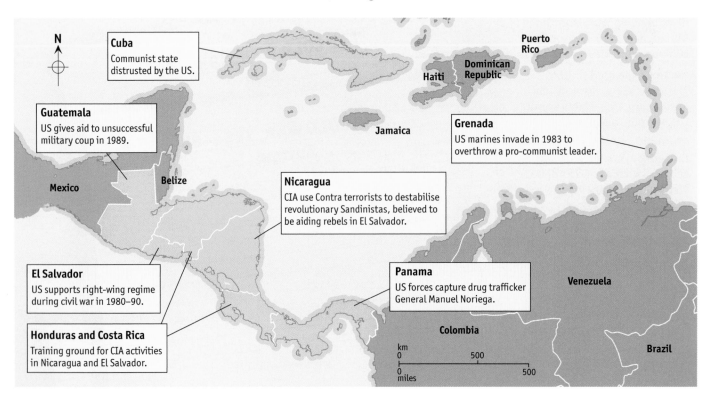

Cuba
Communist state distrusted by the US.

Puerto Rico

Dominican Republic

Haiti

Guatemala
US gives aid to unsuccessful military coup in 1989.

Grenada
US marines invade in 1983 to overthrow a pro-communist leader.

Jamaica

Mexico

Belize

Nicaragua
CIA use Contra terrorists to destabilise revolutionary Sandinistas, believed to be aiding rebels in El Salvador.

El Salvador
US supports right-wing regime during civil war in 1980–90.

Panama
US forces capture drug trafficker General Manuel Noriega.

Venezuela

Honduras and Costa Rica
Training ground for CIA activities in Nicaragua and El Salvador.

Colombia

Brazil

km
0   500

0   500
miles

1 Developments in Europe and the Middle East

Key questions

- Did détente mark the end of the First Cold War, or was it merely a new phase?
- Why did a Second Cold War begin in 1979?
- How did the Second Cold War differ from the First Cold War?

Overview

- Nixon continued the Strategic Arms Limitation Talks (SALT) with the USSR (begun in late 1968). Cold War tensions were eased, as both sides seemed more willing to reach negotiated settlements.
- In 1970, agreements were reached about Germany; 1971 saw a Quadrilateral Agreement on Berlin, and China joined the UN.
- Relations between the US, USSR and China further improved in 1972 – SALT I and an Anti-Ballistic Missiles Treaty were signed.
- In 1973, US involvement in Vietnam ended and, despite war in the Middle East, the US and USSR continued to hold weapons reductions talks; East–West trade increased. When Ford replaced Nixon in 1974, the SALT II outline was agreed.
- In 1975, the war in Vietnam ended, while the USSR signed the Helsinki Declaration on Europe. Good relations continued under Carter (elected 1976) at first, despite civil war in Angola. In 1979, the US and China established diplomatic relations, and Brezhnev and Carter signed SALT II in Vienna.
- However, by the late 1970s, détente was beginning to unravel; it was seriously undermined in December 1979 when Soviet troops went into Afghanistan. This initiated what some historians have called a Second Cold War.
- Carter responded in early 1980 by blocking various exports to the USSR and by suspending ratification of SALT II. In November, Reagan was elected president.
- In August 1981, Reagan announced that the US was stockpiling neutron bombs; later, he imposed economic sanctions on both Poland and the USSR, after martial law had been declared in Poland.
- Some bilateral talks still took place: in June 1982 there were START talks in Geneva. But in March 1983, Reagan made his 'Evil Empire' speech and announced the SDI ('Star Wars') programme. In November, NATO deployed Cruise and Pershing II missiles in Europe.
- The situation began to change in March 1985, when Gorbachev became leader of the USSR. In April, he announced a freeze on Soviet missile development.

Timeline

1969 Jan: Nixon becomes president of the US

Oct: SPD/FPD wins West German elections

1970 Mar: Nuclear Non-Proliferation Treaty comes into force; Moscow Treaty signed

1972 Feb: Nixon visits China

May: SALT I signed

Dec: Basic Treaty

1973 Jun: Brezhnev visits US

Jul: CSCE Conference begins in Helsinki

Oct: Yom Kippur War

1974 Apr: Portuguese Revolution begins

Nov: Vladivostok Summit

1975 Independence for Portuguese colonies in Africa

Aug: Final Act signed in Helsinki

Nov: Franco dies

1976 Oct: Soviet–Angolan Treaty

1977 Mar: Soviet–Mozambican Treaty

1978 Dec: US recognises China

1979 Jan: Iranian Revolution

Jun: Vienna Agreement

Dec: Soviet troops intervene in Afghanistan

1980 Aug: Solidarity crisis in Poland

1981 Jan: Reagan becomes president of US; INF Treaty

1983 Jun: Reagan's 'Evil Empire' speech

1985 Mar: Gorbachev becomes leader of USSR

151

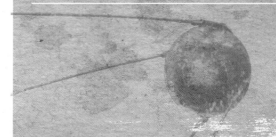

Richard Nixon (1913–94)
Nixon became a Republican senator in 1950, and was a strong supporter of the anti-communist activities of the HUAC during the early 1950s. In 1953, he became vice-president under Eisenhower. He was elected president in 1968, and was re-elected in 1972. He was the first US president to visit Communist China and negotiated US withdrawal from the Vietnam War.

Did détente mark the end of the First Cold War, or was it merely a new phase?

Détente, 1969–79

The period known as détente, or 'relaxation of tensions', is generally seen as starting in 1968–69, although signs of it were apparent before 1968. Certainly by the late 1960s both the US and the USSR came to desire an improvement in Cold War relations, for a variety of reasons. This period is usually seen as ending in 1979–80. In general, it was part of a more complex set of international relations, covering attempts to reduce tensions and increase co-operation between the USSR and the USA, between the USSR and Western Europe, and between the USA and China. However, it is important to realise that détente was just an easing, not the end, of the main underlying Cold War tensions.

Détente and the US

By the late 1960s, several factors had emerged that made the US ready to follow a policy of détente with the USSR. The main reason was the growing impact of the Vietnam War (see pages 130–131), both on the US itself and on its global position. In addition, there was a growing awareness of the dangers of nuclear warfare, and evidence that – at least in some areas – the USSR was beginning to achieve some parity with the US in nuclear weaponry.

In 1968, **Richard Nixon** had won the presidential elections. Although a hardline anti-communist for many years (he had supported McCarthy for a time), he was prepared to limit the US policy of containing communism if the overall consequences were beneficial to US interests. In particular, he believed that continuing the war in Vietnam was having an increasingly negative effect on the USA's ability to maintain its economic and military superiority over the Soviet Union. More immediately, he realised that the American public wanted a withdrawal from Vietnam, and he was worried by signs that the US economy was beginning to decline.

SOURCE A

Henry Kissinger called for a 'philosophical deepening' of American foreign policy. By this he meant adjusting to the changed international order. The Kennedy and Johnson administrations, Kissinger argued, had focused too much on victory in one rather isolated area – Vietnam – at the expense of the global balance of power. The world was shifting from a bipolar balance of power between Washington and Moscow to a multi-polar balance shared among five great economic and strategic centres – the United States, the Soviet Union, Western Europe, Japan and China.

Mason, J. W. 1996. The Cold War. London, UK. Routledge. p. 51.

Nixon thus made détente – and an acceptable withdrawal from Vietnam – the main focus of his foreign policy. Much of the new diplomacy was carried out by **Henry Kissinger**, who had advocated this change based on his belief that the Democrats under Kennedy and Johnson had weakened the USA's global power by concentrating too much on victory in Vietnam. Kissinger and Nixon hoped that the USSR and China could be persuaded to put pressure on North Vietnam too, in a way acceptable to the US and its interests. Kissinger also argued that US foreign policy should take account of the existence of other centres of power, such as China, Japan and Western Europe.

Détente and the USSR

At the same time, three main factors were driving the Soviet Union to seek a better relationship with the USA. First, there were compelling economic reasons. By 1969, the Soviet economy was beginning to show signs of stagnating – in part due to bureaucratic inefficiency, but also because of the heavy burden of defence spending required to match US military developments.

This situation was exacerbated in the 1970s as Soviet spending, both on defence and aid to Developing World countries, was increased; Brezhnev ignored the signs of economic decline. Thus the Brezhnev–Kosygin team wished to import new technology from the more advanced Western economies, and to increase trade generally.

A US cartoon entitled 'Captain Brezhnev runs aground'

Henry Kissinger (b. 1923)
German-born Kissinger was a professor at Harvard University, and acted as a government adviser. In 1969, he became Nixon's national security adviser, and then chief adviser on foreign policy. In 1973, Nixon appointed him secretary of state. In 1973, Kissinger shared the Nobel Peace Prize for his part in negotiating a ceasefire in Vietnam.

153

Fact
Soviet leader Alexei Kosygin, in particular, was worried by increasing problems with the Soviet Union's economy, which was even beginning to show signs of actual decline. This made attempts to further improve living standards in the USSR difficult.

missile gap This was the relative superiority/inferiority in nuclear weapons between the two sides. The US often claimed – incorrectly – that the Soviet Union was ahead, although the USSR did succeed in closing the gap in some areas.

Question

Why was the Soviet Union concerned about the possibility of a diplomatic agreement between the United States and China?

Nixon Doctrine This was a policy of delegation, declared in 1969, which was based on the idea that US 'client' states in the Developing World would be given weapons to fight for US objectives in important regions, thus avoiding the need for direct US military intervention. For example, over the course of the Vietnam War, 300,000 South Korean troops fought in Vietnam (up to 50,000 at one time). The wave of revolutions in the late 1970s, however, led the US to create a Rapid Deployment Force specifically for intervention in the Developing World.

Second, there was a genuine fear that the risk of nuclear war had increased. This Soviet insecurity existed even though by the late 1960s the USSR had managed to close the **missile gap** with the US – or at least had done so in some areas. For instance, the Soviet Union had 1300 ICBMs to the USA's 1054 (although this was no longer so important, as ICBMs had been superseded by SLBMs). Overall, the US no longer had the overwhelming nuclear superiority it had enjoyed since 1945; thus the Soviet leadership believed the US might be prepared to join talks on arms reduction. Previously, such talks had failed because the US had only been prepared to agree to a freeze on armaments, which would maintain a situation of significant Soviet inferiority.

Finally, the Soviet Union was becoming increasingly concerned about the Sino–Soviet split, which had widened since the early 1960s. In 1969, in fact, border disputes and armed clashes along the Ussuri River had almost resulted in war. The particular Soviet fear was the possibility of an anti-Soviet alliance between the USA and China. To help prevent this, an improved relationship with the USA was regarded as important.

China and the Cold War 'Triangle'

Nixon and Kissinger had several reasons (including economics) for desiring a rapprochement with China, but, importantly, they felt it would allow the US to pull troops out of Southeast Asia and to focus attention and resources on the USSR. China (still relatively weak in Asia) could be used to limit actions by the USSR and North Vietnam. When Nixon flew to China to meet Mao in February 1972, the Soviet leaders were afraid that any major disagreements with the US might even result in a Sino–American military pact. The US came to see that improved relations with China would put extra pressure on the USSR to make concessions in areas of special importance to the US.

Détente and the Cold War

Nixon and Kissinger played down the role of ideology in foreign affairs, and were prepared to be more relaxed about military matters. They believed that nuclear sufficiency, not a clear superiority, should be the main aim. However, détente was really an attempt to create a more modern version of containment. The US still wanted to limit Soviet power, while the USSR saw détente as a way of consolidating its European position. Nonetheless, détente was a significant development, and achieved its greatest successes in the early 1970s. Essentially Nixon and Kissinger abandoned the policy of 'rolling back' communism, in favour of a policy of détente and 'linkage'. Linkage refers to the US policy during the 1970s in which the US tried to persuade the Soviet Union and China to co-operate in restraining Developing World revolutions, in return for concessions in nuclear and economic fields. However, while Soviet support was sometimes a factor, a wave of revolutions broke out that were independent of Soviet control, so undermining this strategy.

The US would accept the Soviet Union's closing of the nuclear gap, promise not to interfere in the Soviet sphere of influence, and offer Western technology and investment. The price, or linkage, demanded from the USSR was to include help in extracting the US from Vietnam, and acceptance that both superpowers had a mutual interest in maintaining stability in the Developing World. Nixon believed that direct US involvement in these regions could be replaced by the supply of weapons and training to US 'client' states. This idea – the **Nixon Doctrine** – had been developed as early as July 1969.

SOURCE B

The task at hand, as the Nixon administration saw it, was to get beyond Vietnam without suffering geopolitical losses, and to establish a policy towards the communists that was geared to the relevant battlefields. Nixon saw détente as a tactic in a long-run geopolitical struggle: his liberal critics treated it as an end in itself while the conservatives and neoconservatives rejected the geopolitical approach as so much historical pessimism, preferring a policy of unremitting ideological confrontation.

Kissinger, H. 1994. Diplomacy. New York, USA. Simon & Schuster. pp. 744–45.

Summits and arms limitation

Between 1972 and 1974, four important summit meetings were held between the two Cold War superpowers. Initially, the Soviet Union remained suspicious of US motives in offering arms control just at the point when the USSR was approaching near-parity overall with the US on nuclear weaponry. Some Soviet leaders saw this offer as an attempt to maintain and formalise the USA's superior system of global alliances. The most important agreements are outlined below.

SALT I

In 1969, talks on limiting strategic nuclear weapons (Strategic Arms Limitation Talks – SALT) began hesitantly on arms control, not reduction. New developments in weapons technology that might threaten this new stability (such as computerised guidance systems for ICBMs, MIRVs and ABMs, which undermined the old policy of MAD) would thus be curbed by these arms-control talks. The USSR was particularly alarmed by the USA's big lead in ABM systems, and did not wish to compete in this area because of the massive costs involved.

These talks finished in May 1972, when Brezhnev and Nixon signed SALT I. Though no overall agreement on offensive weapons was reached, progress was made in some areas. Most notably, there was to be a five-year freeze on all ICBMs, SLBMs and long-range bombers. Each side also agreed to having only two ABM sites, with no more than 100 missile launchers each.

SALT I also failed to include limitations on MIRVs. Although the US had developed these first, the Soviet Union soon developed and deployed its own system. However, there was also the Basic Principles Agreement, which committed both sides to work together to prevent conflict and build peaceful coexistence.

Despite its limitations, SALT I was a significant move away from the earlier Cold War hostilities, and marked the beginning of a continuing process of arms control. The USA's acceptance of the narrowing of the missile gap appeased the Soviet Union and did much to reduce tensions between the two nuclear superpowers.

The particular Soviet fear was the possibility of an anti-Soviet alliance between the USA and China. To help prevent this, an improved relationship with the USA was regarded as important.

These negotiations were followed in June 1973 by a visit by Brezhnev to the USA for a second summit meeting. In July 1974, Nixon travelled to Moscow for a third. The summit meetings resulted in agreement on the framework for SALT II talks. In the 1973 Agreement on the Prevention of Nuclear War, both sides promised to contact each other if any crisis seemed likely to threaten nuclear war.

Europe and détente

In Europe, the process of détente was both aided by, and contributed to, developments in West Germany, which prompted agreements on the old problems of Berlin and the division of Germany. As well as pressures from the countries of Western Europe to make Europe a more stable region, the USSR wanted stability, especially after the 1968 crisis in Czechoslovakia. Apart from concerns about Eastern Europe, another persistent worry was that, because of the development of the Cold War, no formal treaty accepting the new borders of Europe after the defeat of Nazi Germany had ever been signed. The Soviet Union was keen to have international recognition and acceptance of the borders of its East European satellites.

In October 1969, the SPD (in alliance with the FPD) won the West German election – the first left-of-centre victory since 1945. This SPD-FPD government, led by Willy Brandt, brought to an end the hardline anti-communist policies associated with the Christian Democrats who had ruled West Germany since its formation. Brandt instead pursued a policy known as *Ostpolitik* (Eastern Policy), intended to reduce the barriers between the FDR and the GDR and to promote contact and trade between Eastern and Western Europe in general.

In August 1970, the Soviet Union and West Germany signed the Moscow Treaty – formally ending the Second World War. The treaty also confirmed the division of Germany and the loss of pre-war East German territory to Poland and the Soviet Union. In 1972, this success was followed by the Final Quadripartite Protocol, which saw the USSR accept West German links with West Berlin, thus ending another long-standing dispute. In December of that year, West and East Germany signed the Basic Treaty, accepting the *de facto* existence of the two German states, although West Germany did not give full diplomatic recognition to the GDR.

So, by 1972, SALT I and *Ostpolitik* had done much to reduce tensions in Europe as far as nuclear weapons and Germany were concerned. However, the Soviet Union also wanted the West to accept the status quo in Eastern Europe. This was partly achieved by the Conference on Security and Co-operation in Europe (CSCE) at Helsinki in July 1973.

The Helsinki Conference and Accords, 1973–75

In 1971, the Warsaw Pact had proposed a conference on European security. Although this did not result in a formal peace treaty, there was a declaration of intent, known as the Final Act, which was eventually signed in 1975.

This contained three 'baskets', or agreements. The first guaranteed the status quo in Europe by recognising as 'inviolable' the current borders of Europe. This was a major breakthrough in relations between East and West Europe. The second co-operation 'basket' called for closer ties and collaboration across a range of activities, such as economic issues, and science and culture.

Fact

Brandt's abandonment of the Hallstein Doctrine, which said West Germany would not recognise any country that recognised the GDR, in fact encouraged the USSR, which had long wanted the West to accept the existence of the GDR and the Soviet bloc in Eastern Europe.

Question

What was *Ostpolitik*?

Kissinger, Brezhnev, Ford and Gromyko (left to right) outside the US embassy in Helsinki in 1973

However, the third and final 'basket' concerned the issue of human rights. This proved contentious and ultimately contributed to the abandonment of détente by the West, because the agreements on the European status quo and increased co-operation were linked to Soviet concessions on human rights in the Soviet bloc. In addition, after Brandt resigned in May 1974, his successor – Helmut Schmidt – restored closer links to the US. In particular, Schmidt accepted the modernisation of NATO's nuclear capacity, which worried the USSR.

Why did a Second Cold War begin in 1979?

The decline of détente

One problem with détente was that, despite the Soviet Union's desire for stability in Europe, it also wanted to extend its influence in the Developing World, which was very limited in comparison with that of the USA. In particular, the Soviet leadership was keen to acquire allies with naval bases. The USSR only had access to six operational bases – all in the Soviet Union. Although the Warsaw Pact outnumbered NATO in terms of the total number of ships and submarines, NATO's access to sea bases around the world meant it could keep twice as many submarines at sea than could the Warsaw Pact countries. For the same reason, the USSR was only able to operate six aircraft carriers, compared to NATO's 20.

157

Watergate This refers to the political scandal involving the Nixon administration, which finally led to Nixon's resignation as president in August 1974. It arose from an attempt to burgle and bug the Democratic Party's national headquarters (the Watergate building) in June 1972. Nixon and his advisers tried to cover up their involvement but, by June 1974, 17 members of his government had been found guilty of various crimes. When Nixon resigned, Ford became president. One of his first acts was to grant Nixon a pardon.

Fact
In fact, as early as May 1972 the USA was trying to weaken the Soviet Union's new position in the Middle East. Immediately after signing SALT I, it asked Iran to persuade Iraq to break its ties with the USSR.

Gerald Ford (1913–2006)
Ford trained as a lawyer and served in the US Navy during the Second World War. He entered the House of Representatives as a Republican in 1948. He became vice-president in 1973, and replaced Nixon as president when Nixon resigned because of the Watergate scandal. He was defeated by the Democrat Jimmy Carter in the 1976 presidential elections.

Also, as Nixon became damaged by the **Watergate** scandal, and Brezhnev's health deteriorated from 1974, those opposed to détente began to come to the fore. Under pressure from the Republicans and Reagan, Ford stopped using the word 'détente' and demoted Kissinger. By 1976, Cold War hostilities were beginning to build again.

The Soviet Union and the Middle East

The USSR had achieved some success in the Middle East. After the Six-Day War between Egypt and Israel in 1967, the Soviet Union replaced all the military equipment Egypt had lost. It also sent thousands of military advisers. In return, Egypt had granted the USSR naval rights in some ports and airbases. Thus, for the first time, the Soviet Union was able to counter US activities in the Mediterranean. During the early 1970s, the Soviet Union built on this, becoming an important ally of several Arab states. This attempt by the Soviet Union to extend its influence into what had long been seen as a Western sphere undermined East–West relations.

However, Anwar Sadat (who replaced Gamal Abdul Nasser as ruler of Egypt) was angered by the USSR's refusal – because of its wish to continue détente – to help recapture territory lost to Israel in 1967. In retaliation, Sadat expelled all Soviet military personnel from Egypt. This deprived the USSR of its most important naval and air bases in the Developing World. Despite sending military supplies to Egypt and Syria when the Yom Kippur War broke out in October 1973, and urging other Arab states to support Egypt and Syria, Soviet influence in the Middle East soon declined. More importantly, the US had been angered by the fact that despite the SALT I and SALT II agreements the USSR had not passed on information about the possibility of an imminent Arab attack on Israel and that, once begun, the Soviet Union had tried to involve other Arab states. As a result, the US deliberately excluded the Soviet Union from the subsequent Middle East peace negotiations.

Détente continued to crumble as the USA made clear its intention to maintain its global power base, while the USSR was equally determined not to accept its inferior position as regards Developing World allies. In addition, and independent of any Soviet actions, a wave of revolutions began to break out in several parts of the Developing World, especially in the Middle East, Africa and Central America. The USSR saw these revolutions as opportunities to improve its international position.

There were also problems with SALT I, which had halted the race in ICBMs and the more important SLBMs (in which the US had a huge lead as far as nuclear warheads were concerned). Several systems, however, were not covered by SALT I, including Trident, MX missiles, the B1 bomber and Cruise missiles. Although relatively short of money, Nixon decided these should be rapidly developed.

In the years 1973–74, Nixon's ability to pursue détente was restricted by the decisions of Congress. The growing Watergate scandal, and the secrecy with which Nixon and Kissinger conducted much of their foreign policy, led Congress to assert its independence and control. Congress insisted that any further agreements with the USSR should only be made if the Soviet Union offered concessions on human rights in Eastern Europe. **Gerald Ford**, who became president in August 1974 after the Watergate scandal, found that Congress placed the same restrictions on his foreign policy, and responded to these developments by refusing to use the word 'détente'. Brezhnev, meanwhile, was increasingly frustrated by the small amount of advanced technology being sold to the Soviet Union by the US.

Another important factor in shifting the US away from détente was its own growing economic problems. The cost of Vietnam, allied to increased competition from the expanding Japanese and West German economies, had produced the USA's first balance of trade deficit since 1900. The situation was made worse by the big increase in oil prices that followed the Arab–Israeli War of 1973. The decline in the US economy obviously had serious implications for the future maintenance of US military power.

Carter and the Democrats

At first, Jimmy Carter – who came to power in 1977 after defeating Ford in the elections – followed a rather inconsistent foreign policy. In part, this was because a wave of post-Vietnam anti-military feeling had contributed to the Democrats' victory. Initially, he avoided the use of anti-Soviet rhetoric, and announced that the US would no longer give automatic support to repressive regimes simply because they were anti-communist.

Carter had had little experience of foreign policy, and relied heavily on two advisers: Cyrus Vance, who was secretary of state, and Zbigniew Brzezinski, who acted as national security adviser. Although both these men considered the Soviet Union as the crucial factor in international relations, they had conflicting opinions on how to conduct negotiations. Vance believed a revival of détente was possible as soon as younger communist leaders were in a position to replace Brezhnev. In particular, he saw SALT II as a way of allowing the US to solve its own economic problems by cutting the defence budget. He was prepared to accept that the Soviet Union should have some influence, along with the US, in the Middle East, and he believed that Africa was not important in superpower relations. Finally, he did not support Nixon's policy towards China, fearing that it might increase Cold War tensions.

Brzezinski, however, had a very different attitude to the Soviet Union. He did not trust its leaders and believed that only superior US strength would force the USSR to make acceptable agreements. He thus advised Carter that the US should begin a drive for overwhelming strategic nuclear superiority, strengthen NATO, undermine Soviet control of Eastern Europe (Brzezinski was Polish), ally more closely with China, and oppose any Soviet initiatives in the Developing World. For Brzezinski, therefore, SALT II had relatively little importance. As a result of this, Carter often received contradictory advice from his two principal advisers.

Soon, developments in the Developing World (especially in the Horn of Africa) led Carter and Brzezinski to conclude that the USSR was attempting to improve its geopolitical position along what was referred to as the 'Arc of Crisis', by taking advantage of the USA's economic problems and its post-Vietnam reluctance to risk involvement in another Developing World regional conflict.

At the same time, Carter alarmed the USSR by giving clear support to the campaign for human rights in the Soviet bloc, and by making far-reaching calls for arms control, which seemed designed to perpetuate the USSR's overall inferiority.

Meanwhile, events in the Developing World resulted in several changes, which took place without Soviet involvement. In April 1978, communists took power in Afghanistan. In January 1979, the shah of Iran (an important regional ally for the US) was toppled by an Islamic fundamentalist revolt. This event increased US concerns about developments in this oil-rich area. In addition, in Central America and the Caribbean, left-wing and pro-Soviet governments took power in Nicaragua and Grenada (see pages 169–70).

James 'Jimmy' Carter (b. 1924) Carter served in the US Navy until 1953, when he began to run his family's peanut farms. He was a Democratic senator and then governor of Georgia, before becoming US president in 1977. He was convincingly defeated by the Republican candidate, Reagan, in the 1980 elections.

159

Fact
Brzezinski believed that a new arms race would ruin the Soviet economy – CIA experts reported that it was extremely weak – and so cause serious problems for the Soviet Union and its control of Eastern Europe. He even believed that a limited nuclear war was winnable.

Arc of Crisis This refers to the region running from Afghanistan, through Iran and the Middle East, to the Horn of Africa (north-east Africa, i.e. Ethiopia and Somalia).

SS-20 These missiles, a retaliatory weapon, replaced the SS-4 and SS-5 missiles. They were inferior to the USA's Pershing I missile, which had been deployed by the US since 1960. US satellites soon discovered all 39 of the SS-20 sites.

The US and SALT II

As early as 1977, Carter had begun to modernise and extend US nuclear superiority. He had cancelled the B1 bomber, but then used the money to develop the new Stealth bomber and Cruise missiles. In fact, US defence expenditure actually increased under Carter. When the West German leader, Helmut Schmidt, told Carter he wanted European theatre (intermediate-range) nuclear weapons included in SALT II, Carter and Brzezinski refused. In March 1977, Vance informed the USSR about this and later that year the USSR began to deploy their **SS-20s** in Eastern Europe.

These developments in the Developing World and Europe caused the Republicans to begin criticising Carter for not resisting what they saw as a new Soviet offensive. This growing pressure soon resulted in a revival of Cold War hostilities. Carter responded by shifting to a more hardline approach. He even began to talk of the possibility of undermining communist rule or Soviet influence in

Test launch of a 'Tomahawk' Cruise missile in the Utah desert, 1985

Despite Soviet concerns at the USA's recognition of Communist China in December 1978, both sides still wanted to slow down the arms race – but each wanted to do so on their own terms.

China, Vietnam, Somalia, Iraq, Algeria and Cuba. Partly in response to pressure from Western European governments, in January 1979 the US decided to deploy Pershing II ballistic missiles in Europe, and ground-launched Cruise missiles in several European countries, including Britain – though the USSR was informed that no action on this would be taken if the SS-20s were removed.

SALT II

The SALT II negotiations, which had begun in 1974, also contributed to the ending of détente. Despite Soviet concern at the USA's recognition of Communist China in December 1978, both sides still wanted to slow down the arms race – but each wanted to do so on their own terms. There was thus a strong desire by both sides to reach agreement, and in fact a draft had been agreed by Ford and Brezhnev at the Vladivostok Summit as early as November 1974. In Vienna in June 1979, they agreed to set a limit of 2400 for missile launchers (both ICBMs and SLBMs) and heavy bombers for each side. A limit on the number of MIRV launchers was also agreed.

However, some in the US began to claim that the USSR had actually achieved ICBM superiority over the US. According to the independent Stockholm International Peace Research Institute (SIPRI), the USSR did have a lead over the US in terms of delivery systems (2501 to 2124) and megatonnage (3:2), but the US had always had a clear superiority as regards technology.

Finally, although SALT II was signed in 1979, the US delayed its ratification when a Soviet combat brigade was 'discovered' in Cuba. In fact, the US had agreed to the presence of a small Soviet force at the end of the Cuban Missile Crisis, but the New Right in the US now pressed Carter to force the USSR to withdraw it. When Brezhnev refused, relations continued to deteriorate. The period of arms control, and thus of détente, was nearing its end. What finally brought it to a close was the Soviet intervention in Afghanistan (see pages 177–78).

> **Fact**
> The initial decision to deploy Pershing II and Cruise missiles had first been taken in 1975, before the USSR had deployed the SS-20s. Although they led to an increase in US expenditure, the significance of these weapons lay in their greatly improved accuracy. Unlike the Soviet SS-20s, these were counter-force (first strike) weapons.

> **Fact**
> The accuracy of US weapons was much superior: the SS-18 was only equivalent to the USA's old Minuteman, while the MX was twice as accurate as the SS 18. Also, 79% of the USSR's ICBMs were on land, compared to 25% for the US; while 54% of the USA's were on submarines, compared to 21% for the USSR.

161

SOURCE C

1980 military expenditures: the strategic balance

(Figures in US$million at 1978 prices)

USA	111,236
Other NATO	82,674
Japan	9,200
China	40,000
Total (US/NATO/anti-Soviet)	**243,110**
USSR	107,300
Other WTO	12,250
Total (USSR and allies)	**119,550**

SIPRI Yearbooks. 1979 (p. 422) and 1981 (p. 156). London, UK. Taylor & Francis.

> **New Right** A conservative, aggressive and right-wing grouping which, according to some historians, began to emerge in the US from the mid 1970s, especially in the south-west. As well as having very conservative views on domestic issues, the New Right favoured a return to a more hardline anti-Soviet foreign policy. Ronald Reagan was particularly associated with this development. More recently, under George Bush Jr, the term usually used is Neo-Cons (new conservatives).

Changes in the US and the Developing World

According to Fred Halliday, the Second Cold War can be explained not so much by Soviet actions as by developments in the USA and in the Developing World. In the US, the south and west became increasingly important economically and demographically during the 1970s, with most of the USA's aerospace and military industry located there. This part of the country had traditionally been the home of more extreme conservative politics, favouring high military spending and a virulent anti-communist foreign policy. In particular, in contrast to the more liberal and Eurocentric east, the south-west believed in military intervention in the Developing World. This region also provided the base for the emergence of the **New Right**, itself a reaction to US economic decline (in 1980, there was no increase in GNP, inflation was at 10% and unemployment at 7.5%).

The New Right (a coalition of Republicans and neo-conservative Democrats) claimed the US was now militarily inferior to the USSR, and took its inspiration from the influential figures of the First Cold War such as Joseph McCarthy. By 1980, this New Right dominated Congress and was allied to the Pentagon and arms manufacturers. In particular the New Right claimed that, since Vietnam, US military strength had declined. However, as early as 1968, the US military had begun to plan Cruise, MX and Trident missiles, as well as the B1 bomber.

With about seven million people directly employed in the armaments industry (and about 10% of the population indirectly employed), a big increase in military spending was seen as a way of at least temporarily halting the economic downturn. It is important to note, however, that Halliday's explanation remains a minority one.

How did the Second Cold War differ from the First Cold War?

The Second Cold War

Carter's reaction to the Soviet intervention in Afghanistan turned out to be the first step in what some historians have called the Second Cold War. In January 1980, Carter demonstrated US anger at the USSR's actions in Afghanistan by blocking various exports to the USSR, including much-needed grain deliveries. He also confirmed the USA's non-ratification of SALT II and called for a boycott of the 1980 Olympics, due to be held in Moscow.

The Carter Doctrine then proclaimed the Persian Gulf to be a vital strategic area for US interests. The USSR was further worried by the US agreeing, for the first time ever, to supply China with military equipment. Fear of such a development had been one of the main reasons that the Soviet Union had earlier signed SALT II.

In July 1980, Carter signed a presidential decree that considered the possibility of a limited war focused on specific military targets. The USSR was vulnerable, as 79% of its ICBMs were land-based, and so easier to detect and hit, while the corresponding figure for the US was only 25%. A Rapid Deployment Force was also set up for intervention in the Developing World, while Carter went back on election promises to withdraw troops from South Korea.

Reagan and the Second Cold War

Despite Carter's increasingly tough stance, **Ronald Reagan** was elected president in November 1980. The Soviet invasion of Afghanistan had played a large part in the growth of the New Right generally, as well as in Reagan's electoral victory. Reagan's Republican administration took office in January 1981, and Reagan had committed himself to 're-establishing' US world power by increasing US nuclear superiority, which would allow greater US intervention in the Developing World. This was linked to expanding the US economy in general, and the Military-Industrial Complex (see page 22) in particular.

SOURCE D

So far, détente's been a one-way street which the Soviet Union has used to pursue its own aims.

Extract from comments made by Ronald Reagan in a news conference, 29 January 1981.

Despite the weakness of the US economy in 1981, Reagan increased US military expenditure by 13% in 1982, and by more than 8% in each subsequent year. He justified this expenditure by claiming there was a 'window of vulnerability'. He asserted that the USSR had greatly increased its expenditure on armaments during the 1970s, and was now outspending the USA. At the same time, the CIA's budget was increased even more, and Reagan's administration began to talk of 'surgical' nuclear strikes. In Europe, he even considered the use of the neutron bomb and chemical weapons.

SOURCE E

US and Soviet nuclear arsenals, 1970–80

	1970	1980
ICBMs		
USA	1054	1052
USSR	1487	1398
SLBMs		
USA	656	576
USSR	248	950
Long-range bombers		
USA	512	348
USSR	156	156
Total warheads		
USA	4000	9200
USSR	1800	6000

SIPRI Yearbooks 1979 (p. 422) and 1981 (p. 273). London, UK. Taylor & Francis.

Ronald Reagan (1911–2004)

An actor and a convinced anti-communist, Reagan played a leading role during the McCarthy period. From 1967 to 1974, he was Republican governor of California and was closely associated with the New Right. He became US president in 1981, and is particularly associated with the start of the Second Cold War. Later he played an important role in the end of the Cold War.

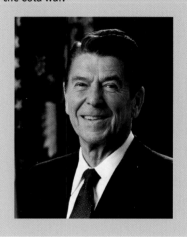

163

Fact

According to the independent Stockholm International Peace Research Institute (SIPRI), the Soviet Union had never outspent the US, and had not made any sudden increase in the 1970s. Soviet military expenditure in the 1970s had increased by 2% per annum, which was less than the annual increase in GNP. Because the USSR's GNP was about half that of the US, it needed to spend double the proportion of its GNP just to match US developments. Overall, in 1980, NATO and other anti-USSR states spent a combined total of $305 billion on defence, compared to a Warsaw Pact expenditure of $201 billion.

Détente was dismissed as a failure, and Moscow was blamed for breaking those agreements that had been reached, especially in relation to its perceived – and actual – increased penetration of Developing World areas, typified by its role in Afghanistan. More importantly, Reagan immediately implemented an extremely vigorous anti-Soviet policy, in tune with his long-held anti-communist views. As a result, US–Soviet relations deteriorated to a low level, especially when Reagan claimed that, despite SALT I and II, the USSR had actually gained nuclear superiority over the US, and that he therefore intended to restore the 'margin of safety'.

In fact, Reagan sent out mixed messages. In 1982, he appointed George Shultz as secretary of state. Shultz was soon calling for new arms controls. In 1983, Reagan referred to the USSR as the 'evil empire' yet, within a year of this, he was offering 'constructive negotiations' – but only when the US had achieved a new superiority. This approach worried Yuri Andropov, the new Soviet leader. He feared that the US policy would risk a real crisis between the two superpowers, especially when Reagan announced a five-year programme of $180 billion to modernise US strategic nuclear forces.

In 1982, at the Intermediate Nuclear Forces (INF) talks, Reagan put forward a new policy known as the 'Zero Option', but the Soviet Union rejected this. In fact, according to SIPRI, this Zero Option (freeze) would have retained a clear US/NATO superiority, as NATO had 1000 medium-range nuclear bombers and 17,000 nuclear warheads, while the Warsaw Pact had, respectively, 550 and 6000. The US also had a large lead in the more important SLBMs. In June 1982, following a vote by Congress, discussions to reduce strategic nuclear weapons – Strategic Arms Reduction Talks (START) – also began in Geneva. Then, in March 1983, Reagan announced the Strategic Defense Initiative – SDI or 'Star Wars' – project. This would have made all offensive nuclear weapons redundant. The USSR feared it would soon have no nuclear deterrent. He saw the improved balance of forces as being wiped out, and believed the US would no longer be interested in arms reduction talks.

In November 1983, NATO began deploying Pershing II and Cruise missiles. As a result, the USSR broke off all further talks. A the same time, the START negotiations were also called off. Overall, 1983 was the worst year in Cold War relations between the two sides since the Cuban Missile Crisis of 1962 (see pages 138–41). In fact, the US deliberately stalled these and subsequent talks, in the hope that the USSR would eventually pull out.

Poland

The Second Cold War, and the situation in Europe, had become more tense after December 1981, when the Polish government imposed martial law in an attempt to stop the growth of the independent Solidarity trade union movement. As with Afghanistan, the Soviet leadership appears to have made decisions without fully considering the likely impact on détente and East–West relations. Though direct military intervention in Poland was finally ruled out, Moscow did put pressure on the Polish leadership for a tough response. In part, this was

Fact
Some Western European states were also alarmed by the Star Wars project, while others were unhappy about the implications of Reagan's belief that all unrest in the world was the work of the USSR. This led the US to increase its support of 'reliable' dictatorial regimes, and to support various terrorist groups, especially in Central America (see page 169).

Question
What was the Star Wars project?

because Moscow feared that if Poland was able to develop a more democratic system, other Eastern European states might try to follow suit. There was also the danger that the people of the Soviet Union itself might try to dismantle the mechanisms which guaranteed the power of the leadership of the CPSU.

The rigid Soviet stance stemmed from its view of Poland as an important part of the Warsaw Pact and hence of Soviet defences. The USSR still felt militarily vulnerable in Europe: although the Soviet Union had an army of 3.7 million as opposed to the USA's two million, the bulk of the Red Army (44 divisions) was deployed on the Soviet Union's borders with China, with only 31 divisions in Eastern Europe. Furthermore, some 60% of Soviet divisions were said by the CIA to be less than half the required size, while 80% were believed not to be combat-ready. In all, the combined NATO armed forces totalled 4.9 million, while the combined figure for the Warsaw Pact was 4.7 million. More importantly, Soviet conventional forces were generally inferior to those of the US and NATO.

Polish soldiers in Gdansk, Poland, in 1981, after martial law was declared

Fact
Though the Warsaw Pact had 45,000 tanks to NATO's 17,000, the Soviet T.62 could only fire six rounds per minute, compared to 30 rpm for the US M. 60. NATO also possessed over 250,000 sophisticated anti-tank missiles.

The Soviet Union continued to be vulnerable to an air attack. Despite the Warsaw Pact's big lead in numbers of fighter-interceptors, NATO had a greater advantage in both numbers and quality of ground-attack planes, with the F.14s, F.15s and F.16s being far superior in range to the MiG 25, which was the USSR's top plane.

The US responded to the USSR's attitude towards Poland by imposing economic and trade sanctions on both countries. The US hoped states in Western Europe would do the same. Yet this conflicted with the interests of several of these states, which still wanted détente – and trade – with the Soviet Union. In particular, Western Europe was keen to maintain the natural gas pipeline which would carry gas from the USSR.

SOURCE F

The imposition of martial law [in Poland] resulted in CIA and American covert action being targeted against Soviet domination in Eastern Europe in a significant way for the first time since the early years of the cold war. ... Most of what flowed out of the CIA and through the intermediaries to Solidarity was printing materials, communications equipment, and other supplies for waging underground political warfare. ...

By the end of 1982, the Reagan administration's covert offensive against the Soviet Union was beginning to take shape. In Central America, Afghanistan, Chad, and elsewhere, often building on programs started by Carter, they confronted Soviet clients with resistance forces now funded and often armed by the United States. ... SDI was a Soviet nightmare come to life. America's industrial base, coupled with American technology, wealth, and managerial skills ... would require an expensive Soviet response at a time [for them] of deep economic crisis.

Gates, R. M. 1996. From the Shadows: The Ultimate Insider's Story of Five Presidents and How they Won the Cold War, New York, USA. Simon & Schuster. pp. 236–64.

The USSR and Gorbachev

Meanwhile, in the years 1982–85, the Soviet Union was going through a tense political transition. Andropov, who had succeeded Brezhnev in November 1982, died in February 1984. His replacement, Chernenko, died in March the following year. These rapid changes in leadership had coincided with increasingly serious economic problems, caused by the USSR's attempt to keep up with US military might. By the late 1980s, the Soviet economy was more like that of a developing country than an advanced industrial nation. In particular, the technological gap between the Soviet Union and the West widened – especially in micro-electronics and computers. Such problems greatly added to the inefficiencies resulting from too much bureaucratic and central control.

The new Soviet leader, elected by the Central Committee of the CPSU on 11 March 1985, was Mikhail Gorbachev, who had already concluded that the USSR could no longer afford to follow each nuclear escalation made by the USA.

SOURCE G

Détente did not prevent resistance to Soviet expansion: on the contrary, it fostered the only psychologically possible framework for such resistance. Nixon knew where to draw the line against Soviet adventure whether it occurred directly or through proxy. ... The United States and the Soviet Union are ideological rivals. Détente cannot change that. The nuclear age compels us to coexist. Rhetorical crusades cannot change that either.

Kissinger, H. 1979. The White House Years. London, UK. Little, Brown. pp. 237–38.

Unit summary

You should now have a good understanding of the main features of, and the main reasons for, the development of détente between the US and the USSR, and of the main agreements that resulted from it. You should also have an appreciation of its limits, and the reasons why it eventually came to an end during the late 1970s. In particular, you should have an understanding of how events in Poland and the Middle East, and developments in the US itself, contributed to the end of détente and the start of the Second Cold War. Finally, you should have an understanding of the main features and developments of this Second Cold War.

End of unit activities

1 Produce a chart to summarise the reasons why both the US and the USSR wanted détente.

2 Draw up a list of the main summits and agreements during the period 1969–79.

Historical debate

Détente remains one of the most keenly debated historical issues – the motives for it, the reasons for its end, and the relative success/failure of the policy. Some, such as Bowker and Williams (*Superpower Détente: a Reappraisal*, 1988), argue that it was a necessary and reasonably successful attempt to reduce superpower tensions. Others, such as Gaddis, stress the limited aims of détente. Critics, however, see it as either a failure – in that a Second Cold War broke out in 1985 – or as a policy of weakness and retreat for the US.

2 Developments in Africa and the Americas

Timeline

For the period 1969–79, the two regions of the Americas and Africa are treated together, as several of the key developments that took place are closely linked. This is mainly because Cuba – which had long been a focus of concern for the US – increasingly gave technical and military aid to left-wing independence movements, especially to Angola, a former Portuguese colony in Africa, and to Ethiopia. This often brought their forces into direct conflict with troops, funded and supported by the US, sent by apartheid South Africa to intervene on the side of pro-Western forces in Angola.

Key questions

- How did the Cold War develop in Africa in the 1970s?
- How did developments in Latin America and the Caribbean affect the Cold War?

Overview

- The Cold War continued to affect other world regions, including the Americas and Africa.
- In addition to aiding anti-communist regimes in Latin America, such as that of Bolivia, which had captured and shot Che Guevara in 1967, the US also played a role in the coup in Chile in 1973.
- In Africa, during the 1970s, Cuba sent troops to help sympathetic governments and movements involved in wars and civil wars against US-backed groups.
- With the growing problems of the Soviet Union, Soviet aid declined and, under Gorbachev, stopped completely. By then, Cuban troops had already returned home.

How did the Cold War develop in Africa in the 1970s?

In the mid 1970s, despite the crippling economic blockade maintained by the US, Fidel Castro grew increasingly prepared to assist Developing World liberation struggles taking place outside the Americas. This was especially true of the former Portuguese colonies in Africa: Mozambique, Guinea-Bissau and, particularly, Angola. All these countries had been granted independence in 1975, following the Portuguese Revolution of 1974. In Angola, a bitter civil war broke out in 1975 between the Popular Movement for the Liberation of Angola (MPLA, backed by the Soviet Union), the FNLA (backed by the US and China) and UNITA (backed by China, South Africa and Israel and, later, the US).

Until the late 1960s, the Soviet Union had had little influence in Africa, although Khrushchev had publicly announced his intention to support 'wars of national liberation' in Africa and elsewhere. But the collapse of the Portuguese empire after the 1974 revolution in Portugal destabilised the area.

The MPLA was initially victorious, and was widely recognised as the legitimate government of Angola. However, these events worried the US to such an extent that Gerald Ford, the US president, dropped the word 'détente' from his vocabulary. Then the MPLA government signed a treaty of co-operation and friendship with the USSR, as did Mozambique the following year.

The US was further alarmed by events unfolding in Ethiopia. In September 1974, Haile Selassie – emperor of Ethiopia since 1930 – was overthrown by a combined revolutionary popular movement and a coup headed by sections of the army. This event had followed an economic crisis, famine and a mutiny in the country. The Derg, a committee of low-ranking officers and ordinary soldiers, rapidly established a dictatorship under Mengistu Haile Mariam, and declared its adherence to 'Marxism'. Despite misgivings about violent aspects of Mengistu's rule, the Soviet Union gave its support to the new government.

US concerns increased when, in 1977, the Soviet Union gave aid to the new Ethiopian government in its struggle to expel Somalia (a former Soviet ally) from the Ogaden region – despite the fact that the US had previously supported Haile Selassie over this issue. In 1978, the Soviet Union also gave its support in the military campaign to suppress the independence movement in the province of Eritrea. Once again, Castro provided about 17,000 Cuban combat troops. All these diplomatic successes enabled the Soviet Union to overcome at last its great inferiority with regard to friendly naval bases outside its own territory. However, according to the Soviet ambassador to the US, Anatoly Dobrynin, these forms of 'ideological bondage' to rebels or governments that called themselves Marxist did not benefit the USSR in the long run.

One result of Cuba's involvement in these areas, however, was that the US became even more determined to find ways to undermine Castro's position. This continued under Jimmy Carter who, in 1980, agreed to the establishment of the Rapid Deployment Force for Developing World interventions.

How did developments in Latin America and the Caribbean affect the Cold War?

In 1973, the US assisted in a military coup in Chile against the democratically elected Marxist president Salvadore Allende and his government, whose social and economic reforms were seen as threatening vital US interests. While the coup and the ensuing repression carried out by the new dictator, General Pinochet, was seen as a success, setbacks were to follow in the second half of the 1970s.

In March 1979, revolution broke out much nearer to the US, in Central America, when the left-wing revolutionary New Jewel Movement took power in the Caribbean island of Grenada. In July, a successful revolution in Nicaragua led to the victory of the **Sandinistas**, a coalition group that contained many Marxists. More importantly, it led to the defeat and expulsion of Somoza, a corrupt and brutal dictator, allied to and normally supported by the USA. In fact, the US had supported the Somoza family in its control of Nicaragua since 1936. Before then, from 1909 to 1933, Nicaragua had been a US protectorate, with US marines

> **Fact**
> During the 1960s, the USSR had been loosely linked to Ghana and Mali. However, in 1966 and 1968 respectively, the rulers of Ghana (Nkrumah) and Mali (Keita) had fallen from power. For most of this time, the USA, the USSR and, increasingly, China, had competed against each other for influence in the region.

> **Sandinistas** The name given to those opposed to Somoza's dictatorship in Nicaragua who, in 1961, set up the Sandinista Front for National Liberation (FSLN). Sandino had led a liberal nationalist uprising in the early 1930s against the Nicaraguan government and the US marines stationed there almost continuously since 1912. The FSLN (a coalition of liberals, radicals, priests and Marxists) took power in 1979. Their government had two broad aims – an 'independent and non-aligned' foreign policy, and the creation of a 'mixed' economy in order to achieve social and economic justice.

Contras Those opposed to the new Sandinista government of Nicaragua, including former members of Somoza's hated National Guard. Claiming that the Sandinistas were using their power to supply weapons to the left-wing guerrillas in El Salvador, Reagan decided to give money and CIA assistance to the Contras. After Congress voted to end any military support when news spread of mounting Contra acts of terrorism against civilians, Reagan attempted to continue his support by using money received from other, non-official, sources – including from arms deals with Iran (also banned by Congress).

permanently stationed there. Also in 1979, the US announced the 'discovery' of a Soviet combat brigade in Cuba – in fact, Soviet troops had been in Cuba for many years, following the failure of a US-sponsored invasion in 1961.

Such developments led Carter and later Reagan to give increased support to the military dictatorship in El Salvador and to the **Contra** terrorist group in Nicaragua. When Congress vetoed support for the Contras, Reagan used illegal methods of funding which, once discovered, led to the Contragate scandal. These attempts to put pressure on states in the Developing World opposed to the US were part of the new Reagan Doctrine. In October 1983, Reagan sent a US invasion force to overthrow the left-wing rulers of Grenada. Despite Castro's fears about the USA's immediate intentions towards Cuba, the Soviet Union did nothing in response to this US invasion.

In all, the years 1974–80 witnessed a whole series of revolutionary upheavals in the Developing World, resulting in 14 changes of regime. It is developments such as these, especially those in Central America and Africa, to which some historians attribute in part the end of détente and the start of the Second Cold War, as the US grew increasingly uneasy at the loss of former allies and the Soviet Union's subsequent increased presence in the Developing World.

US troops guard prisoners during the invasion of Grenada, October 1983

Détente after 1974

Events in Europe also took a worrying turn for the US in the period 1974–77. In 1974, the Portuguese revolution (which overthrew the right-wing dictatorship there) and the fall of the Greek military dictatorship coincided with the growing popularity of 'Eurocommunist' parties in France and, especially, in Italy. In November 1975, Francisco Franco – the semi-fascist pro-Western dictator of Spain – died and Spain also became a democracy.

The series of setbacks and loss of allies in the Developing World, combined with such developments in Europe, seemed to undermine the strength of the USA's global position. Thus, as early as 1976 – after the final victory of North Vietnam in May 1975, and growing Soviet and Cuban involvement in Africa – even Kissinger was saying he would no longer talk of 'détente'.

Unit summary

You should now have a clear understanding of developments in parts of Africa during the 1970s, and of Soviet actions in these areas, as well as of how this impacted US foreign policy. In particular, you should be able to show the significance of events in Angola and Ethiopia. You should also be able to demonstrate how events in the Americas during this same period led to a more aggressive response from the US – especially in El Salvador, Nicaragua and Grenada. Finally, you should be in a position to comment on how much these developments were the result of Soviet intervention.

End of unit activities

1 Make notes on Soviet involvement and actions in Africa during this period, and of US interventions in the Americas.

2 Find out more about the different historical views about the success or failure of détente. Then produce a chart to summarise your findings. Try to mention particular historians where relevant.

3 Developments in Asia

Timeline

Three significant developments took place in Asia in this period. The first was the conclusion of what some historians have seen as the USA's longest war – the Vietnam War, which finally ended in 1975. The second was the US–China diplomatic agreements that helped turn the Cold War from a bi-polar into a multi-polar conflict, and caused particular problems for the USSR, which had a long border with China. The third was the Soviet intervention in Afghanistan in December 1979, which was arguably a turning point in the ending of détente and the development of a new – and final – Cold War.

Key questions

- Why did the US decide to withdraw from Vietnam?
- How important was the US–Sino rapprochement during the 1970s in shaping developments in the Cold War?
- What effect did the Vietnam War have on US foreign policy in the Cold War after 1975?
- Was the Soviet intervention in Afghanistan the main reason for the start of the Second Cold War?

Overview

- After the Viet Cong's and the Viet Minh's Tet Offensive in January 1968, the first peace talks took place between the US and North Vietnam. Nixon, who became president in 1969, promised to end the war, and soon began the process known as 'Vietnamisation'.
- In 1973, partly through combined pressure from the Soviet Union and China, the North agreed to a ceasefire, and US troops began to withdraw from South Vietnam.
- In 1975, the North launched an invasion of the South and the war ended with the defeat of the South in April 1975.
- In 1979, the USSR sent troops into Afghanistan, marking the end of détente and the start of the Second Cold War.

Why did the US decide to withdraw from Vietnam?

Nixon's search for peace

The November 1969 US presidential election was won by Richard Nixon, the Republican candidate. He was determined to end the war, but wanted a peace that would not humiliate the US by forcing it to totally abandon the South. At the Paris Peace Talks, Nixon suggested that North Vietnamese troops should withdraw from the South at the same time as US troops were pulled out. If the North did not agree, he threatened to launch a massive new bombing campaign. The North refused, and Nixon stepped up the bombing of the North, and of Viet Cong strongholds in the South.

Nixon also tried to persuade the Soviet Union and China to put pressure on North Vietnam to agree to a compromise. In return, Nixon promised US economic help for the USSR. Though the Soviet Union made some attempts – for instance, it refused to supply the North with its most effective surface-to-air missiles – the North was reluctant to compromise. More practically, Nixon decided on a policy of 'Vietnamisation' of the war. This involved putting more and more of the burden of fighting the war onto the South Vietnamese army by withdrawing US troops. US financial aid, however, would continue. In April 1969, the number of US troops in South Vietnam was 543,000; by 1971, Nixon had reduced this to 157,000.

By this time, however, the US had been shocked by the exposure of a US war atrocity. In May 1968, a unit of American troops, led by Lieutenant William Calley on a search and destroy mission, massacred about 400 civilians (mostly children and old men and women) in the small village of My Lai. The revelations increased anti-war sentiments and protests, especially as it emerged that the My Lai massacre was not an isolated incident.

Victims of the My Lai massacre in South Vietnam

Vietnamisation The US policy to get the ground fighting in the Vietnam War done by the South Vietnamese army, so that US troops could be withdrawn. The first US troops were removed in 1969. By 1970, the US had mostly ceased its direct involvement in the ground fighting, although it continued to give air support.

Fact
Calley was eventually sentenced to 20 years imprisonment for the murder of 109 civilians. In fact, he only served five years.

Question

What happened at My Lai?

173

Ho Chi Minh Trail A network of jungle routes that runs from North to South Vietnam, through Laos and Cambodia. It was used as a supply route for goods and equipment by the Viet Cong, and later supplied North Vietnamese troops in the South.

Part of the process of 'Vietnamisation' of the war involved increased bombing of the **Ho Chi Minh Trail** in order to prevent fresh supplies of troops and equipment reaching the communists in South Vietnam. In practice, this had little effect on the Viet Cong's ability to wage their guerrilla war, and only resulted in spreading the conflict to the neighbouring countries of Laos and Cambodia, through which the supply trails ran. Between 1969 and 1973 alone, the US dropped over 500,000 tonnes of explosives on Cambodia, and its effect only increased the support for, and determination of, the Cambodian communists, the Khmer Rouge. In Laos, too, the Pathet Lao (see page 126) received increased support.

How important was the US–Sino rapprochement during the 1970s in shaping developments in the Cold War?

Rapprochement with China

As part of his strategy to get the Soviet Union to put pressure on North Vietnam to accept a compromise peace, Nixon tried to develop better relations with China. A former ruler of Vietnam, China was unhappy about Ho Chi Minh's close links with the USSR (though China did give limited support to North Vietnam). Kissinger felt that an agreement with China would enable US troops to leave Vietnam, and Southeast Asia in general. China could also be used as a check on the USSR, and on Vietnam – as Vietnam had little global influence, this policy was not seen as risky for US interests. All this would allow the USA to concentrate its efforts on dealing with the Soviet Union.

SOURCE A

The Soviet leadership simply could not allow the United States and China to develop a relationship independent of and hostile to the Soviet Union. Since reconciliation with Mao was out of the question, the Soviets found themselves compelled to reach out to Washington for a new kind of relationship. ... The second motive ... was the sorry state of the Soviet economy.

Gates, R. M. 1996. *From the Shadows: The Ultimate Insider's Story of Five Presidents and How they Won the Cold War*, New York, USA. *Simon & Schuster. pp. 29–36.*

In 1971, Nixon announced his intention to visit Communist China, which, since its creation in October 1949, the US had refused to recognise. At long last, the US allowed China to join the United Nations. The visit, which took place in February 1972, was a success. Nixon agreed to withdraw US troops from Taiwan and promised to promote the idea of Chinese unification if China would help the US get out of Vietnam without 'losing face', and refrain from any military actions in the Taiwan Straits. However, this improvement in Sino–American relations was slowed by Nixon's growing political embarrassment during the Watergate scandal of 1973–74 (see page 158). It was also hindered by the right wing in the US, whose opposition forced Nixon to delay US recognition of China (it did not take place finally till December 1978), and to keep the defence treaty with Taiwan.

By worrying the USSR at the 'loss' of a communist ally, the US helped create the framework for a settlement over Vietnam in particular, and the process of détente in general. Kissinger favoured the idea of 'linkage' (see page 154) – if the Soviet Union would help the USA out of its mess in Vietnam and agree to 'stabilise' other Developing World tensions, the US would accept its Eastern European sphere of influence and offer it financial and technical assistance.

Ceasefire and withdrawal

Meanwhile, the Vietnam peace talks in Paris dragged on inconclusively. In the summer of 1972, the communists launched another all-out offensive: this time, on the urban centres in the South. This proved to be more successful than the Tet Offensive of 1968 – even though the main population centres were not taken. This offensive resulted in the peace negotiations becoming more serious, with the main negotiators being Kissinger for the US, and Le Duc Tho for North Vietnam.

> **By worrying the USSR at the 'loss' of a communist ally, the US helped create the framework for a settlement over Vietnam in particular, and the process of détente in general.**

People desperately scramble on to the last US helicopters to leave Saigon in 1975; a US Embassy official punches a Vietnamese man trying to get aboard

Fact

Although the new communist government of a reunited Vietnam backed Moscow, signing a Friendship Treaty in 1978, and later joined Comecon, the new Vietnamese regime was critical of détente and at times took an independent line. Also, the USSR was concerned that Vietnam's involvement in Cambodia gave the US and China excuses to step up their interference in the region.

Historical debate

A much-debated issue remains whether the USA's forced withdrawal from Vietnam indicated a complete defeat of its policies and strategy for the region. Some historians argue against this, believing that more significant areas – Malaysia and the 'Asian Tiger' economies – were safeguarded. Through a combination of repressive regimes and booming economies, these states were able to resist the spread of communism. Such outcomes could be seen as in line with the earlier US policies of containment and the Defensive Perimeter.

In January 1973, a ceasefire was agreed. Later that year, Congress refused to give Nixon permission to send US troops to Cambodia to prevent North Vietnamese incursions. It then passed an act to prevent a president from deploying US troops before any declaration of war, ordered an end to the bombing of Cambodia, and ruled that US troops should not be sent to Vietnam again. Once the ceasefire had been signed, the US began to withdraw its remaining troops.

However, the war soon flared up again between communist and South Vietnamese forces. In March 1975, the North launched another major attack. This time, without US air support or troops, the South was unable to withstand the attack. Those critical of détente used this as evidence of the USSR's growing global influence.

The Viet Cong and the Northern army pushed southwards. On 29 April 1975 the communists marched into Saigon, and the war was over. After almost 30 years of warfare, the communists at last controlled the whole of Vietnam. By then, over two million Vietnamese had been killed.

Less than two weeks before, the Khmer Rouge had taken power in Cambodia and, on 9 May, the Pathet Lao finally took over in Laos. Later, in 1978, communist Vietnam sent its army into Cambodia to remove the Pol Pot regime, which had carried out mass killings; it also intervened in Laos. This in turn led to China – which, along with the US, gave support to Pol Pot as he was anti-Soviet – invading Vietnam in January 1979. This was an attempt to limit the power of Vietnam which had signed a treaty with the Soviet Union in 1978.

What effect did the Vietnam War have on US foreign policy in the Cold War after 1975?

The failure of the US to win the war in Vietnam, and the fact that a Developing World nation had forced them to withdraw, was a deep shock for US politicians and public alike. Apart from the billions of dollars it had cost, over 55,000 US soldiers had been killed, and many more seriously wounded or maimed. Yet, despite all this, South Vietnam had been 'lost' to communism, as had the neighbouring states of Laos and Cambodia. More disturbing as far as containment was concerned was the fact that these communist successes seemed to be as much the result of local popular support as of 'outside pressure', which containment had seen as the only significant factor behind the spread of communism.

Consequently, Nixon and his chief adviser, Kissinger, decided to pursue the new policy of détente towards the communist world. In particular, Kissinger argued that the US was focusing too much on communist activity in one region, at the expense of the total global balance of power. He also saw that the world had shifted from a bi-polar international situation to a multi-polar one. Of special significance was the rift between the Soviet Union and China, which gave new opportunities for developing US foreign policy. This approach was continued by Nixon's successors, Gerald Ford and Jimmy Carter, until the end of the 1970s.

The defeat in Vietnam contributed to a US reluctance to commit its own troops to other conflicts in the Developing World. The USSR took advantage of this during the remainder of the 1970s, to increase its influence in those parts of the world where it was weak, especially in the Middle East and Africa.

This cartoon, entitled 'The Myths of Vietnam', appeared in a US newspaper in 1975

Was the Soviet intervention in Afghanistan the main reason for the start of the Second Cold War?

Afghanistan, December 1979

Détente finally reached the brink of collapse due to increased Soviet activity in Afghanistan's internal politics, and then the decision to send in Red Army divisions to support the new pro-Soviet Afghan government. The USSR considered this action to be in line with the Brezhnev Doctrine (see page 118), as Afghanistan had been unofficially accepted by the West as of special concern to the Soviet Union's security, given their common borders, and of no strategic importance to the US.

The first government formed by the People's Democratic Party of Afghanistan had, in fact, been recognised by the West after it had come to power through an internal coup in April 1978. The PDPA, led by Nur Mohammad Taraki, was pro-Soviet and received economic assistance from the Soviet Union.

However, many traditionalist and fundamentalist groups, as well as the powerful feudal landowners, decided to resist the radical social and economic reforms of the new government. These had included land reform, equal rights for women, and secular education for both boys and girls. In September 1979, one faction within the PDPA, led by Hafizullah Amin and with the support of some traditionalists, seized power in another coup.

This sparked off a civil war, in which fundamentalist Muslims set up the Mujahideen and declared a *jihad*, or holy war, against Amin's government. Initially, Amin (who had been a student in the US) was supported by the USSR, but relations later deteriorated. In particular, the USSR became increasingly concerned by Amin's anti-Soviet and pro-Western statements, and especially by his contacts with CIA agents and the US government.

In closed meetings, Amin attacked Soviet policy, and the activities of Soviet advisers, while the Soviet ambassador was in practice expelled from Kabul. This growing political re-orientation to the West – and the danger of the domestic reforms of the earlier Afghan revolution of 1978 – led to growing Soviet concerns.

Carter's reaction (on advice from Brzezinski) to the Soviet military intervention, which he described as 'the greatest threat to world peace since the Second World War', took the Soviet Union by surprise. The USSR claimed it had only intervened after Pakistan – with US support – and Iran had become involved in the civil war.

Fact

April 1978 Taraki and PDPA take power following a coup

September 1979 Amin comes to power after an internal PDPA coup

December 1979 Kamal comes to power after another internal PDPA coup, and requests Soviet intervention

SOURCE B

In this extremely difficult situation, which has threatened the gains of the April [1978] revolution and the interests of maintaining our security, it has become necessary to render additional military assistance to Afghanistan, especially since such requests had been made by the previous administration in the DRA [Democratic Republic of Afghanistan]. In accordance with the provisions of the Soviet–Afghan treaty of 1978, a decision has been made to send the necessary contingent of the Soviet Army to Afghanistan.

Extract from Report on Events in Afghanistan on 27–28 December 1979, *to the Soviet Central Committee, 31 December 1979. CWIHP Bulletin, No. 8–9. 1996–97.*

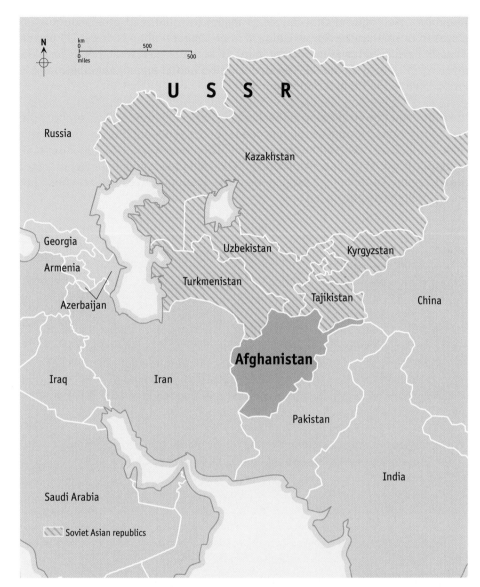

A map showing Afghanistan and the Soviet Asian republics; three of these Soviet republics had common borders with Afghanistan

The Soviet Union attempted to present its intervention as similar to supporting communist governments in Eastern Europe. Moscow feared having a fundamentalist Islamic state so close to its own Islamic central Asian republics – especially if it was allied to either the US or China. It also feared that a victory for the fundamentalist Islamic 'counter-revolutionaries' would result in a bloodbath in Afghanistan.

Fact

Not only did the USSR become involved in a disastrous 'Vietnam-style' military conflict in Afghanistan (at least 15,000 Soviet troops were killed), but its intervention in an Islamic state alienated its allies in the Middle East.

Brezhnev also believed that failure to respond would lead other communist states to think that the Soviet Union was no longer willing to resist US power. The USSR believed it was important to retain as many friendly states as possible, given its inferiority to the US. The Soviet Union had 11 significant allies outside Europe, while the US had more than 50.

In reality, the Soviet decision to back a coup against Amin and to support the pro-Soviet Babrak Kamal as the new leader of the PDPA did it much more harm than good. This new Afghan government then asked the USSR to intervene militarily. It was these interventions in 1979 – not the coming to power of a pro-Soviet regime in 1978 – which provoked the strong US–Western reaction that finally brought détente to an end.

SOURCE C

Outside aggression against the revolutionary Afghanistan perpetuated by counter-revolutionary bands, which were organised and are armed by American special services joined with the Peking militarists, made Soviet assistance necessary in defending the Afghan people's gains. In fact Washington, with the assistance of Peking, provoked the 'Afghan crisis' in order to finally gain a free hand in the policy of anti-détente.

Chernenko's comments on the reasons for Soviet intervention. Quoted in Mendelson, S. 1998. Changing Course: Ideas, Politics, and the Soviet Withdrawal from Afghanistan. Chichester, UK. Princeton University Press. p. 76.

SOURCE D

By 1985, a very complex web of foreign support for the Mujahedin was in place in which the United States worked and co-operated closely with conservative Arab governments and voluntary organizations to jointly fund and operate key initiatives.

Westad, O. A. 2007. The Global Cold War. Cambridge, UK. Cambridge University Press. p. 355.

Even before Soviet intervention in 1979, the US had responded by supplying and training Islamic Mujahideen fighters to combat the new Afghan government and, after 1979, Soviet troops. It also led Carter's administration to issue the 'Carter Doctrine'. This policy stated that the US would intervene in the Persian Gulf if its interests there were threatened. Under Reagan, this US military aid was greatly increased, with much larger amounts of weapons being sent to the Mujahideen via Pakistan, a long-standing ally of both the USA and more recently China. From 1985, during Reagan's second term, this covert US operation to arm the Mujahideen was stepped up – in particular, crucial Stinger anti-aircraft missiles were provide via Pakistan.

One of the countries supporting these US moves was Saudi Arabia. From these Mujahideen bands, even more extremist groups such as the Taliban and al-Qaeda – led by Osama bin Laden – soon emerged. Overall, the Afghan crisis helped bring about a return to a level of Cold War hostility and lack of communication between the USSR and the USA that had not been seen since 1953. In fact, Soviet officials came to believe that the New Right advisers of the US government had used allies such as Pakistan to help provoke the 'Afghan Crisis' in order to end the policy of détente.

Mujahideen fighters in Afghanistan

Discussion point

Working in pairs, use the information in the chapters of this book that you've already read, and any other materials you've used, to produce a couple of paragraphs to support **and** to oppose the Soviet decision to send troops into Afghanistan in December 1979.

 Theory of knowledge

Politics and ethics

The US often gave political support and weapons to repressive governments and terrorist organisations during the Cold War, provided they were hostile to the Soviet Union. Does this mean that the claims of American administrations that they were 'defending the free world' and upholding 'democratic values' during the Cold War were entirely bogus?

Unit summary

You should now have a good understanding of the various reasons for the US withdrawal from Vietnam, and of the significance of Nixon's foreign-policy initiatives towards Communist China as a way of putting pressure on the USSR. You should also be able to assess the role played by Kissinger during and immediately after détente. Finally, you should have a good grasp of how political developments and Soviet actions in Afghanistan in the late 1970s contributed to the development of the Second Cold War – and what the main US actions and reactions were.

End of unit activities

1 Carry out further research on Soviet interventions in Afghanistan, and then produce two brief arguments – one to show how these actions were defensive, and one to show how they were expansionist.

2 Find out more about the reasons for the start of the Second Cold War. Then list them, putting them in the order you think most important. Write a paragraph to explain your choice of the most important reason.

3 Produce a timeline to show the main developments in the Second Cold War from 1979 to 1985.

End of chapter activities

Paper 1 exam practice

Question

With reference to their origin and purpose, assess the value and limitations of Sources A and B below for historians studying attempts to achieve nuclear arms control up to the end of the 1970s.
[6 marks]

Skill

Utility/reliability of sources

SOURCE A

The effort to achieve strategic arms limitation marked the first, and the most daring, attempt to follow a collaborative approach in meeting military security requirements. Early successes held great promises, but also showed the limits of readiness of both superpowers to take this path. ... SALT generated problems of its own and provided a focal point for objection by those who did not want to see either regulated military parity or political détente. ... However, the widely held American view that SALT tried to do too much was a misjudgement: the real flaw was the failure of SALT to do enough. There was remarkable initial success on parity and on stability of the strategic arms relationship but there was insufficient political will (and perhaps political authority) to ban, or sharply limit MIRVs. This failure led in the 1970s to the failure to maintain military parity between the USA and the USSR.

Garthoff, R. L. 1994. Détente and Confrontation: American–Soviet Relations from Nixon to Reagan. Washington DC, USA. Brookings Institution. pp. 96–98. Garthoff is a former American diplomat and was a member of the SALT I delegation.

SOURCE B

The domestic political difficulties of the Nixon administration contributed to the failure to conclude a new SALT treaty to replace the 1972 interim agreement, which was due to expire in 1977. The main obstacle to progress on arms control, however, was the evident unwillingness of both superpowers to abandon the arms race with each other. Behind the public advocacy of détente and disarmament, lay the reality that the freeze on missile numbers in SALT I had never been intended to prevent either side from continuing to develop and modernise existing weapons.

Smith, J. 1998. The Cold War 1945–1991. Oxford, UK. Oxford University Press. p. 106. Smith is a lecturer in American diplomatic history at the University of Exeter in Britain.

Examiner's tips

Utility/reliability questions require you to assess **two** sources over a range of possible issues/aspects – and to comment on their value to historians studying a particular event or period of history. The main areas you need to consider in relation to the sources and the information/view they provide are:

- origin and purpose
- value and limitations.

Before you write your answer, draw a rough chart or spider diagram to show, where relevant, these various aspects. Make sure you do this for **BOTH** sources.

Common mistakes

When asked to assess **two** sources for their value, make sure you don't just comment on **one** of the sources! Every year a few students make this mistake and lose as many as 4 of the 6 marks available.

Simplified markscheme

Band		Marks
1	**Both** sources **linked**, with with **explicit consideration** of BOTH origins and purpose **AND** value and limitations.	5–6
2	**Both** sources assessed, but without consideration of **BOTH** origins and purpose **AND** value and limitations. **OR explicit consideration** of BOTH origins and purpose **AND** value and limitations – **BUT** only for **one** source.	3–4
3	**Limited** consideration/comments on origins and purpose **OR** value and limitations. Possibly only one/the wrong source(s) addressed.	0–2

Student answer

Source A is a book, published in 1994, written by someone who was a US diplomat and a member of their SALT I delegation. While its origin might present both value and limitations, it is difficult to assess its purpose. It might simply be an attempt to truthfully share the insight he gained as a participating diplomat – but it might also be to defend the policy of détente from its critics. It doesn't, though, seem to be an attempt to put just the US view or to blame the USSR alone.

These aspects affect the source's value and point to possible limitations. It certainly provides some valuable 'insider' information about the negotiations and agreements, the motives of both sides and certain problems – and it does so in what seems to be an impartial way, as both superpowers are blamed for the eventual failure of détente. However, it also seems to be a passionate defence of the policy, so might prevent problems and limitations for a historian who would also need to consider the arguments of the critics of détente, in order to arrive at a balanced view. Finally, another limitation is that it really only deals with the first half of the 1970s, and says little about later negotiations and tensions in the period up to 1979.

Examiner's comments

There is good assessment of Source A, referring explicitly to both origin and possible purpose **and** to value and limitations. These comments are valid and are clearly linked to the question (note the remark about it going beyond the mid 1970s). The candidate has thus done enough to get into Band 2, and so be awarded 3 or possibly 4 marks. However, as there are no comments about Source B, this answer fails to get into Band 1.

Activity

Look again at the two sources, the simplified markscheme, and the student answer above. Now try to write a paragraph or two to push the answer up into Band 1, and so obtain the full 6 marks. As well as assessing Source B, try to make a linking comment to show value. For example, do the two sources provide similar information?

185

Summary activities

1 Produce a mind map, with a central circle 'The Cold War, 1969–85', and then 'branches' for each of the **three regions** covered by this chapter: Europe and the Middle East; Africa and the Americas; and Asia. To do this, use the information from this chapter, and any other resources available to you. Remember to make sure you include **all** the main events and turning points.

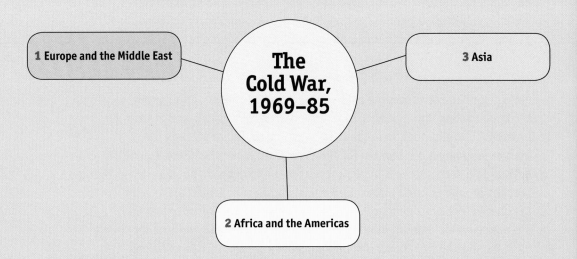

2 Make sure you have attempted all the various comprehension questions that appear in the margins. Many of these are designed to help you understand key events and turning points. There are also questions designed to develop your skills in dealing with Paper 1-type questions, such as comprehension of sources and assessing sources for their value and limitations for historians. Remember, to answer this type of question, you will need to look at a **range** of aspects, such as origin, nature and possible purpose. Don't forget, even if a source has many limitations, it can still be valuable for a historian.

3 Complete the chart below to explain why détente came to an end.

Developments in the US	
Developments in the Middle East	
Unrest in the Developing World	
Nuclear arms race	
Soviet actions in Afghanistan	

4 Use the completed chart to assess who or what was most responsible for its ending.

Practice Paper 2 questions

1 Compare the responsibility of the US and that of the USSR for the ending of détente during the period 1969–85.

2 Examine the reasons behind the decision of the USA to withdraw from the Vietnam War.

3 Evaluate the role of **one** superpower in the Cold War from 1975–85.

4 Analyse the part played by Cuba in the Cold War during the period 1969–85.

5 Compare and contrast the roles of China and Cuba in the Cold War from 1970 to 1985.

6 'The Soviet intervention in Afghanistan was the main reason for the start of the Second Cold War.' To what extent do you agree with this judgement?

Further reading

Try reading the relevant chapters/sections of the following books:

Garthoff, Raymond L. 1994. *Détente and Confrontation: American-Soviet Relations from Nixon to Reagan.* Washington, DC, USA. Brookings Institution.

Gaddis, John Lewis. 2007. *The Cold War: A New History.* London, UK. Penguin Books.

Mann, James. 2000. *About Face: a History of America's Curious Relationship with China, from Nixon to Clinton.* New York, USA. Random House.

MacMillan, Margaret. 2006. *Seize the Hour: When Nixon met Mao.* London, UK. John Murray.

Shlaim, Avi. and Sayigh, Yezid (eds). 1997. *The Cold War and the Middle East.* Oxford, UK. Clarendon Press.

LeoGrande, William. 1998. *Our Own Backyard: The United States in Central America, 1977–92.* Chapel Hill, USA. University of North Carolina Press.

Foot, Rosemary. 1995. *The Practice of Power: US Relations with China Since 1949.* Oxford, UK. Clarendon Press.

Lowe, Peter (ed). 1998. *The Vietnam War.* London, UK. Macmillan.

7 The end of the Cold War (1985–91)

Timeline

Introduction

On Christmas Day 1991, Mikhail Gorbachev resigned as president of the USSR and announced the end of the Soviet Union. This was seen by many as the final act in the Cold War, which had existed in various forms since at least 1946. What was strange about the phenomenon was that not only was it achieved with very limited bloodshed (with the exception of Romania), but also that its outcome was one that most political observers – and indeed most of the general public – had not foreseen.

Very few people had predicted the sudden collapse of a main superpower, although some in the Western security services were well informed about the growing weaknesses of the Soviet Union, both financial and political. However, a small number of political commentators – such as Ernest Mandel, in his 1989 book *Beyond Perestroika: the Future of Gorbachev's USSR* – had earlier stated that the transitional nature of Soviet society (half way between capitalism and socialism) meant it could not remain in that state forever. Instead, it would either have to return to private enterprise or forge a stronger drive to socialism and then move on to communism. In fact, such an idea had been expressed by Trotsky in the 1930s, using the analogy of a person crossing a bridge. He might pause when halfway across, but could not remain there indefinitely: at some point, he would either have to continue to the other side, or return to where he started.

SOURCE A

It would be truer, therefore, to name the present Soviet regime [1937] in all its contradictoriness, not as a socialist regime, but a *preparatory* regime *transitional* from capitalism to socialism. ... To define the Soviet regime as transitional, or intermediate, means to abandon such finished categories as *capitalism* (and therewith 'state capitalism') and also *socialism*. But besides being totally inadequate, in itself, such a definition is capable of producing the mistaken idea that from the present Soviet regime *only* a transition to socialism is possible. In reality a backslide to capitalism is wholly possible. ... The [Soviet] bureaucracy continues to fulfil a necessary function. But it fulfils it in such a way as to prepare an explosion of the whole system which may completely sweep out the results of the [1917] revolution.

Trotsky, L. 1972. *The Revolution Betrayed: What is the Soviet Union and Where is it Going? New York, USA. New Park. pp. 47, 254 and 285–86.*

In fact, in 1970, Brzezinski – later to be US national security adviser to Jimmy Carter – had suggested five possible futures for the USSR: **petrification**, **evolution**, **adaptation**, **fundamentalism** or **disintegration**.

Like most commentators in both West and East, including Gorbachev himself, Brzezinski did not believe disintegration was at all likely. Instead, he believed that the most probable outcome was an amalgamation of petrification and adaptation. Yet between 1989 and 1991, the Soviet satellites gained non-communist governments, the Warsaw Pact was dismantled, Germany was reunited and the USSR broke up into its constituent parts.

The more immediate causes leading up to this truly historic event can be traced back to 1989, when the people in the Soviet satellites in Eastern Europe overthrew their governments in various kinds of 'people or popular power' movements, and left the Warsaw Pact, set up by the Soviet Union for its security 34 years before. An iconic moment was the tearing down of the Berlin Wall in November 1989. However, apart from various long-term factors, the dramatic changes in Soviet–US relations, which had been taking place since 1985, also played a significant part in the eventual collapse of the USSR.

petrification To stay the same.

evolution To change, but in line with the current situation.

adaptation To change to become closer to the Western model.

fundamentalism To revert to early Cold War hostilities.

disintegration To collapse and break up.

The collapse of the communist regimes in Eastern Europe

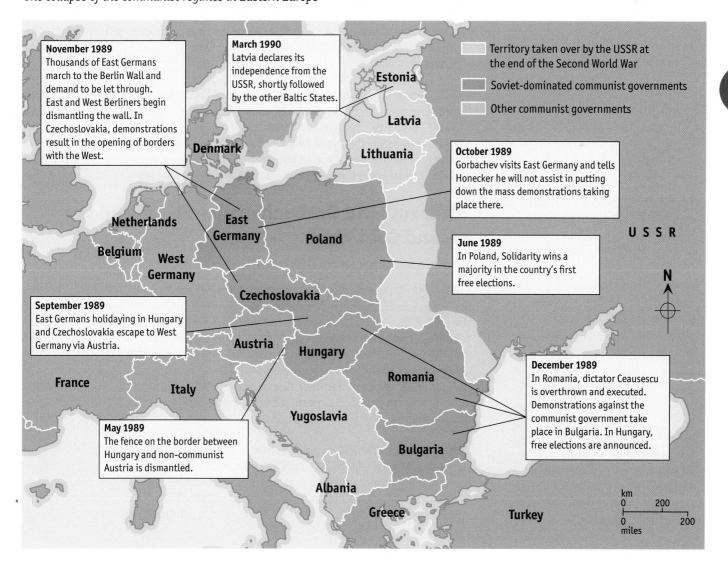

189

Key questions

- What role did Gorbachev play in ending the Second Cold War?
- How significant was the US response and Reagan's role?
- How important were Soviet economic problems?
- How important was the collapse of Eastern European regimes in ending the Cold War?
- How did Gorbachev help end Cold War tensions in Asia, the Americas and Africa?
- Was the end of the Cold War also the end of the 'Great Contest'?

Overview

- In November 1985, Gorbachev and Reagan's first summit took place in Geneva; the second was at Reykjavik, in October 1986.
- Progress was made on arms reductions, although this was partly undermined by US deployment of the new B52 bomber.
- In December 1987, the Washington Summit ended with the signing of the INF Treaty, while 1988 saw the Geneva Agreement on ending the Afghan War, the Moscow Summit, and Gorbachev's unilateral decision to greatly reduce Soviet forces.
- By the end of 1989, most Eastern European regimes had fallen, after Gorbachev announced he would not stop reforms. The US agreed to end most restrictions on US–Soviet trade. In 1990, Germany was reunited, and the CFE Treaty was signed.
- In March 1991, the Warsaw Pact was dissolved; later, START was signed. By the end of the year, Gorbachev and the USSR were gone. The Cold War – in both Europe and the rest of the world – had finally ended.

What role did Gorbachev play in ending the Second Cold War?

The significance of Gorbachev

Mikhail Gorbachev's election as general secretary of the CPSU in March 1985 turned out to be the beginning of the end of the Cold War – and, as it turned out, the end of the Soviet Union itself. Gorbachev is reported to have said, just before taking over as general secretary, 'We can't go on living like this'. As the youngest and the first university-educated leader since Stalin to hold this position, it was unlikely that social and economic, political and foreign policies would remain the same. Gorbachev had few ties to the Soviet military élite and had grown close to reform-minded experts. These experts tended to stress the importance of local issues over global ideological considerations.

Part of Gorbachev's new approach thus involved rethinking Soviet priorities and removing 'Marxist–Leninist' ideology as the main factor in determining Soviet foreign policy. According to one of his closest aides, Gorbachev changed his ideas about international relations early in 1986. Though the collapse of the USSR does not seem to have been Gorbachev's intention, he certainly did set out deliberately to end the Cold War.

Mikhail Gorbachev waves to a crowd in Bratislava, Czechoslovakia, in 1987

Gorbachev's main concern was to end the stagnation of the Soviet economy, then to revitalise it, and to ensure the security of the Soviet system. He realised that the financial burden of maintaining the military power of the USSR was too great, and that its effect on the Soviet economy and on the living standards of consumers would ultimately undermine Soviet security. He also calculated that the USA's huge budget deficit meant that it too could not maintain its increased defence expenditure for much longer. He thus calculated that it might be possible to prevent Reagan from developing his SDI project (see page 164) by initiating a new round of arms-reduction talks.

Gorbachev's New Thinking

While Gorbachev's domestic policy was shaped by his three policies of **glasnost**, **perestroika** and **demokratizatsiya**, he also applied another policy to foreign affairs, known as 'Novoe Myshlenie', or New Thinking. Gorbachev's New Thinking argued that confrontation was counterproductive, and that continuing the arms race was pointless, as one side's advance was simply matched – or even bettered – by the other. He also believed that only political accommodation, not military power, would enable problems to be solved and real security achieved. As part of this approach, he decided to state publicly what had, in fact, long been the reality of Soviet foreign policy: that the ideology and language of class war should not shape the Soviet Union's diplomacy.

191

glasnost This was the policy of 'openness' adopted by Gorbachev. He wanted past mistakes and current problems in the USSR to be voiced in public, including criticism of the leadership of the Communist Party and its policies in the media.

perestroika This was the policy of 'restructuring' launched by Gorbachev. Though it soon came to be used to describe his general intention to modernise the USSR, it was initially aimed at the Soviet economy. His main aim was to make the economic system more modern and to improve productivity.

demokratizatsiya This refers to Gorbachev's attempts to make the Soviet political system more democratic. Under him, elections were reformed to give greater choice to the voters, and political organisations and clubs were allowed to operate outside the control of the Communist Party. Gorbachev also tried to make the government and the Soviet system more independent of party control.

Question

What were the main aspects of Gorbachev's 'New Thinking' as regards Soviet foreign policy?

Fact

These conservative elements in the Soviet Union were determined to maintain the monopoly of power held by the political élite in the USSR, and believed that increased democracy would undermine Soviet control of Eastern Europe. In the main, these hardliners wished to continue with the Stalinist system of rule.

While New Thinking contained elements of traditional Soviet foreign policy, such as aiming for peaceful coexistence and détente with the West, Gorbachev's new policy was also markedly different. In particular, he dropped the dual-track policy of peaceful coexistence as a way of ensuring Soviet security and the peaceful long-term victory of socialism across the world. Gorbachev's stated aim now was simply Soviet security – Khrushchev's idea of a peaceful but competitive coexistence was clearly abandoned.

Gorbachev's new approach was signalled by his appointment of Eduard Shevardnadze as foreign minister. At his first Central Committee meeting in April 1985, Gorbachev announced his wish to reopen arms-control talks and the need to withdraw Soviet troops from Afghanistan. He also spoke of what he called 'reasonable sufficiency' – an early indication of his belief that the arms race need not continue, as all that was needed was the military capacity to threaten an effective counterattack. In particular, unlike the previous Soviet leadership, he was prepared to consider seriously Reagan's 'Zero Option' proposal, which suggested the removal of all intermediate-range missiles from Europe. This was a clear rejection of the policy of parity followed by Brezhnev.

However, while Gorbachev's ideas and approach made him extremely popular abroad, they caused growing criticism from more conservative quarters within the Soviet Union itself.

How significant was the US response and Reagan's role?

Despite following a somewhat contradictory foreign policy in Central America (see page 170), Reagan also contributed to an improved relationship between the two superpowers. The result was a growing and genuine political accommodation between Reagan and Gorbachev in the second half of the 1980s.

SOURCE B

As former Pentagon officials like Casper Weinberger and Richard Perle … and other proponents of the 'Reagan victory school' have argued, a combination of military and ideological pressures gave the Soviets little choice but to abandon expansionism abroad and repression at home. In their view, the Reagan military build-up foreclosed Soviet military options while pushing the Soviet economy to the breaking point. Reagan partisans stress that his dramatic Star Wars initiative put the Soviets on notice that the next phase of the arms race would be waged in areas where the West held a decisive technological edge.

Deudney D. and Ikenberry, G. J. 'Who won the Cold War?', in Foreign Policy, No. 87. Summer 1992. p. 124.

The 'Reagan victory school' viewpoint is based on a stern critique of Carter's détente approach to relations with the Soviet Union, even though it was Carter who initiated the first stages of the Second Cold War after 1979.

The Jimmy Carter–Cyrus Vance approach of rewarding the Soviet build-up with one-sided arms control treaties, opening Moscow's access to Western capital markets and technologies, and condoning Soviet imperial expansion was perfectly designed to preserve the Brezhnev-style approach, delivering the Soviets from any need to re-evaluate (as they did under Gorbachev) or change their policies. Had the Carter–Vance approach been continued. ... the Cold War and the life of the Soviet Union would almost certainly have been prolonged.

Glynn, P. Letter to the Editor, Foreign Policy, *No. 90. Spring 1993. pp. 171–73.*

An arguably more balanced approach is taken by historians such as Rozanne Ridgeway, or M. MacGwire, who stress that Reagan's main contribution to the process was his willingness to move from his strong anti-communist and anti-Soviet position (the 'evil empire') and, instead, to be prepared to engage and negotiate with the new Soviet leader.

This helped a new atmosphere of rapprochement to develop during the four summits that took place between the two leaders. Nonetheless, the US – aware of the increasingly problematic nature of the Soviet Union's economy – drove hard bargains. Soviet weaknesses in Eastern Europe were also exploited, by offering concessions to those satellites that tried to establish greater independence from Moscow, and punishing those regimes (such as Poland under Wojciech Jarulzelski) that stayed loyal.

It became clear that, in the Second Cold War, US strategy had moved from containment and then détente to a policy 'beyond containment', which showed a refusal to simply coexist. Instead, from a position of greater economic, technological and military strength, the US began to demand fundamental change in the Soviet Union and Eastern Europe.

First steps, 1985

As noted above, both Gorbachev's desire to shape a new foreign policy and so bring to an end the Second Cold War, and the fact that Reagan's approach began to moderate at the same time, enabled the processes of negotiation to progress. In particular, it was agreed to resume the arms-control negotiations, which had ended after the Soviet Union walked out in November 1983 (see page 164).

However, Gorbachev was quick to take steps to push the pace. In April 1985, he froze further deployments of the SS-20s; in August he declared a temporary halt to Soviet underground nuclear testing; in September he proposed that the USSR and the US reduce all strategic nuclear weapons stocks by 50%; and in October, he announced plans for a reduction in the number of Soviet missiles in Eastern Europe. Over the next three years, four US–Soviet summits took place on arms control.

The US – aware of the increasingly problematic nature of the Soviet Union's economy – drove hard bargains. Soviet weaknesses in Eastern Europe were also exploited.

> **Overall relations between the two superpowers deteriorated in the first half of 1986. There was increased US agression in Libya and Afghanistan, and in May Reagan announced that the US would not adhere to SALT II.**

Fact
Ever since it had been announced by Reagan in March 1983, the Soviet Union had seen the SDI as violating the ABM Treaty of 1972, and thus escalating the nuclear arms race by rendering impossible any Soviet response to a US first strike.

The Four Summits, 1985–88

Geneva

The first meeting took place in Geneva, in November 1985. Although there were no significant agreements, it was the first such summit for six years. However, any practical agreement on the reduction of Soviet ICBMs was prevented by continuing fear of Reagan's 'Star Wars' plans. Also, Reagan rejected Gorbachev's suggestion that they issue a joint statement promising that neither side would be the first to launch a nuclear attack. This was because the US wanted to keep the option of responding to a conventional attack with nuclear weapons. However, they did agree to promise to prevent any war between themselves and not to seek military superiority.

Nonetheless, after the summit Gorbachev continued to push the pace. In January 1986, he took the US by surprise when he proposed the total elimination of all nuclear weapons by the end of the century. Other offers followed – to eliminate all ICBMs in ten years and to withdraw all tactical nuclear weapons from Europe. Then, in April 1986, he suggested new talks on the reduction of Warsaw Pact and NATO conventional forces. In May, Gorbachev officially launched his New Thinking, despite Reagan's continued refusal to drop the development of SDI.

In spite of this, overall relations between the two superpowers deteriorated in the first half of 1986. There was increased US aggression in Libya and Afghanistan, and in May Reagan announced that the US would not adhere to the still unratified SALT II agreement.

Reykjavik

The second Reagan–Gorbachev summit, which took place in Reykjavik in October 1986, was predictably not as a good-natured as Geneva had been. Once again, the USA's Strategic Defence Initiative was the main item of contention.

At first Gorbachev tried to move the talks from consideration of reductions and limitations to complete nuclear disarmament, and Reagan called for the complete elimination of all ballistic nuclear missiles within ten years. Soviet leaders realised that their ailing economy would not withstand the strain of attempting to keep up with the technological advances of the US.

Agreement was reached in principle that strategic nuclear weapons should be cut by 50%, and that medium-range nuclear missiles in Europe should be withdrawn. However, arguments about SDI finally caused the summit to break up as Reagan refused to abandon SDI, while Gorbachev said further reductions could not happen without this step. As a consequence, no actual agreements were made, and so it seemed a deadlock had been reached. Nonetheless, Gorbachev described the summit as an 'intellectual breakthrough' in relations between the USSR and the USA.

This deadlock was broken by Gorbachev in February 1987, when he offered to accept the NATO policy of the zero-zero option on the deployment of SS-20s and Pershing and Cruise missiles in Europe. In essence, this meant that both sides would withdraw their missiles. Gorbachev's acceptance of NATO's terms

President Reagan announces the initiation of the Strategic Defense Initiative in March 1983

was a complete reversal of what had been Soviet policy on this issue for ten years. It was a huge concession by the Soviet Union, and Gorbachev's critics in the USSR saw this as a dangerous surrender.

In November, Gorbachev acknowledged that human rights needed to be improved in the Soviet bloc and that the 'Iron Curtain' should be lifted. He also spoke of the need to avoid superpower confrontation in the Developing World.

Washington

As a result of Gorbachev's offer, a third summit meeting took place, in Washington in December 1987. This resulted in the signing of the Intermediate Nuclear Forces (INF) Treaty, which agreed that all land-based intermediate- and shorter-range nuclear missiles would be withdrawn from Europe. This was the first arms agreement to be signed since 1979; it was also unique – never before had arms-reduction talks led to the elimination of an entire category of nuclear weapons.

The INF Treaty was also historically important as, for the first time in arms control agreements, the two sides accepted verification procedures, which included access to data and the witnessing of weapons destruction. Thus the arms race was not just slowed down by the INF Treaty, but was actually reversed. At this stage, there were signs that the Cold War would end via a mutually agreed settlement.

Fact
In practical terms, the INF Treaty covered only about five per cent of the total stockpile of nuclear warheads in existence (about 2,500 out of 50,000).

Question

What were the four summits that took place between the Soviet Union and the USA in the years 1985–88?

196

George Bush (b. 1924) George H. W. Bush became vice-president to Reagan in 1980. During this period, he was involved in the Iran-Contragate scandal, when non-lethal aid voted for by Congress was secretly given to the Contras in Nicaragua and to the Mujahideen in Afghanistan. He was elected president in 1988, and took advantage of Soviet weaknesses and Gorbachev's reforms to use US troops to overthrow the government of Panama and, in 1991, to invade Iraq in the Gulf War.

Moscow

The next summit meeting took place in Moscow in May 1988. Prior to this, Gorbachev had taken another step towards easing tensions between East and West by announcing that the Soviet Union would withdraw its forces from Afghanistan without insisting on any guarantees on the type of government which might come to power in that country. This had long been insisted on by the US, and had been resisted by previous Soviet leaders – including Gorbachev himself at first. By April 1988, an international conference in Geneva had resulted in an agreement to end all foreign involvement in the Afghan civil war. Gorbachev even hinted that Soviet troops might soon be withdrawn from Eastern Europe. By February 1989, after almost ten years of fighting, the last units of the Red Army had left Afghanistan.

Despite this, the Moscow Summit achieved little as, once again, arguments about the Star Wars project blocked any agreement on the reduction of strategic nuclear weapons. By then, however, Gorbachev had effectively destroyed Reagan's attempt to depict the Soviet Union as an 'evil empire', and Reagan himself had stated publicly that his earlier view of the USSR had changed, saying that the phrase belonged to 'another time, another era'. However, vice-president Bush commented that 'the Cold War is not over'.

In fact, Gorbachev was soon scoring higher in US opinion polls than US politicians. What became known as 'Gorbimania' hit Western Europe, as people responded to his attempts to end the arms race and his talk of a 'common European home'.

From Reagan to Bush

The November 1988 presidential elections in the US had been won by vice-president **George Bush**. After he took over in January 1989, the pace of improvement in US–Soviet relations slackened off at first, as Bush believed Reagan had made too many concessions. In addition, since the mid 1980s, the US position had been strengthened by a series of developments: new and advanced missiles had been placed in Western Europe, the SDI project continued, and the US had taken various military initiatives to counter political developments overseas – Grenada had been invaded, while support had been given to both the Mujahideen in Afghanistan and the Contras in Nicaragua. In addition, the US was increasingly aware of the political and economic problems of the Soviet satellites in Eastern Europe. Many were in debt, and trade with Western states had made them increasingly dependent on the West. These problems were used as leverage to push for further Soviet concessions, in the knowledge that for Gorbachev's economic reforms to work, the USSR could not afford to match the SDI project. The US also continued to argue that the various agreements did not mean the Cold War was over. In particular, the situation in Eastern Europe, with its links to the USSR, was seen as a major stumbling block.

However, in July 1989, Bush met Gorbachev and was reassured by his statement that the USSR had no desire to challenge the USA's global dominance. This allowed the thaw in Soviet–US relations to resume. Soon, James Baker, the new US secretary of state, developed a good relationship with Eduard Shevardnadze, the Soviet minister of foreign affairs. By now, the Soviet Union was desperate for US financial assistance, and Shevardnadze was instructed to indicate that the USSR was ready to sign the START treaty without any US concessions. In fact, he was criticised by Soviet hardliners for agreeing that the USA could retain 880 submarine-launched Cruise missiles.

How important were Soviet economic problems?

The Gorbachev Doctrine

According to historian and former US ambassador Raymond Garthoff, the Soviet withdrawal from Afghanistan was part of what he has called the 'Gorbachev Doctrine' – a clear policy of disengaging from involvement in the Developing World, in order to avoid any confrontation with the US.

However, Gorbachev's actions here, and in relation to nuclear disarmament and Eastern Europe, have also been described as a 'diplomacy of despair'. This argument maintains that, because of its economic difficulties, the Soviet Union had to make more defence cuts than the US, despite being in an inferior military position. Thus, while the attitudes and policies of individuals such as Gorbachev and Reagan were clearly significant factors in the final stages of the Cold War, there were also important long-term factors involved.

> **Fact**
> Garthoff sees the Gorbachev Doctrine as being achieved by working with the US in order to sponsor the peaceful settlement of conflicts in the Developing World, based on a desire for security via co-operation and improved relations.

SOURCE D

The West did not, as is widely believed, win the Cold War through geopolitical containment and military deterrence. Nor was the Cold War won by the Reagan military build up and the Reagan Doctrine. ... Instead, 'victory' for the West came when a new generation of Soviet leaders realised how badly their system at home and their policies abroad had failed. What containment did was to successfully stalemate Moscow's attempts to advance Soviet hegemony. Over four decades it performed the historic function of holding Soviet power in check until the internal seeds of destruction within the Soviet Union and its empire could mature. At this point, however, it was Gorbachev who brought the Cold War to an end.

Garthoff, R. L. 'Why did the Cold War Arise and Why Did it End?'. In Hogan, M. J. (ed.). 1992. The End of the Cold War: Its Meaning and Implications. 1992. Cambridge, UK. Cambridge University Press. p. 129.

By the time of Brezhnev's death in 1982, the USSR seemed to be more powerful and secure than at any point in its short history. It was under Brezhnev that the Soviet Union finally achieved 'parity' in several areas of nuclear weaponry and technology. At the same time, the foreign policy pursued under Brezhnev had resulted in many more countries with friendly links to the Soviet Union, thus reducing the USSR's global isolation.

However, the deployment of large resources to achieve these results had a very negative impact on the Soviet economy. Most worrying was that Soviet technology was in many vital areas falling behind that of the West. As a result, industrial productivity in the USSR was declining. By the time Gorbachev came to power in 1985, the Soviet economy was in serious trouble, forcing him to make agreements with the West.

> **Question**
> How did the weaknesses of the Soviet economy affect Gorbachev's foreign policy?

197

Several historians critical of the 'Reagan victory' view thus point out that, as these problems existed before Reagan became president, the end of the Cold War was down to other factors, such as internal Soviet weaknesses and/or the earlier US/Western Cold War strategies of containment and détente.

How important was the collapse of Eastern European regimes in ending the Cold War?

The collapse of Eastern Europe, 1988–89

In addition to the economic problems of the USSR, developments in Eastern Europe also played a key role in the ending of the Cold War and the collapse of the USSR. In particular, the period from the late 1970s/early 1980s saw the re-emergence of a new nationalism in many of the Soviet Union's European satellites. The first country to show signs of this was Poland, where dissatisfaction with the poor economic situation in the country had led to industrial unrest and strikes. In Gdansk, a successful strike in the shipyards led to the formation of an independent trade union known as Solidarity, under the leadership of Lech Walesa.

By 1981, Solidarity had claimed a membership of ten million – much to the concern of Brezhnev and other Soviet leaders. In December 1981, a section of the Polish army had been able to get General Jarulzelski installed as prime minister. Jarulzelski, who wanted to maintain links with Moscow, had declared martial law, banned Solidarity and arrested thousands of activists. Order had been restored by 1983, but the economic problems and declining living standards continued, and in the late 1980s trouble reappeared.

Gorbachev made it increasingly clear that he was unwilling to use military force to maintain Soviet influence over the Soviet satellites. Part of his New Thinking was based on the idea that the Soviet Union, and Eastern and Western Europe, shared a 'common European home'.

Of particular importance was Gorbachev's public abandonment of the Brezhnev Doctrine in March 1985. He made it clear that Soviet troops would not be sent into any Eastern European state, either to defend an existing regime or to crush reform communists or mass popular movements. This was reiterated at a Warsaw Pact meeting in April 1985. Yet when Gorbachev came to power in 1985, most regimes in the Soviet bloc seemed reasonably secure and stable. Many of Gorbachev's critics soon blamed the collapse of these states – in a period of only four years – on Gorbachev's policies.

On 7 December 1988, Gorbachev made a speech to the United Nations in which he announced that the number of Soviet troops committed to the Warsaw Pact would be cut by 500,000, and reiterated that he would not use the Soviet army to maintain control of satellite countries.

As part of his approach, Gorbachev also encouraged the policies of *perestroika*, *glasnost* and *demokratizasiya* (see page 191) in the Soviet Union's Eastern European satellites. Some of these were similar to the ideas developed earlier by reform communists in Hungary and Czechoslovakia in the 1960s and 1970s. While many citizens in these countries were keen to enjoy the new freedoms being allowed in the USSR, several Eastern European governments had grave doubts. However, the ruling communists in Hungary and Poland welcomed the new opportunities for reform. Soon, Eastern Europe saw the rise of mass movements which, as well as calling for economic reforms, also demanded greater democracy and various versions of the earlier Czechoslovakian 'Prague Spring' of 1968, which had tried to establish 'socialism with a human face'. Gorbachev's speech to the UN in December 1988, when he declared that ideology should play a smaller part in foreign affairs, and announced major reductions of Soviet forces in Eastern Europe, also encouraged hopes for reform. Some elements in these popular grass-roots movements, however, wanted to go further – to re-establish the power of the Church and to restore capitalism.

The events of 1989

Poland

In Poland, Solidarity was legalised in January 1989 and in April it agreed a package of political and economic reforms with the government. These included elections to be held in June, which resulted in a clear victory for Solidarity. In August 1989, the new Polish parliament elected the first non-communist prime minister to rule in Eastern Europe in over 40 years. The significant aspect of these developments was that Gorbachev, in line with his earlier statements, did not intervene to support the old communist regime. The movements in the rest of Eastern Europe were thus encouraged to continue their demands.

Hungary

In Hungary, reform communists had been carrying out their own Gorbachev-style policies for some time. These moves increased in the late 1980s, and in 1989 it was agreed that multi-party elections would be held. Gorbachev accepted these developments in both Hungary and Poland.

It took developments in the GDR to accelerate the pace of change in the rest of Eastern Europe, but it was Hungary's decision, in August 1989, to open its border with Austria that sparked off the crisis in East Germany. By September 1989, thousands of East Germans were crossing to West Germany via Hungary and Austria, provoking an economic crisis similar to the one that had led to the building of the Berlin Wall.

East Germany

In East Germany, Honecker – unlike Ulbricht in 1961 – could not rely on Soviet support. Although the East German economy was relatively successful, and, like all Soviet bloc countries, provided its citizens with cheap transport, electricity and gas, living standards in many areas were below those enjoyed in the West. Demonstrations in support of democracy spread across the GDR.

On 18 October, Honecker resigned as leader of the communist party and was replaced by Egon Krenz. However, the demonstrations – many of them led by a group known as New Forum – grew even bigger, culminating in a massive protest in East Berlin on 4 November, attended by almost 500,000 people. Gorbachev then made it clear to the GDR that it should form closer ties with West Germany, pointing out that the USSR could no longer afford to subsidise its economy.

On 7 November, the government of the GDR resigned and, on 8 November, Krenz decided to open the Berlin Wall. Thousands of people rushed to the checkpoints and poured through. Soon, people from both East and West Berlin began to demolish the Berlin Wall, which, since its construction in 1961, had come to symbolise the Cold War.

Fact
The Hungarian reformers went beyond liberalisation, and began to encourage nationalism – for instance, during the memorials held on 16 June to commemorate the 1956 reformer Imre Nagy (see page 113).

199

The collapse of the Soviet bloc was a clear indication of the serious decline of the USSR, both internally and externally. In fact, all these Eastern European states had been heavily in debt to the Soviet Union.

> **Fact**
> Gorbachev's only intervention in Eastern Europe was to continue to encourage liberal reforms. Although Gorbachev hoped that the new governments would be made up of reform communists or socialists, who would establish democratic socialism in Eastern Europe, the only certainty in 1989 was that the old-style communist governments had gone.

Czechoslovakia and Bulgaria

The events in East Germany stimulated mass protests in Czechoslovakia and Bulgaria. In Czechoslovakia, people were reminded of the Prague Spring of 1968. The communist government resigned and a multi-party system was established. As a result of this 'Velvet Revolution', led mainly by the Civic Forum group, Vaclav Havel, a dissident and playwright, became president. On 27 October, the countries of the Warsaw Pact, including the USSR, issued a statement condemning the 1968 invasion, promising never again to interfere in the affairs of member states, and guaranteeing that there would be no military intervention to support unpopular governments. In Bulgaria, too, mass demonstrations led to the government's resignation and a multi-party democracy.

Romania

The one exception to these peaceful revolutions was Romania, where Nicolae Ceausescu, the country's leader, tried to use the security forces to crush the demonstrators. On Christmas Eve, the US ambassador in Moscow signalled that there would be no objections if Gorbachev sent in Soviet troops to help the Romanian army against Ceausescu. This suggestion, and the Soviet refusal to intervene, were significant indications that the Cold War was virtually over. Ceausescu and his wife tried to flee, but were arrested by the army, and were executed on Christmas Day 1989.

More significantly, the Soviet Union had allowed the disappearance of a security belt which had been the foundation and main aim of its foreign policy since 1945, and which had played a large part in the start of the Cold War. The hardline communists in these Eastern European states, who had used a form of nationalism to bolster their regimes, soon found themselves outflanked and overtaken by nationalists on the right, who began to stir up ethnic prejudices against minorities such as the Roma and the Sinti, and Jewish people.

Collapse of the Soviet bloc

This new Soviet policy of non-intervention was the result of a combination of Gorbachev's belief in democracy and his recognition that the Soviet Union was politically unable to intervene. The collapse of the Soviet bloc was a clear indication of the serious decline of the USSR, both internally and externally, by the end of the 1980s. In fact, all these Eastern European states had been heavily in debt to the Soviet Union, thus adding to its own economic problems.

SOURCE E

At the beginning of 1989 the Communists had been in complete – and seemingly permanent – control of Eastern Europe. At the end of the year, they were gone. Democratic coalitions, promising free elections in the immediate future, had taken place in East Berlin, Prague, Budapest, Warsaw and even Bucharest. … As a result, the Warsaw Pact had been, in effect, dismantled. The Soviet Union had withdrawn inside its borders. The Cold War in Europe was over.

Ambrose, S. 1991. Rise to Globalism: American Foreign Policy Since 1938. London, UK. Penguin. p. 378.

Most commentators welcomed these developments, but a small minority, while supporting the reforms, nonetheless urged caution. The historian Eric Hobsbawm, for example, warned that the collapse of one-party regimes in Eastern Europe would not necessarily result in tolerant and popular regimes. In particular, he pointed out that before 1945, with the exception of Czechoslovakia, the governments in that area had been authoritarian and often racist, especially towards their Jewish, and the Sinti and Roma, minorities.

He also commented that, as a condition for receiving loans from the West, the new governments would be applying neo-capitalist policies in relatively backward economies, and this would cause great hardship for the majority of their populations. Both jobs and social services would be cut. However, the changes would also provide opportunities for a small minority to become very wealthy.

The final act, December 1989–1991

The Malta Summit

The collapse of the Eastern European regimes – and hence of the Soviet buffer-zone – played a big part in ending the Cold War. At the Malta Summit in December 1989, Gorbachev and Bush officially declared the end of the Cold War. This symbolic statement came about when Gorbachev announced that the USSR no longer saw the US as an enemy.

The US offered economic help, and the two parties reached informal agreements on the future of Eastern Europe, Germany and the Baltic republics. On the latter issue, Gorbachev was prepared to consider a loosening of their ties to the USSR but not, at first, their independence. They also agreed to work towards reducing the size of conventional forces in Europe. After the Malta Summit, Shevardnadze claimed the Cold War had been 'buried at the bottom of the Mediterranean'.

Germany

The question of Germany remained a serious security concern for the Soviet Union. At first Gorbachev hoped to avoid German reunification, believing that, with the uncertain political and diplomatic policies likely to emerge in Eastern Europe, a divided Germany would be less of a possible threat. For a time, both he and Margaret Thatcher – the 'new right' prime minister of Britain who had worked closely with Reagan – tried to restrain the US push for rapid reunification. There were even calls for Soviet troops to remain in Germany for a time. These were supported by the new post-communist regime in Poland. The Soviet Union was also concerned that NATO would extend its membership eastwards, right up to the Soviet Union's borders. However, by February 1990, Gorbachev had accepted that it was up to the Germans to decide whether and when they wanted reunification.

In May, the GDR signed a reunification treaty, and the West German Deutschmark became the common currency in July. In May 1990, Helmut Kohl visited the Soviet Union. The result was Gorbachev's acceptance of reunification in return for German economic aid for the USSR, German acceptance of Poland's western borders, and informal guarantees of Soviet security. In the end, under strong pressure from the West and in a position of economic weakness, Gorbachev finally agreed to reunification of Germany in September 1990. This formally took place on 3 October 1990, and soon came to symbolise the end of the division of Europe itself, which had existed since 1947.

201

> **Fact**
> Gorbachev hoped that, if reunification took place, the new Germany would remain neutral; but US president Bush and Kohl, the West German chancellor, made it clear that a united Germany would join NATO.

Sections of the Berlin Wall are removed by GDR border soldiers in November 1989

Though Gorbachev did obtain some concessions – the former West German army would be reduced, and no NATO forces would be deployed in the former GDR – he was also beginning to negotiate on the withdrawal of Soviet troops from states in Eastern Europe. To ease this process, the US offered much-needed financial assistance. Once again, Gorbachev acted without prior discussion with the Soviet foreign minister or the military.

In November 1990, the Conventional Forces in Europe (CFE) Treaty was signed, which led to a reduction in troop deployments. At the same time, further talks began on the reduction of nuclear weapons. This resulted in the START treaty, which was signed at the Moscow Summit in July 1991, ten years after it was first drawn up. Considerable cuts in the size of US and Soviet strategic nuclear stockpiles were agreed, and talks for a START II treaty were begun.

The collapse of the Soviet Union

Initially, when some Soviet republics – especially the Baltic republics – began to push for independence, the US stated that it was not in favour of the break-up of the Soviet Union, and seemed to prefer Gorbachev's plans for a looser confederation to those of Boris Yeltsin, the newly elected president of the Russian republic – the largest and most important of the 15 republics that made up the USSR. Yeltsin was pushing for a separate Russian republic. Consequently, when violent clashes occurred in Lithuania and Latvia in January 1991 between protestors and Soviet security forces, the US did not break off relations with the Soviet Union.

The CFE treaty was speeded up, resulting in the US announcing $1.5 billion worth of credits for the USSR to purchase grain, but tensions began to resurface.

This stemmed from US insistence that significant economic aid would not be forthcoming unless the Soviet Union moved to a market, or capitalist, economy. Matters were made worse when the KGB claimed to have evidence of US attempts to bring about the disintegration of the USSR.

However, some developments under Gorbachev – especially the loss of Eastern Europe and the acceptance of Soviet nuclear inferiority – continued to alarm his critics in the Soviet leadership. These fears were underlined in July 1991, when the Warsaw Pact was dissolved, leaving NATO unchallenged. In addition, his economic policies had not resulted in any significant improvement, and both Gorbachev and his government, while popular abroad, were losing support at home.

A group of political and military leaders, who were also opposed to plans to give more power to the Soviet republics, decided to overthrow Gorbachev. A new draft Union Treaty, granting such powers, had been given mass support in a referendum in March 1991; the plotters feared it might result in the disintegration of the USSR.

> **Fact**
> The US was not in favour of the break-up of the Soviet Union, partly because it preferred to deal with one central power and feared the possible consequences of the instability that might result from any break up; and partly because it wanted Soviet support for its Gulf War against Iraq (Iraq was allied to the Soviet Union, and several thousand Soviet troops were stationed there).

A map showing the individual states that emerged from the former Soviet Union

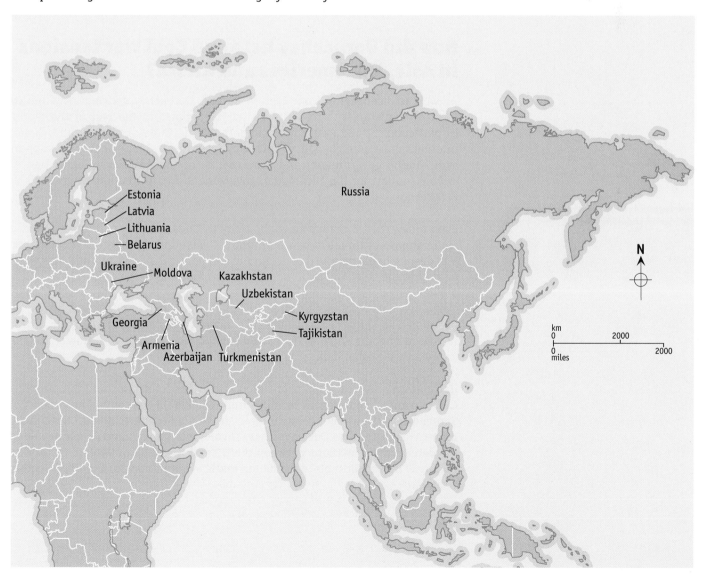

In August 1991, these hardline 'Stalinist' plotters launched their attempted coup while Gorbachev was on holiday. At first, Bush seemed prepared to accept the coup, but he changed his mind and made contact with Yeltsin. The coup failed because the bulk of the army and security forces refused to support it, while Yeltsin soon put himself at the head of popular protests.

Though Gorbachev remained as Soviet president, his position was increasingly undermined by Yeltsin, who used his control of Russia to hasten the collapse of the Soviet Union. In December 1991 Russia, along with the important republics of Belorussia and the Ukraine, declared the formation of the Commonwealth of Independent States (CIS). Perhaps significantly, they informed Bush of their decision before Gorbachev. On 25 December 1991, Gorbachev used a TV broadcast to announce his resignation as president of the Soviet Union.

With this step, the Soviet Union – which had already broken up in practice – was declared formally to have ended. This geopolitical victory topped off the three other aspects of the 'triumph of the West' in the final stages of the Cold War: the ideological Cold War had ended with Gorbachev's speech to the UN in December 1988; the military Cold War had ended at the CSCE talks in Paris in November 1990, where Bush and Gorbachev signed the CFE Treaty; and the economic Cold War had ended at the Malta Summit in December 1989 (see page 201).

How did Gorbachev help end Cold War tensions in Asia, the Americas and Africa?

As well as disengaging from Eastern Europe, Gorbachev decided to withdraw from Afghanistan, and to 'write off' client regimes in the rest of the world. In particular, he reduced Soviet support for the Cuban economy and Cuba's interventionist foreign policy. This rapidly reduced Cuba's ability to support sympathetic governments and movements. In the Americas, Castro had to reduce support for the Nicaraguan government and for the left-wing rebels in El Salvador.

Question

How did the collapse of the USSR in 1991 affect Cuba?

Even today, the US maintains its hostility to Cuba, which – still under Castro's leadership – continues to be a 'communist' island in the western hemisphere. Yet, despite being deprived of economic and political allies, Cuba still acts as an irritant to the USA, and an almost-forgotten footnote to the Cold War.

Gorbachev's new policy also affected Cuba's world role in relation to Africa. He negotiated an agreement with the US concerning the civil war in Angola, which had been ongoing since 1975. In 1991, Cuban troops were withdrawn and the civil war was suspended.

In the Horn of Africa, the Soviet Union also ended its support of Ethiopia, with Cuban combat troops again being withdrawn. The US then ended its support of Somalia, and the war between Ethiopia and Somalia came to an end. Both these military conflicts, and Cuban military involvement, had played a major role in the deteriorating relations between the US and the USSR in the late 1970s. The ending of these 'hot spots' contributed to the eventual conclusion of the Second Cold War.

Was the end of the Cold War also the end of the 'Great Contest'?

The end of history?

The Cold War was clearly at an end, as one of the two superpowers no longer existed. This left the USA with supreme global power after almost 75 years of struggle. Some historians, such as Richard Crockatt, have seen 1991 as the end of what has been described as 'the 50 Years' War' between the US and the USSR – a war that had clearly been won by the US, with its greater economic, technological and military strength.

Other commentators have argued that the end of the Cold War and the collapse of the Soviet Union had an even wider significance, in that these events heralded the end of the 'Great Contest', which had begun in 1917. Or, as expressed by Francis Fukuyama (a US official), the 'end of history' had arrived, resulting in the final victory of 'liberal' capitalism over Marxism and communist or radical movements based to one degree or another on this political philosophy. Certainly, communism remained the official ideology of only a handful of states: apart from China (which was quickly applying capitalist economic policies), the only other communist states were Cuba, North Korea and Vietnam, and Vietnam had also begun moving towards capitalist economic policies once aid from the Soviet Union had ceased.

Conclusion – US power

Certainly, with the collapse of the Soviet Union in 1991, only one superpower from the Cold War remained. Since then, historians have been debating the causes of the collapse of the Soviet Union and thus the end of the Cold War.

In 1992, George Kennan – in many ways the architect of US policy during the Cold War – claimed that the US did not have the power to bring about changes within the USSR. Yet his policy had originally been based on the belief that containment would not just counter Soviet influence in the world, but would also help undermine the Soviet system.

205

This cartoon about the end of the Cold War appeared in the Guardian *newspaper in Britain in June 1988*

There were clearly many long-standing economic and political weaknesses within the Soviet Union itself that played a big part in its eventual downfall. These included bureaucratic control of the economy which resulted in much inefficiency and waste, and to rates of productivity significantly lower than those achieved in the West. In addition, from the late 1980s, the USSR became increasingly drawn into the global capitalist economy. This had not been the case in the 1930s, when the USSR remained largely isolated, undergoing dramatic industrial growth while the US and other Western economies went into decline during the Great Depression. The Malta Summit in December 1989 provided economic aid, but with strings attached, including moves towards a capitalist market economy and political reforms.

Its undemocratic political system had also alienated large sections of Soviet society, and Gorbachev's reforms arguably came too late to save the system. However, it does seem that earlier US policies – especially maintaining and deepening the nuclear arms race – contributed to the distortion and ultimate collapse of Soviet economic and political structures.

Though the collapse of the Soviet Union in 1991 left the US as the only remaining superpower, both China and India are developing rapidly: both are nuclear powers and both have the potential to become rival superpowers in the near future. In addition, the 11 September 2001 attacks on the USA led many commentators to claim that, in place of the Cold War and the 'Great Contest', the new global struggle was a 'War on Terror' – waged against the US and the West, not by those subscribing to a political ideology, but by Islamist fundamentalists whose ideas are drawn from religion.

> **Fact**
> Back in 1947, these possible consequences had been precisely the reasons why Joseph Stalin had rejected participation in the USA's Marshall Plan.

Nuclear stockpiles, 1945–91

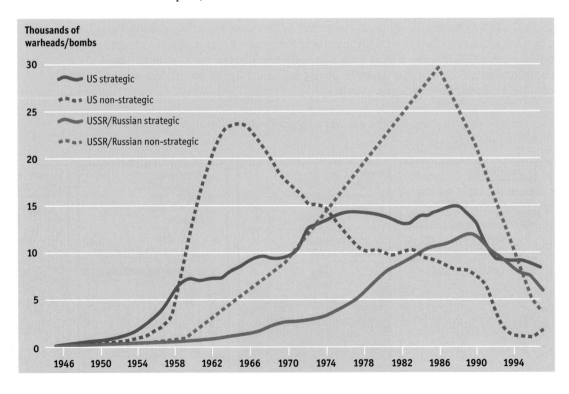

The idea of communism

However, some historians argue that claims that the collapse of the Soviet Union in 1991 marked the end of the 'Great Contest' might be rather premature. In particular, they point out that Marxist theory and communist practice grew from conditions of poverty, the destruction of war, and strong desires for liberty, fairness and equality. While it could be argued that most people in the developed world enjoy these freedoms and conditions, this is hardly true of the majority of the world's population. Thus it is claimed that some version of the early form of communism and global planning is vital to save the world from capitalist and environmental degradation.

With the collapse of the USSR and its Stalinist version of Marxism and communism, commentators have suggested that a newer, more liberal and libertarian version of communism might emerge to challenge the global economic interests of the US or any other new superpower. Thus it may be rather premature for historians – and politicians – to claim that the 'Great Contest' is over.

> ### SOURCE F
>
> We have to take the long view of the historical process. … For as long as contemporary capitalism, a system based on exploitation and inequality and recurring crises, not to mention its impact on the fragile ecology of the planet, continues to exist, the possibility of anti-capitalist movements taking power cannot be ruled out. … The duels between the possessors and the dispossessed continue, taking new forms.
>
> Ali, T. 2009. The Idea of Communism. *London, UK. Seagull Books. pp. 112–14.*

Chapter summary

You should now be able to explain the main elements and significance of Gorbachev's 'New Thinking' for Cold War relations between the USSR and the USA. You should also have a good understanding of the role played by Reagan in contributing to the end of the Cold War, and of the main summits and agreements reached in the years 1985–88.

In addition, you should be able to identify and explain the various factors behind Gorbachev's policies and the collapse of the Soviet Union – including Soviet economic weaknesses, US actions, events in Eastern Europe during 1988–89, and the impact of the new arms race begun by the US.

You should have a sound understanding of how Cold War tensions in Asia, the Americas and Africa were reduced, and of the roles played by Gorbachev and Bush in ending the Cold War. Finally, you should be able to comment on different historians' views about the implications for international relations following the end of the Cold War.

End of chapter activities

Historical debate

One area of debate is whether it was Gorbachev or Reagan who played the most significant role in the ending of the Cold War. Another is whether the final outcome was 'inevitable', or a different result might have been achieved if Soviet leaders had adopted Gorbachev-type reforms in the 1970s – or whether, if Khrushchev had continued in power, the USSR would have avoided many of the economic problems that affected it in the 1970s.

1   Carry out further research on the respective roles played by Gorbachev and Reagan in ending the Cold War.

2   Find out more about the various summit meetings in the period 1985–91. Then draw up a chart to show the main events and outcomes.

3   Produce a timeline to show the main events in the collapse of the regimes in Eastern Europe in 1988–89, including, where relevant, the names of particular historians. Then write a couple of paragraphs showing which factor you think was the most important.

Discussion point

Working in pairs, use the information in the chapters of this book you have already read, and any other materials you have used, to discuss whether you think that Francis Fukuyama was correct to claim that the end of the Cold War and the collapse of the Soviet Union was the 'end of history'.

Paper 1 exam practice

Question

According to Source A below, what was the main reason for the end of the Cold War? [2 marks]

Skill

Comprehension of a source

SOURCE A

The West did not, as is widely believed, win the Cold War through geopolitical containment and military deterrence. Nor was the Cold War won by the Reagan military build up and the Reagan Doctrine. ... Instead, 'victory' for the West came when a new generation of Soviet leaders realised how badly their system at home and their policies abroad had failed. What containment did was to successfully stalemate Moscow's attempts to advance Soviet hegemony. Over four decades it performed the historic function of holding Soviet power in check until the internal seeds of destruction within the Soviet Union and its empire could mature. At this point, however, it was Gorbachev who brought the Cold War to an end.

Garthoff, R. L. 'Why did the Cold War Arise and Why Did it End?'. In Hogan, M. J. (ed). 1992. The End of the Cold War: Its Meaning and Implications. 1992. Cambridge, UK. Cambridge University Press. p. 129.

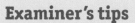
Examiner's tips

Comprehension questions are the most straightforward you will face in Paper 1 – they simply require you to understand a source **and** extract two or three relevant points that relate to the question. As only 2 marks are available for this question, make sure you don't waste valuable exam time that should be spent on the higher-scoring questions by writing a long answer here. All that's needed are a couple of short sentences, giving the necessary information to show you've understood the source. Give one piece of information for each of the marks available for the question.

Common mistakes

When asked to show your comprehension/understanding of a particular source, make sure you don't comment on the **wrong** source! Mistakes like this are made every year. Remember, every mark is important for your final grade.

Simplified markscheme

For **each item of relevant/correct information** identified, award **1 mark** – up to a **maximum of 2 marks**.

Student answer

Source A gives the main reason for the end of the Cold War right at the end, when the historian Garthoff says: '… it was Gorbachev who brought the Cold War to an end.' This is after he has rejected other possible explanations, such as containment or the role of Reagan.

Examiner's comments

The candidate has selected **one** relevant and explicit piece of information from the source – this is enough to gain 1 mark. However, as no other reason/ information has been identified, this candidate fails to gain the other mark available for this question.

Activity

Look again at the source, and the student answer above. Now try to identify **one** other piece of information from the source, and so obtain the other mark available for this question.

Summary activities

1 Produce a spider diagram with a central circle 'The end of the Cold War, 1985–91', and then two main subheadings: '1. Main events and summits' – this one could be further subdivided into 'Summits and treaties' and 'Events' (the latter would cover the political changes in the USSR and Eastern Europe); and '2. Main factors' (here, you will need to look at the role of individuals and various objective factors). To do this, use the information from this chapter and any other resources available to you. Make sure you deal with **all** the main summits, agreements, events and turning points.

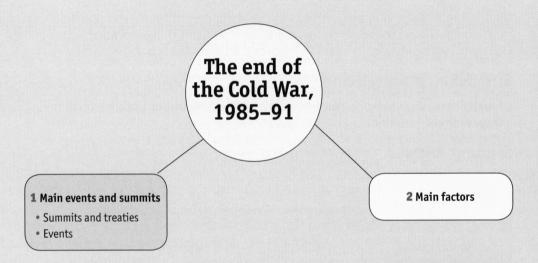

2 Make sure you have attempted all the various comprehension questions that appear in the margins – many of these are designed to help you understand key events and turning points. There are also questions designed to develop your skills in dealing with Paper 1-type questions, such as comprehension of sources, and assessing sources for their value and limitations for historians. Remember – to do these sorts of questions, you will need to look at a **range** of aspects, such as origin, nature and possible purpose. Don't forget – even if a source has many limitations, it can still be valuable for a historian.

Practice Paper 2 questions

1 Compare and contrast the significance of Gorbachev and Reagan for the end of the Cold War.

2 Examine the reasons behind the decision of the USSR to withdraw from Afghanistan.

3 To what extent did economic problems in the communist bloc bring about the end of the Cold War?

4 Assess the social and economic effects of the Cold War on **one** superpower.

5 'The main reason for the end of the Cold War was the superior military strength of the US and NATO.' To what extent do you agree with this statement on the end of the Cold War?

6 In what ways did developments in the Soviet Union affect the final years of the Cold War?

Further reading

Try reading the relevant chapters/sections of the following books:

Hutchings, Robert. 1997. *American Diplomacy and the End of the Cold War*. Baltimore, USA. John Hopkins University Press.

Gaddis, John Lewis. 2007. *The Cold War: A New History*. London, UK. Penguin Books.

Chernyaev, A. 2000. *My Six Years with Gorbachev*. Translated and edited by R. English and E. Tucker. Pennsylvania State University Press.

Laver, John. 1999. *Eastern and Central European States, 1945–9*. London, UK. Macmillan.

Njolstad, Olav (ed.). 2004. *The Last Decade of the Cold War*. London, UK. Routledge.

8 Exam practice

Introduction

You have now completed your study of the main aspects and events of the Cold War from its origins to its end. In the previous chapters, you have had practice at answering some of the types of source-based question you will have to deal with in Paper 1. In this chapter, you will gain experience of dealing with:

• the longer Paper 1 question, which requires you to use both sources and your own knowledge to write a mini-essay
• the essay questions you will meet in Paper 2.

Exam skills needed for IB History

This book is designed primarily to prepare both Standard and Higher Level students for the Paper 2 Cold War topic (Topic 5). However, by providing the necessary historical knowledge and understanding, as well as an awareness of the relevant key historical debates, it will also help you prepare for Paper 1. The skills you need for answering both Paper 1 and Paper 2 exam questions are explained in the following pages.

The example below shows you how to find the information related to the 'W' questions that you will need to evaluate sources for their value and limitations.

SOURCE X

I cannot conceal from you the concern with which I view the development of events since our fruitful meeting at Yalta. So far there has been a discouraging lack of progress made in the carrying out of the decisions we made at the Conference, particularly those relating to the Polish question. I am frankly puzzled as to why this should be and must tell you that I do not fully understand the attitude of your government.

Extract from a letter *written by* Roosevelt *on* 1 April 1945, *criticising Stalin for the lack of progress over Poland. Quoted in McAleavy, T. 1996.* Modern World History. *Cambridge, UK. Cambridge University Press. p. 100.*

letter WHAT? (type of source)
Roosevelt WHO? (produced it)
1 April 1945 WHEN? (date/time of production)
criticising WHY? (possible purpose)
Stalin WHO? (intended audience)

Paper 1 exam practice

Paper 1 skills and questions

This section of the book is designed to give you the skills and understanding to tackle Paper 1 questions. These are based on the comprehension, critical analysis and evaluation of different types of historical sources as evidence, along with the use of appropriate historical contextual knowledge.

For example, you will need to test sources for reliability and utility – a skill essential for historians. A range of sources has been provided, including extracts from official documents, personal diaries, memoirs and speeches, as well as visual sources such as photographs and cartoons.

In order to analyse and evaluate sources as historical evidence, you will need to ask the following **'W' questions** of historical sources:

- **Who** produced it? Were they in a position to know?
- **What** type of source is it? What is its nature – is it a primary or secondary source?
- **Where** and **when** was it produced? What was happening at the time?
- **Why** was it produced? Was its purpose to inform or to persuade? Is it an accurate attempt to record facts, or is it an example of propaganda?
- **Who** was the intended audience – decision-makers or the general public?

This will help you to become familiar with interpreting, understanding, analysing and evaluating different types of historical sources. It will also aid you in synthesising critical analysis of sources with historical knowledge when constructing an explanation or analysis of some aspect or development of the past. Remember, for Paper 1, as for Paper 2, you need to acquire, select and deploy relevant historical knowledge to explain causes and consequences, continuity and change. You also need to develop and show an awareness of historical debates and different interpretations.

Paper 1 questions will thus involve examining sources in the light of:

- their **origins** and **purpose**
- their value and limitations.

The **value and limitations** of sources to historians will be based on the **origins and purpose** aspects. For example, a source might be useful because it is primary – the event depicted was witnessed by the person producing it. But was the person in a position to know? Is the view an untypical view of the event? What is its nature? Is it a private diary entry (therefore possibly more likely to be true), or is it a speech or piece of propaganda intended to persuade? The value of a source may be limited by some aspects, but that doesn't mean it has no value at all. For example, it may be valuable as evidence of the types of propaganda put out at the time. Similarly, a secondary – or even a tertiary – source can have more value than some primary sources, for instance, because the author might be writing at a time when new evidence has become available.

origins The 'who, what, when and where?' questions.

purpose This means 'reasons, what the writer/creator was trying to achieve, who the intended audience was'.

Remember, a source doesn't have to be primary to be useful. Remember, too, that content isn't the only aspect to have possible value. The context, the person who produced it, and so on, can also be important in offering an insight. Finally, when in the exam room, use all the information provided by the Chief Examiner about the five sources, as it can give some useful clues to help you construct a good answer.

Paper 1 contains four types of question. The first three of these are:

1 Comprehension/understanding of a source – some will have 2 marks, others 3 marks. For such questions, write only a short answer (scoring 2 or 3 points); save your longer answers for the questions carrying the higher marks.

2 Cross-referencing/comparing or contrasting two sources – try to write an integrated comparison, e.g. comment on how the two sources deal with one aspect, then compare/contrast the sources on another aspect. This will usually score more highly than answers that deal with the sources separately. Try to avoid simply describing each source in turn – there needs to be explicit comparison/contrast.

3 Assessing the value and limitations of 2 sources – here it is best to deal with each source separately, as you are not being asked to decide which source is more important/useful. But remember to deal with **all** the aspects required: **origins, purpose, value and limitations**.

These three types of questions are covered in the chapters above. The other, longer, type of Paper 1 question will be dealt with in this section.

Paper 1 – judgement questions

The fourth type of Paper 1 question is a judgement question. Judgement questions are a *synthesis of source evaluation and own knowledge*.

Examiner's tips

- This fourth type of Paper 1 question requires you to produce a mini-essay to address the question/statement given in the question. You should try to develop and present an argument and/or come to a balanced judgement by analysing and using these **five** sources **and** your own knowledge.
- Before you write your answer to this kind of question, you may find it useful to draw a rough chart to note what the sources show in relation to the question. This will also make sure you refer to all or at least most of the sources. Note, however, that some sources may hint at more than one factor/result. When using your own knowledge, make sure it is relevant to the question.
- Look carefully at the simplified markscheme opposite. This will help you focus on what you need to do to reach the top bands and so score the higher marks.

Common mistakes

When answering Paper 1 argument/judgement questions, make sure you don't just deal with sources **or** your own knowledge! Every year, some candidates (even good ones) do this, and so limit themselves to – at best – only 5 out of the 8 marks available.

Simplified markscheme

Band		Marks
1	**Developed and balanced** analysis and comments using **BOTH** sources **AND** own knowledge. References to sources are precise; sources and detailed own knowledge are used together; where relevant, a judgement is made.	8
2	**Developed** analysis/comments using **BOTH** sources **AND** some detailed own knowledge; some clear references to sources. But sources and own knowledge not always **combined together**.	6–7
3	**Some developed** analysis/comments, using the sources **OR** some relevant own knowledge.	4–5
4	**Limited/general** comments using sources **OR** own knowledge.	0–3

Student answers

The student answers below have brief examiner's comments in the margins, as well as a longer overall comment at the end. Those parts of the answers that make use of the sources are **highlighted in green**. Those parts that deploy relevant own knowledge are **highlighted in red**. In this way, you should find it easier to follow why particular bands and marks were – or were not – awarded.

Question 1

Using Sources A, B, C, D and E on pages 216–217, **and** your own knowledge, explain why the Cold War began in the period 1941–49.
[8 marks]

SOURCE A

A communist rally in Germany, 1918

SOURCE B

Stalin's postwar goals were security for himself, his regime, his country, and his ideology, in precisely that order. He sought to make sure that … no external threats would ever again place his country at risk. The interests of communists elsewhere in the world, admirable though those might be, would never outweigh the priorities of the Soviet state as he had determined them.

Gaddis, J. L. 2005. The Cold War. London, UK. Penguin Books. p. 11.

SOURCE C

I cannot conceal from you the concern with which I view the development of events since our fruitful meeting at Yalta. So far there has been a discouraging lack of progress made in the carrying out of the decisions we made at the Conference, particularly those relating to the Polish question. I am frankly puzzled as to why this should be and must tell you that I do not fully understand the attitude of your government.

Extract from a letter written by Roosevelt on 1 April 1945, criticising Stalin for the lack of progress over Poland. Quoted in McAleavy, T. 1996. Modern World History. Cambridge, UK. Cambridge University Press. p. 100.

SOURCE D

After only eleven days in power Harry Truman made his decision to lay down the law to an ally which had contributed more in blood and agony than we had – and about Poland, an area through which Russia had been invaded three times since 1914. The basis for the Cold War was laid on 23 April in the scourging which Truman administered to Molotov [the Soviet foreign minister], giving notice that in areas of the most vital concern to Russia our wishes must be obeyed.

Extract from Fleming, D. F. 1961. The Cold War and its Origins, 1917–1960. Quoted in McAleavy, T. 1996. Modern World History. Cambridge, UK. Cambridge University Press. p. 102.

SOURCE E

This cartoon appeared in the British magazine *Punch* at the time the Marshall Plan was announced

THE TRUMAN LINE

Student answer

There are a number of reasons why the Cold War began in the period 1941–49, and these five sources between them offer a range of reasons for this. Firstly, Source A shows a rally held by the German Communist Party in 1918 – although this is well before 1941, it relates to the fear of communism that was widespread in capitalist countries in the West after the Bolshevik Revolution in 1917. From then on, according to some historians, there was a 'Great Contest' between capitalism and communism that never went away – even when the USA, the USSR and Britain formed the Grand Alliance in 1941 to resist Nazi Germany. Once the Second World War was over, the 'marriage of convenience' soon began to turn into the Cold War.

Examiner's comment
This is a good, well-focused, start – Source A is referred to and used, along with a little own knowledge.

Sources B, C and D all relate to the same factor, though in slightly different ways. Source B, in a way, also connects to Source A in that it says that the West needn't have been so fearful of the USSR spreading communism, as Stalin was much more concerned with Soviet security from further attacks (the USSR had been invaded via Poland three times since 1900).

It was these security fears that led Stalin to ignore the agreements about the make-up of the post-war Polish government and the holding of free elections made at the Yalta Conference in February 1945. Source C shows that even Roosevelt, who was quite sympathetic to Soviet security concerns, was becoming unhappy about events in Poland after Yalta. However, Source D shows that once Truman took over as president of the US, events in Poland became a much more serious issue, which played a big part in the start of the Cold War. This source also comments on Truman's harsh attitude – this made relations even worse.

Examiner's comment
The sources (B, C and D) are again clearly referred to and used, showing good understanding, and there is a little own knowledge. There is also a comment at the end which hints at why the Cold War may have started.

Finally, Source E refers to the two US policies of the Truman Doctrine and the Marshall Plan – both introduced into Europe in 1947. These policies show the strong anti-Soviet line taken by Truman, which is mentioned in Source D. In a way, these policies can be seen as forming a Western version of the 'Iron Curtain' that Churchill said the USSR had set down along the borders of Eastern Europe. This is especially true as, although Marshall Aid was offered to the USSR and its satellites in Eastern Europe, Truman made sure the terms would be rejected by Stalin by insisting on 'free markets' and help for private enterprise companies in any country receiving the aid.

Examiner's comment
As before, the sources (E and D) are clearly used and, in this case, linked. There is also some relevant own knowledge. However, there are no explicit explanations/comments on how these policies led to the start of the Cold War.

So, in conclusion, these five sources touch on all the main reasons why a Cold War had begun by 1949. Overall, the main reason was probably the one shown in Source A – the great struggle between two opposed social and economic systems, which began from the moment the Bolshevik Revolution took place in November 1917.

Examiner's comment
The brief conclusion shows the student has kept the question in mind and has attempted to make a judgement.

219

Overall examiner's comments

There is good use of the sources, with clear references to them. However, although there is some own knowledge, which is mainly integrated with comments on the sources, there are some omissions. For instance, own knowledge could have been used to give other factors not mentioned by the sources, such as the issue of the second front, the US nuclear bomb, the question of German reparations, Stalin's actions in Eastern Europe, the Berlin Blockade and Airlift, and the setting up of NATO. Also, while explaining the sources, there are few explicit explanations as to why these issues caused the start of the Cold War. Instead, reasons tend to be merely listed. Hence this answer fails to get into Band 1 – but this is a reasonably sound Band 2 answer and so probably scores 6 marks out of the 8 available.

Activity

Look again at all the sources, the simplified markscheme on page 214, and the student answer above. Now try to write a few paragraphs to push the answer up into Band 1, and so obtain the full 8 marks. As well as using all/most of the sources, and some precise own knowledge, try to integrate the sources with your own knowledge, rather than dealing with sources and own knowledge separately. And don't lose sight of the need to use the sources and your own knowledge to *explain* why the Cold War began.

Question 2

Using Sources A, B, C, D and E, **and** your own knowledge, analyse the reasons for the start of a Second Cold War in 1979.   [8 marks]

SOURCE A

Revolutionary upheavals in the Developing World, 1974–80

Country	Event	Date
1 Ethiopia	Deposition of Haile Selassie	12 September 1974
2 Cambodia	Khmer Rouge takes Phnom Penh	17 April 1975
3 Vietnam	NLF takes Saigon	30 April 1975
4 Laos	Pathet Lao take over state	9 May 1975
5 Guinea-Bissau	Independence from Portugal	9 September 1974
6 Mozambique	Independence from Portugal	25 June 1975
7 Cape Verde	Independence from Portugal	5 July 1975
8 São Tomé	Independence from Portugal	12 July 1975
9 Angola	Independence from Portugal	11 November 1975
10 Afghanistan	PDPA military coup	27 April 1978
11 Iran	Khomeiny's government installed	11 February 1979
12 Grenada	New Jewel Movement comes to power	13 March 1979
13 Nicaragua	FLN takes Managua	19 July 1979
14 Zimbabwe	Independence from Britain	17 April 1980

Halliday, F. 1989. The Making of the Second Cold War (2nd ed.). London, UK. Verso. p. 92.

SOURCE B

So far, détente's been a one-way street which the Soviet Union has used to pursue its own aims.

Extract from comments made by Ronald Reagan, printed in the International Herald Tribune, 31 January 1981.

SOURCE C

Détente did not prevent resistance to Soviet expansion: on the contrary, it fostered the only psychologically possible framework for such resistance. [President] Nixon knew where to draw the line against Soviet adventure whether it occurred directly or through proxy. ... The United States and the Soviet Union are ideological rivals. Détente cannot change that. The nuclear age compels us to coexist. Rhetorical crusades cannot change that either.

Kissinger, H. 1979. The White House Years. New York, USA. Little, Brown. pp. 237–38.

SOURCE D

Outside aggression against the revolutionary Afghanistan perpetuated by counter-revolutionary bands, which were organised and are armed by American special services joined with the Peking militarists, made Soviet assistance necessary in defending the Afghan people's gains. In fact Washington, with the assistance of Peking, provoked the 'Afghan crisis' in order to finally gain a free hand in the policy of anti-détente.

Chernenko's comments on the reasons for Soviet intervention. Quoted in Mendelson, S. 1998. Changing Course: Ideas, Politics, and the Soviet Withdrawal from Afghanistan. Chichester, UK. Princeton University Press. p. 76.

SOURCE E

Mujahideen fighters in Afghanistan

221

Student answer

There were several main factors behind the start of the Second Cold War – only some of these are mentioned by the five sources. The main ones are the outbreak of revolutions in those areas of the Developing World that were seen by the US as being in its 'sphere of influence'; growing dissatisfaction in the West with the policy of détente; economic problems and developments in the USA; the USA's determination to push ahead with new nuclear weapons; the failure of the USSR to deliver fully on its promises about human rights; the USSR closing some aspects of the 'missile gap'; the rise of the 'New Right' in the US; and the Soviet military intervention in Afghanistan.

Examiner's comment
This is a good introduction, showing a clear understanding of the topic and the question.

Source A, which lists 14 revolutions that broke out in the Developing World after 1974, shows one important reason for the start of the Second Cold War. Particularly important was the revolution in Iran in 1979, which deprived the US of the important Middle Eastern alliance with the shah; and, also in 1979, the loss of Somoza, the dictator of Nicaragua and another important US ally in the Cold War in the Americas (the USA's 'own backyard'). Also important were developments in the Horn of Africa – especially the loss of Haile Selassie in Ethiopia in 1974. Although the USSR did not start these revolutions, it was keen to use them as opportunities to extend its global influence and so improve its geopolitical position, which was much less than that of the US. This both angered and worried many US politicians and strategists – those such as Brzezinski and Carter talked of an 'Arc of Crisis', and recommended that the US take action to counter this.

Examiner's comment
There is good use of Source A, and the use of some precise own knowledge which is integrated in the answer.

Sources B and C touch on another important reason – the growing opposition to détente within the US. In part, this was connected to the various revolutions and loss of US allies from 1974. Some came to argue that the USSR was taking advantage of this policy to increase its influence around the world, and was not delivering on the promises made at the Helsinki Conference and in the Helsinki Accords (1973–75) to respect human rights. As Kissinger (the adviser most associated with détente) noted in Source C, détente had never meant making significant concessions to the USSR. However, in the late 1970s and early 1980s, 'New Right' Republicans such as Reagan tried to put pressure on Carter by saying that the USA was giving away too much for nothing in return, and was thus 'falling behind' the Soviet Union (Source B). In fact, this rise of the 'New Right' had much more to do with the economic problems of the US after the 1973 Arab–Israeli War and the costs of the wars in Indochina (such as inflation, unemployment and zero growth rates); and with the growing importance of the south-west part of the US. These factors pushed the 'New Right' into wanting a more interventionist foreign policy in the Developing World, and a big increase in US military spending. In part, this was justified by the fact that, under Brezhnev, the USSR had begun closing the missile gap in some areas – although at great long-term cost to the Soviet economy. The 'New Right' then called for a new generation of nuclear weapons. This was started under Carter and taken further once Reagan became president.

Examiner's comment
There is good understanding and clear use of two more sources, and also the integration of plenty of sound and relevant own knowledge.

The final reason for the Second Cold War, suggested by Sources D and E, *is the USSR's decision, in December 1979, to send troops into Afghanistan. In fact, this action can be seen as more an excuse than a real reason for the end of détente and the start of a new Cold War.* Afghanistan had long been seen as unimportant by the West, which had in practice accepted it as falling within the Soviet 'sphere of influence', given its borders with the Soviet Union's Asiatic Muslim republics. **Furthermore,** as stated by the *Soviet leader Chernenko in Source D, the US had already begun arming and training extremist Muslim terrorist groups (such as those seen in Source E), via bases in Pakistan, to cause trouble for the USSR and its ally. Chernenko and his advisers felt that such US actions threatened their security, as is stated clearly in Source D.*

Examiner's comment
Once again, there is a good synthesis of both sources and some precise own knowledge to produced an analytical explanation of the reasons for the Second Cold War.

Consequently, the most important reasons for the start of the Second Cold War appear to be revolutionary developments in the Developing World in the period 1974–80, and also economic and political developments in the US itself. Soviet actions around the world, and even its military intervention in Afghanistan, appear to be much less important reasons.

223

Examiner's comment
A concise summary of what has been an analytical argument throughout, and making a clear judgement.

Overall examiner's comments

There is good and clear use of sources throughout, and constant integration of precise own knowledge to both explain and add to the sources. The overall result is a sound analytical explanation, focused clearly on the question. The candidate has done more than enough to be awarded Band 1 and the full 8 marks.

Activity

Look again at the all sources, the simplified markscheme on page 214, and the student answer above. Now try to write your own answer to this question – and see if you can make different points with the sources. Try to use different/ additional own knowledge to produce an answer that offers an alternative explanation to that given above.

Paper 2 skills and questions

For Paper 2, you have to answer two essay questions from two of the five different topics offered. Very often, you will be asked to comment on two states from two different IB regions of the world. Although each question has a specific markscheme, you can get a good general idea of what examiners are looking for in order to be able to put answers into the higher bands from the 'generic' markscheme. In particular, you will need to acquire reasonably precise historical knowledge in order to address issues such as cause and effect, or change and continuity, and to learn how to explain historical developments in a clear, coherent, well-supported and relevant way. You will also need to understand and be able to refer to aspects relating to historical debates and interpretations.

Make sure you read the questions carefully, and select your questions wisely. It is a good idea to produce a rough plan of **each** of the essays you intend to attempt, **before** you start to write your answers. That way, you will soon know whether you have enough own knowledge to answer them adequately.

Remember, too, to keep your answers relevant and focused on the question. For example, don't go outside the dates mentioned in the question, or answer on individuals/states different from the ones identified in the question. Don't just describe the events or developments – sometimes, students just focus on one key word or individual, and then write down all they know about it. Instead, select your own knowledge carefully, and pin the relevant information to the key features raised by the question. Also, if the question asks for 'reasons' and 'results', or two different countries, make sure you deal with **all** the parts of the question. Otherwise, you will limit yourself to half marks at best.

Examiner's tips

For Paper 2 answers, examiners are looking for clear/precise analysis, and a balanced argument, linked to the question, with the use of good, precise and relevant own knowledge. In order to obtain the highest marks, you should be able to refer to different historical debate/interpretations or historians' knowledge, making sure it is relevant to the question.

Common mistakes

- When answering Paper 2 questions, try to avoid simply describing what happened. A detailed narrative, with no explicit attempts to link the knowledge to the question, will only get you half marks at most.
- If the question asks you to select examples from **two** different regions, make sure you don't choose two states from the same region. Every year, some candidates do this, and so limit themselves to – at best – only 12 out of the 20 marks available.

Simplified markscheme

Band		Marks
1	Clear analysis/argument, with very specific and relevant own knowledge, consistently and explicitly linked to the question. A balanced answer, with references to historical debate/historians, where appropriate.	17–20
2	Relevant analysis/argument, mainly clearly focused on the question, and with relevant supporting own knowledge. Factors identified and explained, but not all aspects of the question fully developed or addressed.	11–16
3	**EITHER** shows reasonable relevant own knowledge, identifying some factors, with limited focus/explanation – but **mainly narrative** in approach, with question only implicitly addressed **OR** coherent analysis/argument, but limited.	8–10
4	**Some limited/relevant** own knowledge, but **not linked effectively** to the question.	6–7
5	**Short/general** answer, but with very **little accurate/relevant knowledge and limited understanding** of the question.	0–5

Student answers

Those parts of the student answers that follow will have brief examiner's comments in the margins, as well as a longer overall comment at the end. Those parts of student's answers that are particularly strong and well-focused will be highlighted in red. Errors/confusions/loss of focus will be highlighted in blue. In this way, you should find it easier to follow why marks were – or were not – awarded.

Question 1

Assess the role of **two** non-superpower states on the development of the Cold War in the period 1950–70, each chosen from a **different** region.
[20 marks]

Skill

Analysis/argument/assessment.

Examiner's tip

Look carefully at the wording of this question, which asks for the role/impact of **two non-superpower** states, each from a **different** region, in the **development** of the Cold War. All aspects of the questions will need to be addressed if high marks are to be achieved. Remember, don't just describe what happened; you need to provide explicit analysis and explanation, with some precise supporting own knowledge.

Student answer

Although the Cold War began as a conflict in Europe between the USA and the USSR immediately after the end of the Second World War, it soon spread to other regions of the world. Both Korea (in Asia), and Cuba (in the Americas) played significant roles in the development and deepening polarisation of the Cold War. The conflicts or crises involving these two states (the Korean War and the Cuban Missile Crisis) also led to the development of the nuclear war strategy known as 'Mutually Assured Destruction' (MAD).

Examiner's comment
This is a clear and well-focused introduction, showing a good grasp of the key requirements of the question.

After 1945, Korea was split into North and South along the 38th parallel. As the Cold War began, this division into two states became permanent – the North became a communist one-party state, allied to the Soviet Union, while the South was an undemocratic capitalist state, supported by the US. Both states wanted to bring about reunification – but on their own terms. After several border clashes, the North invaded the South in June 1950.

This war involved the UN, as the US was able to get UN approval for its military action in support of the South. This was because the USSR was boycotting the UN Security Council in protest at the USA's refusal to allow Communist China a seat in the UN. The involvement of the UN – with several member states, including Britain, sending troops under US command – polarised the Cold War. At first, the USSR gave military equipment to the North and then began to send military advisers. However, both superpowers tried to avoid direct conflict between their military personnel. Relations worsened when the US ignored Chinese warnings not to invade North Korea (this was an act beyond the original UN brief) and approach the border with China. Communist China then sent in thousands of military 'volunteers' to fight US/UN forces. For a time, this brought the Soviet Union and China closer together, and so made the divisions between capitalist and communist countries even deeper. Eventually, a stalemate developed and an armistice was signed in 1953 – but not a permanent peace.

Examiner's comment
There is accurate supporting own knowledge, explicitly linked to the significance of the effects/results of the Korean War on the Cold War.

226

Cuba's role in the Cold War also helped deepen Cold War suspicions and hostilities. This began in 1959, after Castro led a successful revolution against Batista, the dictator of Cuba, who had been a US ally. The US did not accept Cuba's right to complete independence, and increasingly came to see developments in Cuba as part of a Soviet plot for extending its influence in the world. As disagreements between Cuba and the US deepened, following Castro's economic policies and his increasingly close relations with the Soviet Union, the US decided to take action. The US – which saw the whole of the Americas as its sphere of influence (its 'own backyard') – at first applied economic sanctions. In 1961, in the Bay of Pigs fiasco, it tried to overthrow Castro via a plan originally drawn up by the CIA under Eisenhower, but actually given the go-ahead by Kennedy, the newly elected US president. *The failure of this attempted invasion, by US-trained and equipped anti-Castro Cuban exiles, led Castro to appeal to the USSR for protection – so increasing Cold War tensions.*

Khrushchev's decision to install nuclear weapons on Cuba, to protect Castro and to counter US missiles close to the USSR in Turkey, sparked off the Cuban Missile Crisis in 1962, when US spy planes noticed the new sites.

Though the crisis was eventually averted without a nuclear Third World War, and actually led to a Test-Ban Treaty and the establishment of a hot-line between Washington and Moscow, its net result was to deepen Cold War suspicions on both sides.

Examiner's comment
Again, there is accurate supporting own knowledge, with explicit comments on the effects/results of developments in Cuba on the Cold War as a whole.

227

In addition, both the Korean War and the Cuban Missile Crisis had an impact on military strategy, resulting in the emergence of MAD (Mutually Assured Destruction). This policy (similar to Eisenhower's 'massive retaliation') came to replace the idea of 'counterforce', which had earlier been developed by Kennedy's advisers. MAD was based on the idea that no nuclear war would take place because both superpowers knew that if they fired nuclear weapons, the other side would retaliate with such force that both sides – and the world – would be destroyed.

In fact, both superpowers had adopted a similar approach, as both feared nuclear war. In Korea, Truman had dismissed MacArthur when he had suggested using nuclear weapons against China, and Khrushchev had decided not to place warheads in Cuba once he knew Kennedy had put US ICBMs on nuclear alert.

Examiner's comment
There is more accurate supporting own knowledge, clearly focused on the impact of these crises on nuclear weapons strategy.

Examiner's comment
There is then a brief but well-focused conclusion, drawing out the impact of these two states on the development of the Cold War.

Overall, both Korea and Cuba, though quite different crises in different regions of the world, helped increase Cold War polarisation and contributed to the development of new nuclear strategies. These two crises showed the Cold War had become truly global.

Overall examiner's comments

This is a good, well-focused and analytical answer, with some precise and accurate own knowledge to support the points made. The answer is thus good enough to be awarded the mark at the very top of Band 2 – 16 marks. However, not all aspects are addressed. To reach Band 1, some comments on the effect of the Korean War in gaining the support of the US Congress for the big increases in military expenditure and a more aggressive US Cold War policy, suggested by NSC-68, would have been useful, as would comments about it helping to spark off a more serious arms race – both nuclear and conventional. More importantly, it would have been very useful to have some mention of **relevant specific historians/historical interpretations**.

Activity

Look again at the simplified markscheme on page 225, and the student answer above. Now try to write a few extra paragraphs to push the answer up into Band 1, and so obtain the full 20 marks. As well as making sure you address **all** aspects of the question, try to integrate some references to relevant historians/historical interpretations.

Money from the Marshall Plan was used in the rebuilding of Berlin

Question 2

For what reasons, and with what results, did the Second World War allies become post-war enemies?
[20 marks]

Skill

Analysis/argument/assessment

Examiner's tip

Look carefully at the wording of this question, which asks for consideration of a **range** of reasons and results in relation to the emerging tensions between the allies after 1945. Just focusing on one reason will prevent you scoring top marks.

Student answer

The Second World War allies – Britain, the USA and the USSR – joined together in a Grand Alliance in 1941 solely to defeat Nazi Germany; thus it was a 'marriage of convenience'. The two Western powers were capitalist states, and before 1941 had been hostile to the Soviet Union, which had the opposing ideology of communism. *It was mainly these ideological differences which broke the allies up after 1945. This clash of ideologies created two polarised and opposed superpowers. Policies such as the Truman Doctrine and the Marshall Plan, and crises such as the Berlin Blockade and Airlift, created further divisions and rifts between the former allies.*

Examiner's comment
This is a well-focused introduction, clearly identifying ideology as an important factor, and identifying some results – though rather lacking in specific information/dates in relation to the policies and crises mentioned.

229

The political ideology of the West was based on individualism and individual rights (such as free speech, free elections), with the minimum of state intervention in the economy. This capitalist economy was based on private ownership and free trade, and was actively promoted by the US after 1945. Although Roosevelt shared these views, he also appreciated Soviet security fears – but ideological differences became greater after Truman took over.

Until 1953 the Soviet Union was led by Stalin, who had developed his own version of communism, called 'Marxism–Leninism'. Under him, the USSR was a one-party dictatorship and the beliefs about individual rights and the economy were completely different to those in the West. In particular, the USSR was based on state ownership and control of the economy. Although the constitution spoke of individual rights, these were often ignored by the state, and there was only one party to vote for in elections.

Although these ideologies were diametrically opposed, they did not affect the wartime coalition against fascism, which was the common enemy. Despite the terror which had existed for some time in the USSR, Stalin was portrayed as 'Uncle Joe' in the West during the war. This was because defeating Nazi Germany was the main priority.

Tensions began to appear once Germany was defeated, and the question of who was to control Europe became an issue. The first issue was over Germany itself, including Berlin. Eventually, both Germany and Berlin were split into four sectors, controlled by the US, Britain, France and the USSR. The Cold War proper can be seen as starting when Stalin began his blockade of Berlin, to try to force the West out of their part of Berlin, which was in the Soviet sector of Germany. The US and its allies then organised the Berlin Airlift to deliver food to the Eastern bloc and West Berlin. This was all the result of clashing ideologies.

Examiner's comment
There is some supporting own knowledge to describe the different ideologies but it is not always fully relevant, and is rather narrative-based in sections. In addition, there are errors, and the answer lacks precision on the actual disagreements – for instance, the early disputes of 1945–46 are muddled up with the later Berlin Crisis of 1948–49.

This clash of ideologies can also be seen as the two superpowers tried to impose their respective spheres of influence in Europe. In the Marshall Plan of 1947, the USA provided aid to a war-devastated Europe. The public reason for this was to get Europe back on its feet, but there were many other motives. Firstly, in line with the Truman Doctrine, it was a way to contain communism, and to counter the growing popularity of communist parties in states such as France and Italy. In fact, it mostly aided Greece and Turkey, which were both facing strong challenges from their communist parties. In addition, it was a way to ensure customers for US companies and, according to the USSR, was also a way of ensuring US political as well as economic dominance over Western Europe. For this reason, the Soviet Union rejected Marshall Aid for itself and its Eastern European satellites, because of the pro-capitalist policies acceptance of it entailed.

Examiner's comment
Again, there are some inaccuracies in supporting own knowledge, and the approach is rather narrative-based.

In conclusion, differing ideologies were the main reason for the tensions between the USSR and the USA (along with the other former allies). These differences resulted in mutual distrust and the attempt to extend their respective spheres of influence in Europe, especially in Germany. The result of these ideological clashes was the Cold War, **which was vastly different from the Second World War in which the two superpowers had fought side by side.**

Overall examiner's comments

This answer attempts to explicitly address both reasons and results, but it is not well-supported by precise/correct own knowledge; in addition, the approach is too narrative in several places. There are also some confusions/errors and it is rather unbalanced, in that differing ideologies is the main focus – the other reasons are not really touched on. The answer is good enough to be awarded a mark at the top end of Band 3 – probably about 10 marks. To reach the higher bands, some **specific details on other reasons** (such as the second front, Poland, German reparations, the US nuclear monopoly and Soviet actions in East Europe) would be helpful. More importantly, for Band 1, it would be necessary to have some **mention of relevant specific historians/historical interpretations** – there are several to choose from on this topic.

Activity

Look again at the simplified markscheme on page 225, and the student answer above. Now try to write a few extra paragraphs to push the answer up into Band 1, and so obtain the full 20 marks. As well as making sure you address **all** aspects of the question, try to integrate some references to relevant historians/historical interpretations.

Question 3

Assess the part played by differing ideologies in the origin of the Cold War. [20 marks]

Skill

Analysis/argument/assessment

Examiner's tip

Look carefully at the wording of this question, which asks for the part played by differing ideologies in the origin of the Cold War to be assessed – this means that **other factors** also have to be addressed. **All** aspects of the question will need to be covered to achieve top marks. Remember, don't just describe what happened; what's needed is explicit analysis and explanation, with some precise supporting own knowledge.

Student answer

The Cold War was certainly due to differing ideologies, and this contributed to the collapse of the wartime alliance and the emergence of the Cold War. However, it is also true to say that other factors were important – such as mutual distrust, and clashes over what should happen in Europe at the end of the war.

Examiner's comment
This is a clear and well-focused introduction, and suggests that ideology will be assessed alongside 'other factors' in a multi-causal approach, which is exactly what this question requires.

231

The differences in ideology between the capitalist USA and communist USSR played a part in the origins of the Cold War, but not necessarily a very important one. Stalin was a realist in foreign affairs, and put Soviet security above the spreading of communist revolution elsewhere. However, he was also an opportunist, ready to take advantage of any opportunity to further the cause of communism in another country – provided it didn't risk Soviet security. This increased the concerns of the capitalist states of the West, who feared the spread of communist revolution to war-devastated Europe, and to countries in the rest of the world where they had important economic or strategic interests.

Examiner's comment
This is still focused on the question, but the treatment of differing ideologies is rather too brief here.

However, there are many other reasons why the Cold War began. Before 1941, relations between the USSR and the West (the US and Britain) had often been poor. This was in large part the result of the intervention of Britain and the US on the side of the Whites in the Russian Civil War, and of the USA's refusal to recognise the USSR until 1933. Britain's appeasement of Hitler, and then Russia's Non-Aggression Pact with Nazi Germany in 1939, also caused bad feeling. After 1941, although these three countries joined in a Grand Alliance to fight Nazi Germany, they all remained suspicious of each other's motives. In particular, Stalin's repeated calls for a second front from 1942 were ignored until 1944 – making him think the West wanted the USSR weakened more than it wanted to defeat Nazi Germany. Thus the history of relations between 1917 and 1945, and the various suspicions each side had about the other, all contributed to poor relations.

Examiner's comment
There is accurate supporting own knowledge here, referring to the historical context before 1945, and identifying several other reasons for mutual mistrust and so why the Cold War began.

Another reason for the start of the Cold War was the Soviet Union's desire for reparations and a 'buffer zone' in Central and Eastern Europe. Unlike the USA and Britain, the USSR was the only one of the 'Big Three' allies to have been invaded and occupied. About 30 million Russians died in the war, and much of the industry developed in the 1930s had been destroyed, or shipped back to Germany by the Nazis. As Russia had been invaded through Poland three times since 1914, Stalin insisted on a buffer zone of friendly states along the USSR's western border. However, the West saw – or said it saw – this as the first step in spreading communism to the whole of Europe. While Roosevelt, at the Yalta Conference in February 1945, had been prepared to accept some steps in this direction, the Potsdam Conference in July 1945 – where Truman replaced Roosevelt – saw greater differences emerge over Poland. In particular, Stalin was determined to have Poland firmly in the USSR's sphere of influence, even if this meant not carrying through his promises to hold free elections and to accept the 'pro-Western London Poles' as well as the 'pro-Russian Lublin Poles' as part of a coalition government.

Potsdam also saw Truman go back on Roosevelt's idea of withdrawing US troops from Europe within two years of the end of the war. Truman decided to keep them present. There was also the issue of the US nuclear weapons monopoly after August 1945, and Truman's decision not to share the technology with the USSR. In general, Truman's attitude to the Soviet Union and its representatives was much colder and harsher than Roosevelt's had been. All these issues helped start the Cold War.

Examiner's comment
Again, there is accurate supporting own knowledge, with explicit references to a range of 'other factors', such as Soviet security concerns and the significance of the West's anger over Poland, leading to the start of the Cold War.

233

However, the factor that was probably the most important one in starting off the Cold War was Germany. The USA and Britain, as capitalist countries, wanted an economically strong Germany to trade with – and as a block to the USSR. However, Stalin wanted to keep Germany weak, so it would never be a threat to the Soviet Union again (as it had in 1914 and again in 1941). The introduction of the Marshall Plan in 1947, and then the unilateral introduction of a new currency in the Western zones of Germany, made Stalin very suspicious. These issues led to the Berlin Blockade and Airlift, and it was these events that led to the real start of the Cold War.

Examiner's comment
There is accurate supporting own knowledge, clearly focused on yet another factor, which is judged to be the most important. However, some aspects of this are not touched on or developed (for example, de-Nazification, reparations, and so on).

> *Overall, although differing ideologies contributed to the origins of the Cold War, the most important factor in my opinion was mutual distrust and fear, and the lack of understanding of each other's motives, which caused the former allies to drift into the Cold War. Also important was the past history of the 'Big Three', and the fact that both the West and the USSR were determined to set up their own spheres of influence in Europe and the rest of the world. To a large extent, their aims were incompatible.*

Examiner's comment
There is then a brief but well-focused conclusion, which makes a judgement about the most important factor(s).

Overall examiner's comments

This is a good, well-focused and analytical answer, with some precise and accurate own knowledge to support the points made – the student has clearly understood the demands of the question. However, it is rather unbalanced, in that **ideology is not sufficiently developed, and not all aspects of the 'other factors' are sufficiently dealt with**.

The answer is thus good enough to be awarded a mark towards the bottom of Band 2 – probably about 12 marks. To reach Band 1, some **developed comments on aspects of these other factors, and greater depth on ideology**, are needed. In addition, a topic like this calls for some **mention of relevant specific historians/historical interpretations**.

Activity

Look again at the simplified markscheme on page 225, and the student answer above. Now try to write a few extra paragraphs to push the answer up into Band 1, and so obtain the full 20 marks. As well as making sure you address **all** aspects of the question, try to integrate some references to relevant historians/historical interpretations.

234

Further information

Sources and quotations in this book have been taken from the following publications.

Ali, Tariq. 1988. *Revolution From Above: Where Is the Soviet Union Going?*. London, UK. Hutchinson.

Ali, Tariq. 2009. *The Idea of Communism*. London, UK.

Blechman, Barry M. and Kaplan, Stephen S. 1978. *Force Without War*. Washington, DC, USA. The Brookings Institution.

Deudney Daniel and Ikenberry, G. John. 'Who won the Cold War?', in *Foreign Policy*, No. 87. Summer 1992.

Deutscher, Isaac. 1969. *Stalin*. Oxford, UK. Oxford University Press.

Dobrynin, Anatoly. 1995. *In Confidence: Moscow's Ambassador to America's Six Cold War Presidents*. New York, USA. Times Books.

Eastman, Max. 1955. *Reflections on the Failure of Socialism*. New York, USA. Devin-Adair.

Gaddis, J. L. 2005. *The Cold War*. London, UK. Penguin Books.

Gaddis, J. L. and Etzold, T.H. (eds). 1978. *Containment: Documents on American Policy and Strategy, 1945–1950*. New York, USA. Columbia University Press.

Garthoff, R. L. 1994. *Détente and Confrontation: American-Soviet Relations from Nixon to Reagan*. Washington DC, USA. Brookings Institution.

Gates, Robert M. 1996. *From the Shadows: the Ultimate insider's Story of Five Presidents*. New York, USA. Simon & Schuster.

Glynn, P. 'Letter to the Editor', *Foreign Policy*, No. 90. Spring 1993.

Halliday, Fred. 1989. *The Making of the Second Cold War*. London, UK. Verso.

Hogan, Michael J. (ed.). 1992. *The End of the Cold War: Its Meaning and Implications*. Cambridge, UK. Cambridge University Press.

Hunt, M. (ed.). 1996. *Crises in US Foreign Policy: An International History Reader*. New Haven, USA. Yale University Press.

Khrushchev, Nikita and Crankshaw, Edward (ed.). 1970. *Khrushchev Remembers*. New York, UDSA. Simon & Schuster.

Kissinger, Henry. 1979. *The White House Years*. New York, USA. Little, Brown.

Kissinger, Henry. 1994. *Diplomacy*. New York, USA. Simon & Schuster.

Lewin, Moshe. 2005. *The Soviet Century*. London, UK. Verso.

Mason, John W. 1996. *The Cold War: 1945–1991*, London, UK. Routledge.

McAleavy, Tony. 1996. *Modern World History*. Cambridge, UK. Cambridge University Press.

Mendelson, Sarah E. 1998. *Changing Course: Ideas, Politics, and the Soviet Withdrawal from Afghanistan*. Chichester, UK. Princeton University Press.

Rayner, E. G. 1992. *The Cold War*. London, UK. Hodder Murray.

Sewell, Mike. 2002. *The Cold War*, Cambridge, UK. Cambridge University Press.

SIPRI Yearbooks. 1979 and 1981. London, UK. Taylor & Francis.

Smith, Joseph. 1998. *The Cold War 1945–1991*. Oxford, UK. Blackwell.

Trotsky, Leon. 1972. *The Revolution Betrayed: What is the Soviet Union and Where is it Going?* New York, USA. Pathfinder Press.

Truman, Harry S. 1956. *Years of Trial and Hope, 1946–1953*. London, UK. Hodder & Stoughton.

Westad, Odd Arne. 2007. *The Global Cold War*. Cambridge, UK. Cambridge University Press.

Williams, William Appleman. 1972. *The Tragedy of American Diplomacy*. London, UK. Norton.

Williamson, David. 2001. *Europe and the Cold War, 1945–91*. London, UK. Hodder Murray.

Index

Acknowledgements

The volume editor and publishers acknowledge the following sources of copyright material and are grateful for the permissions granted. While every effort has been made, it has not always been possible to identify the sources of all the material used, or to trace all copyright holders. If any omissions are brought to our notice we will be happy to include the appropriate acknowledgement on reprinting.

p. 12 Alexander, A. 'The Soviet threat was a myth'. © Guardian Newspapers Limited 2002.

Picture Credits

Cover © Corbis; p. 5 DANJAQ/EON/UA/The Kobal Collection; p. 6 © Corbis; p. 17 Getty Images; p. 24 Thinkstock/© Getty Images; p. 25 Thinkstock/© Getty Images; p. 29 © Bettmann/Corbis; p. 30 Yugoslav People's Army; p. 32 Popperfoto/Getty Images; p. 35 NASA/JPL; p. 37 HMSO (Open Government Licence); p. 38 © Trinity Mirror/Mirrorpix/Alamy; p. 46 Getty Images; p. 50 US Embassy; p. 51 National Archives and Record Administration; p. 52 © Topfoto; p. 57 Getty Images; p. 59 David King Collection; p. 61 US Department of State; p. 70 Archives Charmet/ Bridgeman Art Library; p. 70 US Department of State; p. 71 © Associated Newspapers Ltd./Solo Syndication; p. 73 (t) US Department of State; p. 73 (b) Library of Congress; p. 75 William Augustus Sillince/Punch; p. 80 The Truman Library; p. 81 Krokodil/SSEES University of London; p. 82 Popperfoto/Getty Images; p. 84 UK Government; p. 86 © Topham Picturepoint; p. 89 Hung Chung Chih/Shutterstock; p. 91 AFP/Getty Images; p. 96 National Archives and Record Administration; p. 99 Getty Images; p. 106 © Bettmann/Corbis; p. 108 National Archives and Record Administration; p. 109 White House Press Office; p. 114 © Topfoto; p. 115 White House Press Office; p. 116 (t) © Bettmann/Corbis; p. 116 (b) National Archives and Record Administration; p. 124 Getty Images; p. 125 Time & Life Pictures/Getty Images; p. 126 (t) White House Press Office; p 126 (b) White House Press Office; p. 127 © Bettmann/Corbis; p. 128 NASA Headquarters/GReatest Images of NASA; p. 131 AFP/Getty Images; p. 134 Library of Congress; p. 137 Pravda 1960; p. 141 © Bettmann/Corbis; p. 152 Nixon Presidential Library and Museum; p. 153 (l) Shoe Cartoons; p. 153 (r) Library of Congress/US News and World Report; p. 157 AFP/Getty Images; p. 158 Library of Congress/US News and World Report; p. 159 National Archives and Record Administration; p. 160 Time & Life Pictures/Getty Images; p. 163 United States Government; p. 165 Popperfoto/Getty Images; p. 170 © Bettmann/Corbis; p. 173 Time & Life Pictures/Getty Images; p. 175 SZ Foto; p. 177 Doug Marlette Foundation; p. 181 © Reuters/Corbis; p. 191 Popperfoto/Getty Images; p. 195 © Corbis; p. 196 US Department of Defense; p. 202 © dpa/Corbis; p. 205 Doonesbury © 1988 G.B. Trudeau. Reprinted by permission of Universal Uclick. All rights reserved; p. 215 Getty Images; p. 217 © William Augustus Sillince/ Punch; p. 221 © Reuters/Corbis; p. 228 © Bettmann/Corbis.

Produced for Cambridge University Press by

 White-Thomson Publishing
+44 (0)843 208 7460
www.wtpub.co.uk

Series editor: Allan Todd
Development editor: Margaret Haynes
Reviewer: David L. Evans
Editor: Sonya Newland
Designer: Clare Nicholas
Picture researcher: Amy Sparks